STRUGGLING READERS

Solving Problems in the Teaching of Literacy

Cathy Collins Block, Series Editor

Struggling Readers

ASSESSMENT AND INSTRUCTION
IN GRADES K–6

Ernest Balajthy

Sally Lipa-Wade

THE GUILFORD PRESS
New York   London

© 2003 The Guilford Press
A Division of Guilford Publications, Inc.
72 Spring Street, New York, NY 10012
www.guilford.com

Printed in the United States of America

This book is printed on acid-free paper.

Last digit is print number: 9   8   7   6   5   4   3   2   1

Library of Congress Cataloging-in-Publication Data

Balajthy, Ernest, 1951–
    Struggling readers: assessment and instruction in grades K–6 /
Ernest Balajthy, Sally Lipa-Wade.
        p.   cm. — (Solving problems in the teaching of literacy)
    Includes bibliographical references and index.
    ISBN 1-57230-852-4 (pbk.)
    1. Reading—Remedial teaching.   2. Reading disability.   3. Reading
(Elementary)   I. Lipa-Wade, Sally.   II. Title.   III. Series.
LB1050.5.B29 2003
372.43—dc21
                                                            2002151198

11/22/04

To Janet

For 15 years, my wife and best friend: "Her worth is far above rubies." Her love and support of me professionally and personally have made this book possible. Our mutual roles in establishing a home and in childrearing have given my life meaning and joy. "A cord of three strands is not easily broken."

And to David and Sara—two great kids.

—Ernie Balajthy

I dedicate this book to my children, Bruce and Amy, who shared my whole career with me. They learned to wait—until I finished one more sentence, until I graded one more paper, or read one more article. They never faltered in accepting my career demands as part of their childhood. I appreciate their love and trust. I also dedicate this book to my husband, Durlyn, who took up where my grown children left off. He, too, supported me, waited while I finished projects, and shared my enthusiasm for this book.

—Sally Lipa-Wade

About the Authors

Ernest Balajthy, EdD, is Director of the Reading and Literacy Center and Assistant Director for Graduate Studies of the School of Education at the State University of New York at Geneseo. He teaches reading, literacy, and educational computing courses. His specializations include technology applications in reading and writing, comprehension processes and strategies, and secondary and college literacy instruction. Dr. Balajthy is the editor of the "Issues in Technology" column that appears in the journal *Reading and Writing Quarterly* and the author of two books on computer applications in reading and language arts.

Sally Lipa-Wade, PhD, is the recently retired Director of the Reading and Literacy Center at the State University of New York at Geneseo. She continues to teach undergraduate and graduate reading and literacy courses as an adjunct faculty member at the University of South Florida. During her time at Geneseo, the Reading and Literacy Center became well known for the training provided to elementary classroom teachers and reading/literacy specialists. Rather than centering on specific reading programs or methodologies, the center stresses a "what's right" approach for individuals' reading development.

Acknowledgments

A special thanks to the extensive editorial work carried out by Margaret Ryan and Anna Brackett of The Guilford Press. Their suggestions were of invaluable help in improving this book.

Contents

PART TWO. CATCH-UP READERS

PART THREE. STALLED READERS

STRUGGLING READERS

Introduction

How does a child learn to read? What roles do I, as a teacher, play in encouraging a child's growth in reading and literacy?

Those questions have long been at the center of teachers' concerns as they engage in the wonderful, challenging world of teaching children how to learn. Teaching reading and facilitating literacy are at the heart of the classroom and of children's early lives. Our responsibilities as teachers of reading are a blend of the awesome and the mundane. We experience the enervating glow radiated by children who are discovering more about themselves and their world even as we enact the routine day-to-day disciplines of lesson planning and class preparation. In our classrooms we read books that bring joy and wonder into children's lives and, at the same time, we acknowledge that the pedagogical foundations of word recognition and comprehension knowledge and strategies are essential to academic growth.

Balance and *perspective,* in life and in the classroom, comprise the ethic we try to follow as teachers and the gift we try to pass on to our students. "To everything there is a season," it is written in Ecclesiastes, "and a time to every purpose under heaven." There is a time for books that allow us to escape into other times and worlds through transactional creations of reader and author. There are other times for plowing through a science text and learning the mechanics of some physical process.

The purpose of this text is to provide cohesion and balance to our thinking about the confusing array of research and theories on struggling readers which can seem like a formidable obstacle for teachers. So much of this writing is transitory: tentative findings and hypotheses that receive brief moments of fame, only to be discarded as new theories and research appear in print.

In this text we take a unique approach to thinking about struggling readers and their teachers. Although we provide discussions of the causes of reading and literacy difficulties, our focus is on *instruction.* We suggest that struggling readers in the elementary grades can be grouped into one of three broad categories: the Catch-On Reader, the Catch-Up Reader, and the Stalled Reader. Although individuals within each category differ in some ways, by and large they share most characteristics of the particular category and respond to particular instructional strategies.

THE THREE TYPES OF READERS

Catch-On Readers are primary-grade children who are having difficulty understanding what readers do. They experience difficulty (1) acquiring basic sight vocabulary, (2) applying language cueing systems for word recognition, or (3) in comprehension. Often these children have not acquired basic concepts of print, such as word boundaries, left-to-right progression during reading, letter and word groupings, or even the concept that print contains a message. These children are candidates for early intervention programs, but alert classroom teachers may also meet their needs.

Catch-Up Readers are elementary-grade children having difficulty meeting the demands of reading at their grade level. These children are reading below the level exhibited by their peers in terms of word recognition, vocabulary development, and/or comprehension. These children are sometimes known as "remedial," "corrective," or "adaptive" readers.

Stalled Readers are children or young people in elementary or secondary school who have made very limited progress in reading, despite the best efforts of classroom teachers. Their development of word-recognition and comprehension skills has remained unsatisfactory, even with the added efforts of remedial or special education teachers. Some of these children are known as "severely remedial readers" or "dyslexics."

It is often hard for a teacher to pinpoint the exact causes of a child's reading difficulty. It is critically important that teachers recognize that our use of the terms Catch-On Reader, Catch-Up Reader, and Stalled Reader would be very inappropriate if they were used to permanently label children with some sort of academic malady. Children with reading problems can become children who read on grade level, with the help of the kinds of interventions described in these chapters.

RECENT CHANGES IN THE ASSESSMENT AND INSTRUCTION OF STRUGGLING READERS

A major shift in our understanding of the reading process and the teaching of reading was brought about in the 1980s and 1990s as teachers realized the importance of instruction that was centered on the needs of children and that emphasized authentic reading and writing. A hallmark of this realization was a promotion of the view that development in reading, writing, listening, and speaking is an integrated and interrelated process, not a collection of discrete skills. Acquiring reading skills and literacy involves interrelated social, cognitive, and linguistic developmental processes that are bit effectively engaged via direct sequential instruction in a collection of isolated skills.

These shifts in beliefs about reading and literacy influenced assessment procedures as well as instructional emphases. Some significant changes include the assessment of oral reading behaviors through miscue analysis; the assessment of reading skills in terms of what the child can, rather than cannot, do; the evaluation of miscues in terms of meaning changes; the use of new criteria for determining independent, instructional, and frustration levels or eliminating the use of instructional levels altogether; and the assessment of students' progress through portfolios and other informal measures.

In the last decade these viewpoints have continued to mature into what has become known as "social constructivist approaches" to reading and literacy assessment. Attention has veered away from the use of tests that are unrelated to students' classwork and toward authentic measures that include observation and interpretation of students' classroom behaviors and examples of their work as carried out in the classroom community of learners.

At the same time that constructivist approaches to assessment have come to prominence within the field of reading and literacy, pressure from the public sphere has reemphasized the need for a clear understanding of formal, standardized testing. "High-stakes" tests, administered by state governments, have placed new demands on schools. It is clear that teachers must be aware of a variety of assessment instruments, understand the purposes of those instruments, and learn to select, administer, and interpret them as another source of information about students' reading and literacy needs.

Our hope is that this text provides a framework that will enable classroom teachers and reading/literacy specialists to make effective strategic and curricular decisions about the children who struggle with reading and literacy development. Reading and literacy difficulties may stem from a wide variety of social, emotional, physical, and cognitive factors. Today's schoolchildren reside in culturally and linguistically diverse households. In our experience, they respond well to caring, sensitive adjustments in curriculum that are tuned to meet their needs.

As a result of this diversity in our student population, approaches to assessment and instruction should be multidimensional. In this text, the assessment process reflects a child-centered philosophy in which we examine (1) what a child *can* do, (2) any special abilities that could be engaged to foster reading and literacy growth, and (3) the instructional objectives that will lead to that growth. Interviews, observational checklists, attitude inventories, planned observations, reflective teaching, and structured perusal of student work are advocated as valid instruments for assessing individual differences in reading and literacy development. Assessment issues are then placed in an instructional context that provides guidance to teachers and specialists who work with these varied students.

A THEORY OF READING AND READING DIFFICULTIES

Comprehending written text is the goal of reading. A reading difficulty is present when (1) comprehension is impeded because of inability to recognize and/or understand the meaning of printed words or sentences and longer discourse, (2) strategies for word recognition and comprehension are inefficient and inappropriate, or (3) the reader believes that saying words without understanding them is sufficient.

This textbook is based on the assumption that efficient reading involves word recognition and comprehension as well as fluency and reader self-monitoring. The teacher's task is to teach all aspects of the reading process, regularly monitor reading and literacy behavior, and actively assess growth. Adequate understanding of the complexities involved in the reading process and in how children learn to read is essential to the successful accomplishment of this challenging task. The reflective teacher must be aware of the factors that interfere with learning to read and be able to select and administer appropriate assessments to effectively teach students the strategies and techniques needed for effective reading.

Our ideas are based on a balanced, interactive, social constructivist theory of reading. This interactive theory provides for different ways of processing print and comprehending text. The theory is reader-centered, in that it allows for individual differences in readers' abilities to select and use cue systems. The reflective teacher using this theory recognizes and utilizes opportunities to constructively observe and analyze the cues readers use under different conditions. The interactional aspect of the theory implies that a relationship or action develops between and among reading and literacy variables: the reader, the text, and the instructional setting.

The social constructivist theory is the most useful theory for understanding reading difficulties and for planning effective, child-centered instructional strategies for struggling readers. This interactive theory best reflects our belief that there is no "right way" to read. We cannot assume that struggling readers approach or process print in the same manner as those who do not struggle. Nor can we assume that beginning readers use the same strategies as fluent reader.

FORMAT AND ORGANIZATION

As noted, we explore three types of children who struggle with reading and literacy: the Catch-On Reader, the Catch-Up Reader, and the Stalled Reader. We recognize that there are a wide variety of causal factors in reading and literacy dysfunction. We also recognize that the results of these dysfunctions are highly individual and varied. Yet research results suggest the presence of significant patterns among children experiencing difficulty in learning. The intent of our typology is to offer a balanced, comprehensible approach to understanding reading and literacy difficulties.

We provide a detailed examination of each learning type: Part One discusses the Catch-On Reader, Part Two the Catch-Up Reader, and Part Three the Stalled Reader. An appendix containing informal assessment instruments developed by the authors is also included.

Parts One, Two, and Three are organized in parallel formats. The first chapter in each part deals with the characteristics of the particular reader type. It includes background research on the etiology of the reading and literacy difficulties, suggestions for assessment, and general goals of instruction. A central focus of these initial chapters in each part is to provide case studies that contain practical examples. Readers might find it useful to read or skim all three introductory chapters as the first step in reading this book.

The next chapter in each part deals with instruction. Chapters discuss major instructional goals and methods for each type of reader. The final two chapters in each part provide instructional support for teachers. The first of these two chapters offers feedback and discussion of the case studies provided in the first chapter of the part. The second of these two chapters provides a review of the part, an annotated bibliography of key research on the type of learner, descriptions of important commercial materials and curricula designed to meet the needs of this type of learner, and descriptions of technology resources.

PART ONE

Catch-On Readers

CHAPTER 1

Who Are the Catch-On Readers in Your Classroom?

JOSHUA'S STORY

Joshua, a 5-year-old kindergartener, was referred to a university reading clinic by his mother. It was February of the school year, and Joshua's teacher had just reported to his parents that she was worried about their son's academic growth. He was not learning the skills associated with literacy. Joshua did not recall letter names or letter sounds that had been incorporated into lessons throughout the school year. He had not acquired a memory for predictable text, even though the teacher conducted daily shared reading lessons using big books. His handwriting samples revealed drawn forms that resembled letters but did not include the characteristics of well-constructed letters (see Figure 1.1).

Joshua's mother asked for early school intervention for him. His older brother, in third grade, had had similar problems in kindergarten. He had continued to have difficulty learning to read as a first grader and was classified as learning disabled at the end of second grade. As a student classified as learning disabled, he was eligible for resource room help.

FIGURE 1.1. *Joshua's handwriting.*

But even with that help, he had not progressed beyond the preprimer level (see Sidebar 1.1). Joshua's brother had developed a serious attitude problem towards reading. Joshua's mother hoped that she could prevent her younger son from having these problems by securing early intervention for him.

However, the school refused her request for help on the grounds that Joshua would have to be tested and classified before he could receive special services. Furthermore, school policy contended that Joshua was too young to be tested with the needed degree of validity and reliability. Frustrated, his mother then asked for help from the after-school reading program at the university reading clinic. She was rewarded with an open door.

The clinic's program began with an evaluation to determine why Joshua was having so much difficulty learning letter names and their sounds and recalling predictable text. Initial reading experiences at the clinic included having him read books at a very easy level, helping him learn to focus on the distinctive features of letters, and teaching him strategies for successful reading.

During the first three tutoring sessions, Joshua's mother stayed with him because he did not want her to leave. In fact, he spent part of the time on her lap. Although the parent's participation is not a common occurrence in the reading clinic, the staff believed that Joshua's mother would benefit from observing the strategies being taught and the interaction taking place between Joshua and his tutor. Soon Joshua was so involved in the lessons that he forgot his need for his mother's presence. Joshua's interactions with his mother and her comments to the tutor and clinic director suggested that, on the one hand, she was overprotective of both her sons, but on the other hand, she seldom made a decision without their permission.

Several conclusions became apparent from observing Joshua during the time he attended the reading clinic:

1. He was manipulative in his attempts to control the tutoring. For example, if the tutor decided to play a game with letters or words, Joshua would change the rules so

Sidebar 1.1. What Are Levels in Reading?

Teachers of reading have a variety of methods available with which to identify children's achievement levels. One such method is based on the traditional basal series, the commercially published reading texts that have served as the centerpiece of most schools' reading programs for well over a century. Although each series offered unique variations on the basic system, most were very similar. Today's basal reading series are usually more flexibly constructed than those used in the past, but the terminology referring to the traditional levels is still often used.

A primer, the first formal text used for the teaching of reading, is typically introduced to children in first grade. A child who is able to read materials at this level, with some teacher help, is said to be reading at the primer level. Stories using the vocabulary and sentence structure common to this level are said to be written at the primer level. The following sentences are typical of those found in a primer:

Look at the man.

The man is big.

Prior to primer instruction, in kindergarten and early first grade, children are introduced to reading in a basal series through easier books. Often these books are very short paperbacks that feature pictures providing most of the story content. A single word, or two or three, may appear on a page.

See. See.

See Daddy.

See Mommy.

See Mommy and Daddy.

As children in first grade advance beyond the basal level, they are given the first set of graded readers. The 1-1 reader represents early and mid-first-grade reading, and the 1-2 reader represents later first-grade reading. A child who is reading at the 1-2 level is successful in reading material similar to the following, with some teacher help:

We saw the ball.

It was red and blue.

Mother threw the ball.

The 2-1, 2-2, 3-1, and 3-2 basal readers are provided for second and third graders. From the fourth grade on, students receive only one text per year—the 4, 5, or 6 readers.

Levels of reading are sometimes determined in tenths. A 2.2 level, for example, would represent the reading level of the average second grader in the second month of the academic year, October. This usage is typical of standardized tests.

that he would not be responsible for recalling the letters and words. If the tutor selected several books from which he was to choose one to read, he would ask for one that was not available or one that was too difficult for him to read.

2. He had difficulty recalling information that was not meaningful to him.

3. He changed the words in predictable text to match his own language patterns. He did not see the need to try to match the author's language but strongly asserted his personal views of the print.

4. He focused on the pictures, not the print, during shared reading and when reading by himself.

Joshua's mother was convinced that he was learning disabled due to a cognitive processing impairment. However, the clinician's observations and examination of the data supplied by the parents and the school suggested that maturity was an important factor: Perhaps Joshua had not yet reached the level of maturity that would allow him easy recall of print, especially nonmeaningful print such as letter names. His reading and literacy behaviors resembled those of a younger child.

How would you teach Joshua? What can you suggest to his teachers?

KWESI'S STORY

Kwesi came into Mrs. Suarez's second-grade class in mid-March. According to his results on the Metropolitan Achievement Test (MAT) administered by the school in early September, he had begun second grade with a reading ability at the preprimer level. Kwesi's school was in a disadvantaged area of a large, urban Southwestern school district that was widely recognized as suffering from underachievement. Even so, Kwesi's reading was well below the average reading ability in his class.

Kwesi's district had recently instituted annual administration of the MAT as a means of closely monitoring student achievement. State legislators and the public exerted intense pressure on the district due to its low scores on the new state "high-stakes" testing program that involved periodic assessments over the school years, culminating in a high school test that all students had to pass in order to get a high school diploma. Kwesi's school was one of the lower scoring schools in the state on the fourth-grade administration of the state test.

Kwesi's reading ability had not improved to any discernible extent during the first 6 months of second grade. He often cried in the morning, complaining of headaches or stomachaches, before going to school. His mom had contacted the principal on three occasions to express her concern that Kwesi's attitude toward school was getting worse because of his poor performance, as he compared himself to the other students in his class. "The other kids laugh at me," he cried. "School is boring. My teacher is always mad at me."

The situation had boiled over in a tense conference held in February, with Kwesi's mom bringing in the pastor of her church to help her discuss the matter with the classroom teacher, guidance counselor, and principal. The anger and frustration toward the school on the mom's part was evident. She felt that her earlier expressions of concern had been ignored by the school. A generally trusting and friendly person who felt uncomfortable challenging authority figures, she was helped by her pastor to express herself when words failed her. At one or two points, tears came into her eyes as she described how Kwesi was responding emotionally to the difficulties in school.

The principal, who had visited enough classrooms in his school to have a sense of what might be part of the problem, proposed a plan to resolve the tension. First, he acknowledged that his own conflicted role had contributed to the problem. Teachers throughout the school had been instructed to adapt their classroom instruction to incorporate spending large amounts of time preparing their students for the MAT. In Kwesi's class, as in the others, time that was once spent on creative activities that fostered students' self-expression and involvement with children's literature was now spent on vocabulary drills and comprehension exercises similar to those that would appear on the MAT.

The principal had played the central role in redirecting instructional focus toward improving reading scores on standardized tests. He certainly recognized the downside of such instruction, but there had been little choice on the matter: These new policies had been instituted by the state in an effort to improve instruction for all students (see Sidebar 1.2). Schools that failed to improve their scores would face the dire possibility of administrational takeover by state authorities.

A clear example of the downside of state policies was Kwesi's teacher's approach, which included little or no effort to adjust instruction to a struggling student's reading level. Kwesi needed instruction and reinforcement on basic sight words and on the structure of words; instead he was confronted by drills that were far too hard for him—drills based on the difficulty level of materials the class would encounter on the standardized test.

"Enough is enough," the principal said to himself, and he agreed to a rare mid-year transfer of Kwesi to a teacher who better understood principles of teaching diverse students. He met with Mrs. Suarez to explain the situation, and she agreed to bring Kwesi into her classroom and teach him reading with a small group of her students who also experienced reading difficulties, though none as severely as Kwesi. This group focused on language experience activities for their instruction, while the rest of the class worked out of a basal reader and did the school's standardized test practice exercises. In addition, the principal arranged for the school's reading specialist to conduct assessments of Kwesi's reading and literacy abilities.

We continue our analysis of Kwesi's experience in Chapter 6.

CHARACTERISTICS OF THE CATCH-ON READER

The Catch-On Reader is one who remains at the emergent level of literacy in spite of consistent instruction and repeated opportunities to engage in literacy activities. This reader might be described as one who is not aware of print activities, does not fully participate in the literacy experiences that are provided, and does not understand the literacy processes in which readers must engage.

Many Catch-On Readers have not yet developed an awareness of the basic functions of print and textual materials, often called "concepts about print," or CAP, skills, that are necessary for reading. Among the basic CAP prerequisites to acquiring literacy are letter and number identification, as well as awareness that:

Different spoken words look different in print.
Print is read from left to right and top to bottom.
Print conveys a message.
Words are separated by spaces.
Words are composed of letters that are often similar in form.
Words are composed of sounds that are often similar.

Sidebar 1.2. What Is High-Stakes Testing?

High-stakes tests have become a part of most teachers' and students' lives in the past decade. Teachers and schools are expected to demonstrate student achievement in a variety of academic areas, including reading and writing.

High-stakes tests are designed to provide information that will be used to make key decisions about schools, teachers, or students. For example, common areas in which test results have significant bearing include:

- Promotion and retention of students
- Improvement of instruction
- State takeover of failing schools
- Guidance of students into academic, general, or remedial tracks

Guthrie (2002) surveyed research on reading tests and concluded that actual reading ability accounts for about 40% of a child's test score. Content knowledge accounts for 20% and motivation for 15%. Intrinsic test factors—the format of the test and the degree of statistical measurement error—account for another 25%.

To the dismay of many teachers who would like greater control over their own curriculum, test preparation has become an important part of reading and literacy instruction. One key component of preparing struggling readers for high-stakes tests is obviously to help them improve their overall reading ability. Teachers can focus specifically on strategies that will help students deal with test questions. Those questions often emphasize plot, character, and other story grammar elements (see Chapter 11). Tests of writing often use standard questions about describing a major character or contrasting two points of view.

In addition, time spent familiarizing students with the format of the test is helpful. If speed in answering questions is a test component, giving students guided practice will help then develop the focus to work more rapidly. An important factor in test taking is motivation. Teachers can mirror the needed motivation by preparing students and administering the test enthusiastically; students should be informed of the test's importance but encouraged to be confident and secure at the same time.

Many teachers are justifiably concerned that focusing on the needs dictated by high-stakes tests may impoverish the reading and language arts curriculum. Schools may require excessive amounts of practice testing to prepare students for the test format. In addition, the curriculum may suffer in terms of creativity and depth if teachers and schools allow these tests too much influence.

(See a more detailed list in the Print Awareness Checklist in the appendix, and principles for instruction with methodologies in Chapter 2.)

The Catch-On Reader has difficulty learning letters and sounds, as well as difficulty identifying letter–sound correspondences. Discriminating similar letters, such as r-h, f-t, b-d, and q-p, and sounds, such as /b/ and /p/, /v/ and /f/, /j/ and /dr/, is another common problem. Applying letter and sound cues to word identification also can be challenging for this reader.

Typically, the Catch-On Reader learns a few basic sight words but does not transfer common elements in these words to learning new words. This student often has difficulty remembering words from one day to the next and recalling sight words when they are presented in a setting different from the one in which they were learned. For example, the student might recognize the word *giant* in *The Hungry Giant* but fail to recognize the same word when he/she reads *Jack and the Beanstalk*.

Children entering school obviously possess differing levels of growth and development. Children have unique patterns of development, just as they are differentially exposed to opportunities for acquiring literacy. Some, for example, excel in motor development, others in language development, and others in social interaction of a nonverbal nature. Some children are anxious to engage in literacy activities, whereas others prefer large motor activities such as block building, gymnastics, or play that involves trucks or dolls.

The wide range of development among children entering school suggests that inevitably, some will be introduced to formal literacy activities before their physical and cognitive abilities are well developed. These students might not "catch on" to the processes involved in reading and writing. Inflexible teaching assumptions about children's normal growth and development in literacy can limit the child's ability to profit from instruction.

REASONS FOR DIFFICULTY

It is unusual that a single factor is powerful enough, in and of itself, to bring about the achievement failures typical of those experienced by Catch-On Readers. Most often, a teacher who is interested in finding out causes of the difficulty will be able to spot multiple factors that are sometimes obvious and sometimes elusive. In some cases these factors constitute an ongoing set of challenges to be overcome; in other cases the factors converged at one point in the past to present difficulties that the child has not been able to overcome, even when the factors themselves are no longer an issue in his/her life.

In the education of reading specialists or special education teachers, etiology (a study of the cause of difficulties) is often a focus. Learning about the etiology of reading and literacy problems can be valuable. For example, learning that maturational or developmental delays (see below) can create reading difficulties leads teachers to the understanding that their classroom instruction must be flexible. Struggling children who fail to learn key concepts about literacy because of their maturational delay, can assimilate the unlearned material—provided a teacher supplies it—once they have sufficiently matured.

In this text, we focus on instruction rather than on detailed investigations of causation. In general, effective instruction contains the same elements for all Catch-On Readers, no matter what the etiology of their struggles. As stated earlier, however, an awareness of common sources of difficulty, such as those summarized below, is important and can inform instruction.

Maturational or Developmental Delay

A specific delay in visual, auditory, neurological, social–emotional, or cognitive development can interfere with a child's literacy acquisition. Rate of development varies widely among young children. The Checklist for Oral Language Assessment (see Appendix) can help teachers structure their observations of oral language development, for example. Usually these delays are not serious, and by the end of kindergarten or first grade, the child has caught up to his/her peers. With Catch-On Readers, however, the delays can play a more critical role.

Phonological Problems

According to Keith Stanovich's Matthew effect model (Stanovich, 1988, 2000), lack of phonological awareness (i.e., awareness of the sounds that make up words) is at the heart of young children's reading difficulties. This model posits that poor phonological awareness leads to failed development of decoding abilities. Young children facing such problems fall further and further behind their peers as the years progress. Children with effective decoding ability, on the other hand, have a better attitude toward reading, read more, and, as a result, improve in their ability. Stanovich's emphasis on decoding was reinforced by the 1990 publication of Adams's highly influential research review *Beginning to Read*, as well as by a substantial body of research on phonological processing (Snider, 1995; Torgesen & Mathes, 2000; Yopp & Yopp, 2000). The emphasis on decoding and phonological awareness in recent years has been so great that Richgels has called this "the Age of Phonemic Awareness" (2001).

Frustration

Attempting to engage a child in formal literacy instruction at too early an age can instill a sense of frustration. Students may learn not to take risks or to rely on only one strategy for word identification or comprehension.

Inadequate Instruction

Misunderstandings about the strategies and processes involved in reading and writing can develop from inadequate instruction. Developing literacy and literate behavior in the school setting requires that teachers carefully and flexibly consider the needs of their students when choosing teaching strategies and textual material.

Home and Preschool Experiences

Students' ability to profit from formal schooling can be affected by their home environment and early school experiences, which create variability in their reading acquisition and influence their school performance (Ehri, 1991; Meyer & Wardhop, 1994). Literacy difficulties are more likely to occur when children have had little exposure to literacy activities prior to school. Early literacy development is often exhibited in a rudimentary fashion as children learn to associate common commercial symbols with meaning. A Pepsi logo, for example, can represent soda in general, cola in particular, or the word *Pepsi* itself. The animated Kool Aid pitcher comes to represent a juice drink or the words *Kool Aid*. Evaluation of this early ability to associate logos with words and meaning can be carried out using a teacher-made assessment device. In the Lipa Logo Test, a teacher creates a series of flashcards, each of which has a commercial logo on it. The student is then shown the flashcards and is asked what each one means. (See Appendix for the Lipa Logo Test—Scoring Guide.) Such a device, which can be modified to contain currently or locally popular logos, can provide insight into the child's meaning making and understanding of symbols.

Factors Related to Disadvantage

Many of the factors discussed here are closely related. For example, factors related to social and economic disadvantage may well affect the home and preschool experiences of children

(Neuman & Roskos, 1993). Children attending schools burdened by lack of finances may receive inadequate instruction (Duke, 2000). Physical and health problems may affect children from poor families more than those from the middle class. Thus those students from poor urban and rural areas have a higher risk of reading failure (Currie, 2000; Snow, Burns, & Griffin, 1998).

Discourse Styles

The factor of discourse styles has received considerable attention recently from researchers investigating factors that might explain why some groups of students do much worse in schools than others. It may be that the interactions between students and teachers (often called "discourse styles" or "literacies" by researchers) create barriers to learning. Effective teachers strengthen their instruction by taking seriously their students' speech patterns and avoid giving subtle cues that certain styles of speaking and interaction are less valid than others (Foster & Peele, 2001). They work to overcome the stereotypical representations of minorities that, even in the early grades, begin to diminish some students' access to opportunities and life choices (Grant, 2001).

Other Difficulties

Orthographic problems (Leslie & Thimke, 1986), verbal deficits (Vellutino, 1977; Vellutino & Scanlon, 1982), lack of adequate print exposure (Cunningham & Stanovich, 1991), and an underdeveloped oral vocabulary (Carver, 1994, 2000) are additional factors associated with difficulties in early reading.

INSTRUCTIONAL GOALS

We recommend direct teaching (National Reading Panel, 2000) within meaningful contexts of authentic reading and writing to help Catch-On Readers acquire literacy. This instruction should be designed to accomplish the following:

1. Provide students with a schema (or set) for learning.
2. Model the strategies to be learned.
3. Involve the students in the lesson by having them interact and participate in the activities with the teacher.
4. Provide practice for the intended learning.

These teaching goals are especially important for Catch-On Readers because their literacy difficulties are often related, at least in part, to their lack of awareness about the purpose and process of reading. That is, without explicit and direct teaching, they might not be aware of what they are supposed to learn, how they are supposed to interact with text and teacher in the lesson, and what they are supposed to do when working independently (Cunningham & Allington, 1999). Many of these children do not know how to do literacy tasks or why they *should* be doing them in the first place.

Observing students' reactions to direct instructional strategies provides a yardstick for determining the effectiveness of such teaching methods. Strategies that are very effective with one student may be ineffective with another, according to their abilities and predispositions to learning certain tasks. Likewise, some teachers function better with one strategy and less well with another. Furthermore, the teacher's unique presentation style as well as his/her interaction with the student and the materials also affect the success of the strategy.

The selection of materials to be used with Catch-On Readers should carefully ensure successful literacy experiences for the children. Print size should be large for easy identification of letters and words. Words should be spaced far enough apart so that children can easily see the word boundaries (where one word ends and another begins). Pictures enrich stories and provide visual images that help students understand the content and focus on word identification instead of comprehension difficulties.

READING RECOVERY
AND EARLY INTERVENTION APPROACHES

Until recently, children with emergent literacy difficulties often received little or no help beyond what the classroom teacher could provide. Few schools could afford programs to provide extra instruction to Catch-On Readers. Like Joshua, they were left to fend for themselves until the second or third grade, when they might receive a special education classification or be placed in a remedial reading program.

In the early 1990s, a program called Reading Recovery, developed in New Zealand schools by Marie Clay (1985), began to garner a great deal of attention in the United States. Since that time, a variety of similar programs, called "early literacy intervention programs," have been introduced (see Chapter 7 for sources of additional information on Reading Recovery and similar programs).

Reading Recovery is a tutorial program for first-grade children who are identified as being at high risk for failure in learning to read. The program involves a balanced immersion in reading and writing experiences, in which whole text is used as reading material and accompanied by strategy instruction.

Clay observed good readers' behavior and described the strategies they used to read: operating on print (i.e., understanding and using print conventions), self-monitoring, cross-checking, searching for cues, and self-correction. She hypothesized that poor readers do not use these strategies and therefore need to receive instruction *while* they are reading and writing. The goal of the early literacy intervention teacher is to guide children in the simultaneous use of several strategies during reading.

Reading Recovery is cost-intensive; the program provides 30 minutes of daily tutorial instruction and extends over a 20-week period. Other intervention programs, striving to provide instruction to more students with the resources available, often use small groups or less frequent sessions. The goal is to enable each child to read at the first-grade reading level and to function well in regular classroom instruction. The daily lesson is structured in two parts (Clay, 1985):

1. *Shared book experiences,* during which children read familiar stories aloud and then are introduced to a new story. The teacher makes a running record—a simple recording of oral reading quality—each day to monitor progress (see the Running Record Summary Sheet in the appendix).
2. *Strategy activities,* including phonemic awareness, letter and word identification, and writing activities.

Emergent literacy intervention lessons all incorporate this framework and pattern, yet within each similar pattern is the unique interaction of child and teacher as they engage in reading and writing activities. For example, Reading Recovery children often read different books. Book selection is determined by the student's reading ability when he/she starts the program and as he/she makes progress through the program. Although the teacher does have a lesson plan, he/she also has to be a keen observer during the lesson, seizing opportunities to praise the child for attempting to use strategies and guiding the child in using each particular strategy.

Reading Recovery lessons are difficult to describe because the rich interaction between teacher and child changes with each lesson and with each child. Clay has written that teaching "can be likened to a conversation in which you listen to the speaker carefully before you reply" (1985, p. 6). It is this attitude of careful listening and observation that makes the difference in any emergent literacy instruction. An astute teacher, well trained in working with young children, learns to observe and interpret children's reading behaviors so that they can be affirmed and utilized in a positive way.

Data from Reading Recovery procedures have shown that children enrolled in this program with a well-trained teacher make significant gains. These gains appear to be maintained at least through the third grade (Pinnell, 1989), though other researchers question the long-term effects of early intervention (Hiebert, 1994; Shanahan & Barr, 1995). Some teachers suggest that follow-up programs be instituted to maintain the gains achieved (MacKenzie, 2001). The effectiveness of Reading Recovery, as it is presently designed, was demonstrated by Pinnell, Lyons, Deford, Bryk, and Seltzer (1994) in a study that included several abbreviated versions of Reading Recovery and a one-to-one skills practice model. The authors concluded that the essential components of Reading Recovery included tutorial instruction, the Reading Recovery lesson framework, and the Reading Recovery staff development model. They described this staff development model as one that provides both a network for teachers to continue their learning and a link between the school and teacher education experts in the university.

SUMMARY

Catch-On Readers function at the emergent level of literacy despite consistent instruction and rich opportunities to engage in reading and writing. They do not understand the foundational principles involved in literacy, including basic print concepts, letter-sound relationships, and basic sight words. Their difficulties may stem from any of a wide range of challenges, including maturational or developmental delays, lack of phonological awareness, inadequate instruction, effects of the home environment or early schooling, factors related to economic disadvantage, or a mismatch of discourse styles between home and school. Instruction for Catch-On Readers involves a balance between direct instruction and authentic reading and writing experiences within the context of individualized attention. Early intervention approaches based on Reading Recovery principles, for example, include both strategy instruction and reading of simple predictable books.

Chapters 2 through 5 provide details on key components of instruction for Catch-On Readers: basic print concepts, word recognition instruction, language experience, and integrated reading and writing.

CHAPTER 2

Helping Catch-On Readers with Basic Print Concepts

As young children observe literacy activities modeled in the world around them, they gradually develop an awareness of the characteristics of written language. This print awareness includes the recognition of such basic print concepts as print/speech mapping, print direction, and the understanding that print carries a message. It has long been known that children who have a more sophisticated understanding of these concepts are more successful in early reading, but the recent popularity of early intervention approaches has renewed teachers' awareness of their importance.

The Print Awareness Checklist in the appendix provides a comprehensive list of print conventions that are important for the emergent reader. Terms such as "literacy conventions," "print conventions," and "print concepts" are used to describe the aspects of printed text that young children gradually come to recognize. Many teachers use the term "concepts about print," or "CAP skills," used by Marie Clay in her writings on the Reading Recovery program (1993).

Children coming into kindergarten or first grade with insufficiently developed print concepts are often from disadvantaged homes. Researchers have paid some attention to possible factors, outside the control of schools, in creating this problem. Neuman and Celano (2001), for example, compared the amount of exposure to printed materials available to children from low-income and middle-income communities. They found that children in the low-income communities had fewer opportunities to be exposed to all forms of print, including signs, labels, periodicals, and books. Concern also has been raised about differences in classroom environments across socioeconomic levels. Duke (2000) compared low and high socioeconomic status first-grade classrooms. She found that these schools spent the same amount of time on print-based and writing activities, but that the disadvantaged classrooms provided:

Fewer printed materials on the walls
Fewer books and magazines in the classroom library
Fewer teacher references to environmental print
Fewer opportunities to use the library
A smaller amount of time dealing with extended forms of text, such as whole stories
Fewer opportunities to choose books or to choose topics for writing
More time in copying, taking dictation, and completing worksheets

In the light of these findings, teachers may need to consider the richness of the classroom literacy experience as a vehicle for helping children *avoid* becoming Catch-On Readers.

PRINT/SPEECH MAPPING AND PHONEMIC AWARENESS

Understanding that there is a correspondence between spoken words and printed words is called speech-to-print mapping. Young children, not realizing that this correspondence exists, learn to say common phrases as if they were one word, as in

Peanutbutterandjellysandwich

or

IpledgeallegiancetotheflagoftheUnitedStatesofAmerica.

Most children acquire the speech/print match as parents or teachers point to words while reading. Gradually, children assimilate the concepts that words are composed of letters and that sentences are composed of words. However, some Catch-On Readers need more than the usual amount of exposure to word boundaries in written language. This kind of modeling can be done by the teacher taking care to point to each printed word as it is said during oral reading, rather than sliding a finger or pointer across the line, as is commonly done. This pointing is called "tracking."

In working with Catch-On Readers who do not yet recognize print conventions, teachers can employ the following suggestions for improving the children's speech-to-print concepts.

Tracking

Use a big book (i.e., a book printed in a large format so that all children in the class can see the words as you read) or a book with large print and wide spaces between words. If necessary, you might even use word-processing software to type out a story in large print with extra spaces between words. Read a sentence or two to the student while you point to the words you are reading. Then ask the student to point to the words as you read them. Read slowly so that the student can follow your voice as well as the print. Additional support can be offered by guiding the student's hand under each word as it is said. Remind the student to look at the print as each word is spoken.

Highlighting

If the student does not respond to simple tracking practice, take a colored highlighter and mark over each of the words in the first sentence as you read, leaving sufficient white space between words. Then go back to the beginning of the sentence to continue the exercise of pointing to words as they are read aloud.

Boundary Marking

In some cases, highlighting the words does not adequately demonstrate the concept of word boundaries. If the student requires additional support, the spaces between each word can be marked as another means of showing where one word ends and the other begins (see Figure 2.1).

PRINT DIRECTION

Another important basic print concept involves directionality. English print is read from top to bottom and left to right, with a return sweep at the end of each line. Children who do not acquire this concept from observing others reading to them need more direct modeling. First, in a teaching session, model the process during reading by tracking. Next, ask the students to move their hands under the print as you read. Finally, ask the students to read the sentences, pointing to each word, and following the left-to-right progression and return sweep.

You also can use a directional line under the text (see Figure 2.2). Students practice tracing the line with a finger to the arrowhead as a first step. Then you read the print while tracing the line to the arrowhead. Finally, the students read the print, following the line with a finger to the arrowhead.

A diagnostic teaching exercise in which students are given several sentences and asked to highlight or underline each word, or mark between each word, can identify those who have not developed the concept of word boundaries or print directionality. Circulate among the students as they work, observing them and asking them to mark the words or word boundaries as you read them and to demonstrate the return sweep.

|The| boys| wanted| to |play| baseball| in| the| lot.|

FIGURE 2.1. *Marking the spaces between words in a sentence.*

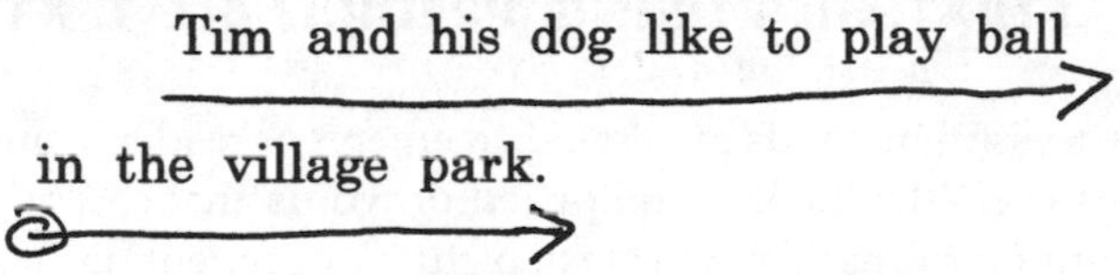

Tim and his dog like to play ball

in the village park.

FIGURE 2.2. *Modeling print direction.*

THE MESSAGE CONTAINED IN PRINT

Understanding that print contains a message is a third basic concept necessary for literacy acquisition—one that is often unclear even to first graders. Understanding that the words within sentence units "say" what the author intends is basic to understanding the processes of reading and writing. Addressing the issue "Why do some students fail to learn to read?" Cambourne (2001) suggested that "they get faulty demonstrations of how to read or write" (p. 784) as his number one reason. One example he provided was the use of nonsense text in instructional materials that use decodable text—that is, text that is composed mostly of phonic elements that students have already learned. Students might learn to focus solely on the graphic clues in the text, disregarding meaning, which gives them an incorrect sense as to what reading is all about. For example:

He ran.

He ran to the man.

Nan ran.

Nan ran to the man.

Nan ran to the tan man.

A similar problem, having to do with the message contained in the print, might very well occur in approaches that use whole language methods with authentic text. On occasion, some children may be misled by the storybook reading practice of looking at and discussing the story's pictures in a prereading activity. They may conclude that the pictures represent events in stories and fail to realize that the print is the message that is being read.

If a Catch-On Reader consistently "reads" pictures, cover them prior to reading a story. Then, while reading, ask the child to visualize the scenes and retell the story. Reread parts of the story if the student needs help in recalling details or sequencing. Discuss the story and ask the student to draw a picture about it. Finally, show the student the illustrated pictures of the story. Compare the illustrator's version with the student's version. Discuss how the two pictures are alike and different and which picture best represents the information in the text. Be sure the story is short and does not contain too many details or complex sequencing.

STRATEGIES USING PREDICTABLE TEXT

One of the most successful methods of helping an emergent reader acquire literacy is that of reading predictable text—that is, text comprised of words that can be predicted based on prior knowledge, prior information in the text, pictures, or repetition. Text for younger readers is usually more predictable. As readers' literacy improves, the texts gradually incorporate more and more nonpredictable elements.

Predictable text typically contains a series of lines and phrases that are repeated; some texts also use rhyme to enhance predictability. Predictable text makes reading easy when two conditions are present: (1) the student's language base is sufficiently developed to predict upcoming words, and (2) the student's memory can support the recall of repetitive phrases.

Use of predictable text is an excellent way to help emerging readers feel and act like readers. Catch-On Readers, however, will require more direct modeling of print concepts than the normally developing readers. Some Catch-On Readers will need direct instruction to accomplish the transition from an early understanding that reading is a matter of memorizing stories or making guesses about predictable text (sometimes called "pseudo-reading") to the point of understanding that reading is a multifaceted process that involves word recognition and comprehension.

Strategies that use predictable text include:

- Choral reading
- Assisted reading
- Shared reading

Choral Reading

Choral reading is a strategy in which the teacher models how to read a selection with a group of students. In this nonthreatening means of engaging in reading, students can participate in the comforting context of a strong support group and do not need to read every word accurately. Songs, nursery rhymes, and poems are often chosen for choral reading because of students' familiarity with these formats. Nursery rhymes and songs such as "Baa, Baa, Black Sheep," "Row, Row, Row Your Boat," and "Lazy Mary" can be printed on chart paper or displayed on an overhead projector so that all the students can see the print as they participate in reading aloud.

In choral reading, the teacher first reads the selection while tracking each word. Next, both teacher and students join in the reading. Participation in the reading will vary, since not all of the students will know all of the words. As the students become more familiar with the selection, increased participation can be expected.

Choral reading also can serve as a vehicle for the teacher to help students develop intonation and dramatic interpretation. Once sufficiently rehearsed, choral readings are often presented to an audience, such as another class or during parent visits to the classroom. Choral reading performances are one way for students to feel successful about reading aloud without the stress of soloing.

In addition, choral reading selections can be used to help children identify specific words. For example, in "Row, Row, Row Your Boat," the teacher might ask one student to point to the word *boat* on the chart. Another child can be asked to find two words that are the same, or to find and name the word that starts with the letter *b*. These activities help students focus on the specific features of words and provide practice in recognizing words.

Assisted Reading

Hoskisson (1979) described assisted reading as a one-to-one teaching situation similar to the supportive environment that parents offer their children when they read to and with them. Assisted Reading is a classroom version of a parent's lap reading, where the parent provides a warm, supportive reading environment as the child sits on his/her lap during story reading. Although teachers usually do not hold children on their laps, a warm, comfortable environment can be provided within the classroom. The teacher offers support, guidance, and modeling to the child engaged in the reading task, thereby helping him/her, through unobtrusive modeling, to understand what one does when one reads.

Reading environmental print, telling the child the captioned words on television screens or under pictures, stopping the reading of a story at a place in which the child can predict upcoming words—all are forms of assisted reading. Modeling comprehension strategies through questioning and predicting what will happen in the story are also part of assisted reading. This one-to-one interaction can be a very supportive and rewarding experience for Catch-On Readers.

Shared Reading

Don Holdaway (1979) introduced the "big book" to classroom teachers around the world and popularized this reading experience. Although not originally developed specifically for struggling readers, the method of shared reading has proved to be very effective with all types of emergent readers. As is the case with assisted reading, Holdaway's "shared book experience" simulates the experiences that young children have at home as their parents read to them and interact with them about the stories.

Holdaway used big books that contain large print so all children in the classroom could see. Such books are available from many publishers, or teachers can make their own using large sheets of heavy-duty paper. Seeing the print promotes better participation in the reading lesson; children are not only memorizing repeated text but are also (1) visually following the left–right progression of print, (2) identifying the special features of words within a story, and (3) noting the word boundaries of individual words as the teacher points to them.

Shared reading lessons involve children in orally rereading one or more familiar stories and the repeated reading of a "new" story until it becomes familiar. Each lesson begins with students rereading aloud one or more familiar stories. Then the teacher introduces a new story by reading and discussing it. This story is reread several times; students read predictable sections right from the start and become increasingly active in the reading. After several days of shared book experiences with the new story, students are able to read it independently and fluently.

Holdaway proposed a five-step process for the shared book experience.

1. *Discovery.* Point to each word as you read the book aloud to your students.
2. *Exploration.* Students participate in repeated readings of the book. One student

points to the words during reading. Others predict, ask questions, and request that parts of the book be reread.

3. *Independent experience expression*. Students store in memory a clear model of the language structure of the book. The students predict words and phrases and carry out self-correction of mistakes.

4. *New story*. Students increasingly participate in reading new books.

5. *Independent practice*. Students work alone or in small groups independently of the teacher. They reread their new books as well as favorite books that were introduced in earlier lessons.

Holdaway's (1979) technique for using shared book experiences can be modified to teach word recognition more directly to Catch-On Readers. This modification is intended for tutorial or small group instruction;

1. Select a book that has a highly repetitive pattern for high predictability.

2. Read the story to the student; then read the story *with* the student. In both cases, point to words as they are read.

3. Select one or two words in the story that the student wants to learn.

4. Reread the story, stopping at the targeted word(s) so that the student can supply it.

5. Make a T-scope type mask* to fit the size of the words in the story you are reading. Reread the text. Move the mask across the page as you and the student read. Stop at the targeted word. Let the student supply the word.

6. Write the student's word on an index card. Turn to the beginning of the story. Ask the student to find the word that looks just like the targeted word. Do this throughout the story.

7. Reread the text. Using the T-scope mask, let the student supply the targeted word to the text. Again, ask the student to match the targeted word to the word in the text.

8. Place the word card in a word box (a collection of word cards). Review the story by discussing or rereading. Review words by daily practice.

9. Repeat the above steps by using the same story and selecting a new targeted word.

Holdaway (1979) recommended several reinforcement activities to help students develop their sight-word knowledge:

1. Tape-record the story so that the child can listen to it and read along during independent reading.

2. Dramatize the story; make puppets and act out the story.

3. Ask the student to draw pictures of his/her favorite parts of the story; be sure to label the pictures and read the labels with the student.

---

*This mask is a simple device made of two pieces of cardboard fit together in a T-shape. The bottom piece serves as a handle. The horizontal top piece has a rectangular hole that is the size of a typical printed word in the story. The child can see the word through the rectangular hole when the mask is placed on top of the text, but other words are concealed.

EARLY INTERVENTION APPROACHES

Marie Clay's Reading Recovery program (1993) was designed for use in schools that provide whole language emphases on authentic reading and writing experiences. First graders experiencing difficulties in acquiring literacy would receive intensive tutorial instruction in Reading Recovery. In the United States, Clay's program catalyzed a rethinking of school policies, in which almost all funds for struggling readers were devoted to instruction of older elementary children in remedial reading settings. In the mid-1990s, many schools began to shift funds into newly established early intervention programs that provided instruction to young children, though they may have used very different approaches to instruction than Reading Recovery (Hiebert & Taylor, 2000).

Clay (1993) took the position that most children would learn their basic print concepts naturally, a viewpoint common to whole language teachers:

> In learning to read the child making normal progress picks up and organizes for himself a wealth of detailed information about letters, print, words and reading with a spontaneity that leads teachers to believe that many things do not have to be taught. (p. 9)

Clay warned strongly against overuse of what she called "teaching for detail"—an overemphasis on print concepts or other early reading skills outside of the context of real reading and writing. She allowed for brief excursions into skills teaching but emphasized that it should be a brief "detour from a program whose main focus is reading books and writing stories" (p. 10).

As a result, the bulk of any given Reading Recovery lesson was devoted to shared reading and to writing activities, including the language experience approach (see Chapter 4). However, teachers were able to use a wide variety of activities to develop basic print concepts, as necessary, with individual children. For directional difficulties, for example, Clay suggested use of a green "Go" sticker placed at the part of the page where the student was to start reading. A colored marker could be used to draw a vertical line down the left margin to assist in orientation. For speech-to-print mapping and recognition of word boundaries, she suggested having the child use a long pointer for tracking, because the greater length would require more effort to control movement. She also used a two-finger framing technique, in which the child places one finger to the left and one to the right of each word encountered.

SUMMARY

Achievement delays experienced by Catch-On Readers often stem from a lack of understanding of the basic functions of print language and the basic print concepts such as an understanding that print conveys a message, of print direction, and of print/speech mapping. Teachers convey these concepts to students in classroom environments that provide many rich experiences with reading and writing. Teaching strategies can include use of predictable text, repeated choral readings, assisted reading, and shared reading. Teachers should keep in mind that the language experience activities in Chapter 4 and the integrated reading–writing strategies in Chapter 5 can be very useful alternatives in helping students acquire basic literacy.

As students engage in the experiences necessary to understand the function of print, they can begin to learn word recognition, the focus of our next chapter, Chapter 3. Until Catch-On Readers understand these functions, however, they will have great difficulty acquiring a flexible, effective repertoire of word-recognition strategies.

CHAPTER 3

Helping Catch-On Readers
in Word Recognition

While debates rage over the most appropriate methods of teaching children beginning reading, there is no debate over the importance of fluent word recognition nor of the key role of repeated, engaged exposures to words in developing that fluency. Judging from the heated debates among advocates of whole language, traditional phonics approaches, other approaches to decoding, and balanced instruction, there is a wide variety of methods that can be effective. The key for all emergent readers, Catch-On Readers included, is that they experience motivation and success in reading achievement, through engagement with words, that is repeated often enough to yield an ability to recognize those words when encountered in text. Adams (1990), in her extensive review of methods used to teach beginning reading, concluded that "the most critical factor in fluent reading is the ability to recognize letters, spelling patterns, and whole words effortlessly, automatically, and visually" (p. 54).

Repetition has long been known to play a key role in the development of word recognition. Edmund Burke Huey (1908/1968), one of the foremost early psychologists who studied reading, wrote:

> Repetition progressively frees the mind from attention to details, makes facile the total act, shortens the time, and reduces the extent to which consciousness must concern itself with the process. (p. 104)

Yet repetition for the Catch-Up Reader need not consist solely of the all-too-frequent drudgery of worksheets and drills. Engaged exposure to words during real reading can be effective, as long as those words occur frequently and in close temporal proximity so that they can be learned. Even drills, which offer the advantage of repeated exposures in a short period of time, can be enhanced by presentation in game-like computer formats.

DEVELOPING AN EARLY SIGHT-WORD VOCABULARY

A sight-word vocabulary—a set of words that can be recognized instantly—is necessary for fluent reading, given that words need to be recognized both quickly and accurately. Beginning readers' sight-word vocabularies include words that are commonly seen in print. High-frequency words include *go, come, up, down, what, they,* and so forth. Many of these words are irregular in spelling and cannot be readily analyzed either phonetically or structurally. They are best learned as whole words (see Sidebar 3.1).

Catch-On Readers often have difficulty developing an automatic sight-word vocabulary—too often, a word learned one day is forgotten the next day, and a word that is read in one selection is not recalled in another. Helping young children establish a base of sight words that is recalled in any setting often demands novel approaches to teaching, in which the children are given many opportunities to see the same word and learn its characteristics.

Organic Reading

One approach to developing a sight-word vocabulary has its roots in Sylvia Ashton-Warner's "organic reading" (1963). Warner taught Maori children in New Zealand to read by selecting words they wanted to learn. These chosen words were used in writing activities and other practice exercises. Gradually, children moved into what Warner called "transitional reading," reading another author's text. The key to organic reading is the selection of words by the children themselves—an act that provides both motivation and context for learning.

David, a second grader, used invented spelling to create a list of words, shown in Figure 3.1, that he wants to learn to recognize and use in writing. These words reflect his interests in armies (the first word on the list), sports and the local professional soccer team, spaceships, animals, and pioneers such as Davy Crockett; the words will evoke a high level of motivation and will also be useful in his journaling, since on many days he writes about such favorite topics.

Key Vocabulary

Jeannette Veatch (Veatch, Sawichi, Elliott, Barnette, & Blakey, 1973) modified Ashton-Warner's (1963) organic reading approach by developing an instructional sequence for learning self-selected words. The following five steps comprise the basics of Veatch's key vocabulary approach:

1. Elicit a key word from a student by asking: "What is the best word you can think of?"; ". . . the scariest word you can think of?"; ". . . the nicest word?"
2. The student whispers a word into the teacher's ear and then watches while the teacher prints the word on paper.

Sidebar 3.1. Word Recognition or Word Identification?

What is the difference between the terms *word recognition* and *word identification?*

Whereas in the past some educators have distinguished between the two terms (*word identification* referred to identifying words that were unknown, and *word recognition* referred to recognizing words to which readers had already been exposed), today they are used as synonyms (Harris & Hodges, 1995). Both *word recognition* and *word identification* refer to the processes involved in pronouncing an unknown word as well as identifying its meaning, to some degree. Word-identification abilities include sight-word reading, phonic analysis, structural analysis (use of word parts), and awareness of context clues.

Word discrimination, on the other hand, has a singular definition: It involves the processes used in noting the differences between two or more words, usually in print. (*Auditory discrimination* is the term usually used to refer to noting differences between spoken words.) For beginning readers, for example, discriminating between *w* words (such as *were, where, when, was, went*) and *th* words (such as *the, then, their, there, than*) presents a significant challenge.

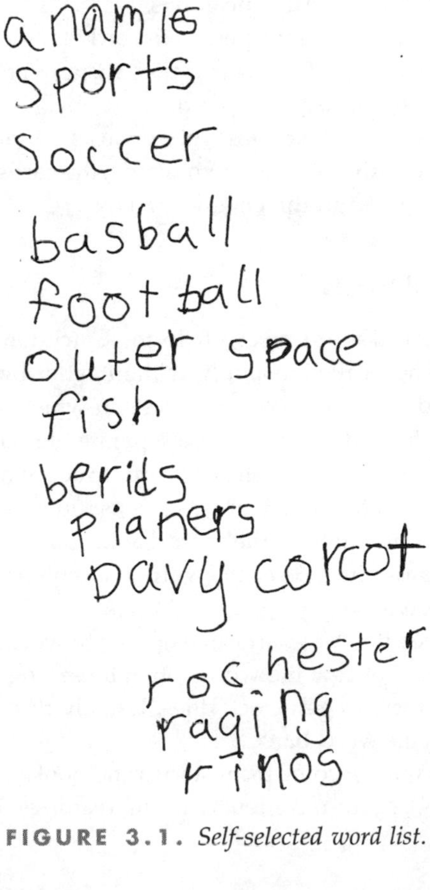

FIGURE 3.1. *Self-selected word list.*

3. The student traces over the word.
4. The student carries out an activity with the word. Veatch recommended that the student write the word, draw a picture of it, or copy it on the chalkboard.
5. Review words with the student. The student reads the words to the teacher to determine if they are recognized instantly. If not, the words should be placed in a classroom word box for further review. If the child continues to have difficulty with given words, they should eventually be discarded as not appropriate for the student's key vocabulary.

Veatch suggested the use of several reinforcement activities for learning key words, such as dictating and writing sentences in which key words are included, forming key words out of modeling clay, and making alphabet books.

Once children have acquired a variety of key words, they seem to better understand the relationship between oral language and print (Veatch et al., 1973). Children have better recall of self-selected words than words selected by the teacher for instruction.

Organic reading/key vocabulary approaches can also be used for whole class instruction:

1. Students each select a personal word they want to learn and write their words on index cards.
2. Students tell the class about the personal words. For example, they might share experiences that reflect the words' meanings.
3. Students make sentences with the personal word cards and practice reading them.
4. The teacher collects the word cards and uses them in an activity in which each student must identify his or her own word.
5. Students file the words in their own word boxes. If students continue to have problems immediately identifying their own words, the cards are removed from the personal file box and placed in the class word box.

Word Banks and Word Walls

Word banks (sometimes called word boxes) help the Catch-On Reader develop a stock of basic sight words that can be recalled instantly, without letter-by-letter analysis. These sight words are often composed, at least in part, of words in which students have an interest in learning and recalling. Each word is written on a separate file card, and a sentence using the word is written on the opposite side of the file card. Practice activities with the file cards help students learn special features of words, such as letter sequence and distinct letters within words. As words accumulate in the word bank, some will have very similar visual features. If the student is not quite sure of the word, the sentence on the back can be read to help the student make a decision.

Word banks are divided into two parts: one of known words and one for words still being learned. Students should review the words often by saying them, reading them within sentences, and practicing them in game activities. Usually three to five words are selected per lesson to be added to the word bank.

Words for the word bank can come from stories and books being read, language experience stories (see Chapter 4), or from content learning readings for science or social studies.

Using words from the word bank, children can create an "All about Me" book with the teacher's help, or an "I Like" book in which each sentence starts with "I like" and is completed by the individual student. These are good resources for utilizing words that the children are highly motivated to learn.

Incentives for continuing to learn words and place them in a word bank include:

- Counting them to determine the number of words learned
- Printing them on specially shaped paper (e.g., cut in the shape of dinosaurs, flowers, or Mickey Mouse)
- Taping them on a wall (as in a word worm—a picture of a worm in which each segment has a separate word printed on it)
- Charting or graphing them to show how many have been learned
- Using them in game situations

A wide variety of activities can be used to give Catch-On Readers the extensive exposure to each word that will be needed for long-term retention:

- Alphabetizing activities
- Making sentences from the words
- Carrying out word sorts (see below)
- Playing games (the Memory Game is always a favorite)

Children can play Go Fish or Crazy Letters (a version of Crazy Eights in which seven word cards are dealt, with one turned face up; the student and other players must lay down a card that has the same beginning sound, ending sound, or vowel sound as the one face up on the board). Game boards can be created for Sight Word Soccer or Baseball.

A word wall is a collection of sight words that have been chosen for the entire class. Large cards with the words printed on them are posted on the classroom bulletin board. Children are encouraged to use the word wall to help in word recognition during reading and to help in spelling. Words are often placed on an ABC word wall (Cunningham, 2000), in alphabetical order, all the words beginning with *d*, for example, listed underneath a large *Dd* on the board. Sometimes different types of words are placed on different types of cards. Nouns, for example, might be placed on red cards and verbs on yellow.

A typical use of a word wall goes as follows: The class recites this target line from a story: "There was an old lady who swallowed a fly." After the reading, the teacher goes back to the word *there*—an irregularly pronounced word that is high frequency. She prints the word on a card and posts it, drawing the children's attention to it by using it in another sentence and by having them repeat it several times. The word is posted because of its frequency of occurrence in English text. She also prints the word *an* on a card and posts it, again drawing the children's attention to it. This word can be used as a clue word (sometimes called an anchor word or a key word—though this type of key word is not to be confused with Veatch's key vocabulary described above) when the children later attempt to identify unknown words that have the -*an* rime in them, using the decoding-by-analogy strategy: "If *an* is /an/, then *plan* must be /pl/ and /an/: /plan/."

Pinnell and Fountas (1998) warned that word walls will be of little help unless they are used regularly. They can be used for spelling tests, writing activities, I Spy games, and word sorts (see below). In working with individual Catch-On Readers, a smaller version of the word wall can be created on cardboard sheets that can be posted nearby during tutoring sessions.

DEVELOPING DECODING STRATEGIES

Learning sound–symbol relationships (i.e., phonics) to recognize words in print is an important language ability that is one of the first steps toward independent word recognition. Just *how much* phonics should be taught—and *how* it should be taught—have long been issues in the field of education. There is little doubt but that the role of phonics in beginning reading instruction has increased in recent years. Two recent extensive surveys have been carried out on experimental research in teaching decoding; one by the National Reading Panel (2000) and one by the National Research Council (Snow et al., 1998). Both surveys indicated that explicit, systematically organized instruction in phonics is a key factor in initial stages of learning to read. Various major approaches to teaching phonics are discussed in Chapter 9, and methods specifically appropriate for readers with very serious reading difficulties are provided in Chapter 16. In the section below, we focus on the development of phonological and phonemic awareness (see Sidebar 3.2 for a discussion of the differences between these terms), important prerequisites to learning phonics and to success in reading.

Catch-On Readers need direct teaching in phonics instruction to understand that words are composed of individual sounds (*phonemes*, which are commonly represented in print as a letter or letters between slash marks, as in /d/ and /t/), which are represented in print by letters (*graphemes*). The student's name might be used to teach the concept of sound–symbol relationships, since one's name is usually the first word that a child learns to read and write. For example:

1. Ask Dan to write his name. Then say, "Listen to me as I say your name. . . . D-d-d-d-a-a-n-n-n. What sound do you hear at the beginning of *Dan*?"

   The student will usually be able to identify the /d/. He might say, "D—an, D-D." Then ask what letter is associated with that sound. He may or may not know that the letter *d* corresponds to the beginning sound in *Dan*. However, since he has just written his name, point out that the letter is *d*.
2. Ask Dan, "How does your name end? Let's say your name and listen to the last sound we make: Da—n-n-n." He should reply with the sound "N-n-n."

   Say, "That's right. Let's look at your name and locate that letter."

While this type of teaching is sometimes criticized for isolating and distorting individual phonemes, it provides a clearly recognizable sound–symbol relationship for those children who have not caught on to the concept that spoken words are composed of individual phonemes (a concept known as phonemic awareness) or to the processes involved in decoding. Students at risk for learning to read need more guided instruction in learning letter–sound relationships than is typically given to normally developing students (Juel & Minden-Cupp, 2000).

Taping an alphabet strip to Catch-On Readers' desks can help them as they learn sound–symbol associations. Although identifying initial or final sounds is usually easy

Sidebar 3.2. How Is Phonemic Awareness Different from Phonics . . . and So Forth?

Terms such as *phonemic awareness, phonics,* and *phonological awareness* are used loosely by most educators to mean more or less the same thing—study of sound–symbol relationships in beginning reading. When reading this book, though, and when reading high-caliber professional literature, it is important to recognize that the terms have distinct meanings. As is often the case, appropriate use of terminology can make quite a difference. In the complex world of reading and literacy education, with new terms coming into use and older terms that mean more or less the same thing remaining in use, semantic caution and care are warranted. The International Reading Association has published an extremely useful reference tool, *The Literacy Dictionary: The Vocabulary of Reading and Writing* (Harris & Hodges, 1995), that should be an important part of every reading professional's library.

Note that in the explanations below, we follow the convention of indicating the sound(s) made by the letter(s) or word(s) with slash marks. /Sat/, then, does not have the meaning of the printed word *sat*; instead it signifies the sounds that comprise the word *sat* when it is spoken aloud. This convention is used throughout this textbook as well as in most professional literature dealing with reading.

Phonological awareness is a general term referring to an awareness (i.e., an ability to focus on and manipulate) of the sounds of words and their components. ("Phon" is a morpheme referring to sounds, and "ology" refers to the study of a topic; thus *phonology* refers to the study of sounds.) Phonological awareness includes phonemic awareness (see below), as well as such aspects of language as onsets (the initial letter sound[s] in a word, such a /b/ in *book* or /spl/ in *splash*), the sounds of syllables, and rhymes.

Phonemic awareness is one component of phonological awareness and refers to phonemes, minimal sound units in a language that affect the meaning of words. In English, for example, the /v/ in *vat* differentiates that word from *fat*. Thus both /v/ and /f/, though similar in sound, are distinct phonemes in English.

Phonemic discrimination is easier for children to achieve than phonemic awareness. Phonemic discrimination simply involves the ability to tell whether two spoken words that differ by only one phoneme are alike or different. Are /red/ and /bed/ the same or different? Even children who cannot manipulate phonemes within words can usually discern that the two words are different.

Phonics, on the other hand, is quite a different term altogether. It refers to the variety of methodologies involved in teaching students to make associations between speech sounds and printed letters.

for these students, matching these sounds to the appropriate letter name or grapheme is difficult. It is not unusual to hear a student say the sound in a word, as in "Dad, D—d—d—d," then look at the alphabet strip and say the letter names in order, "*A, B, C, D.*" Then they might say, "D-d-d-d" repeatedly to verify that the sound matches the grapheme *d*.

Phonemic Awareness

Many Catch-On Readers, however, have not yet reached the point in their literacy development at which phonics can be taught successfully. In recent years, understanding phonemic and phonological awareness has become increasingly recognized as a prerequisite or corequisite to word recognition. These types of awarenesses are seen as important not only to the learning of decoding but to development of a large sight-word vocabulary as well.

Phonemic awareness reflects the ability to focus on and manipulate phonemes in spoken words. Phonemic awareness tasks are often quite difficult for Catch-On Readers, to an extent that is hard for proficient readers to understand. A major difficulty arises from the fact that *phoneme* is an abstract concept. Proficient adult readers may perceive three different "sounds" in the spoken word /hat/—the /h/, the /a/, and the /t/, its three phonemes. In fact, however, there are no concrete boundaries between the three phonemes in the actual pronunciation of the word. Phonemes are blended seamlessly into one another in speech.

A variety of tasks can be used to teach and to assess phonemic awareness.

Phonemic Isolation Tasks

The student must recognize an individual phoneme within a word. For example:

"What is the first sound in the word *sell*?"
"What is the last sound in the word *hard*?"

Phonemic Identity Tasks

The student must recognize the same sound in two different words. For example:

"Tell me the sound that is the same in *sell*, *Sue*, and *soap*."
"Tell me the sound that is the same in *bread*, *pad*, and *sod*."
"Tell me the sound that is the same in *man*, *more*, and *same*."

Phonemic Categorization Tasks

The student must recognize the word with a sound that does not fit the dominant pattern in a group of words. For example:

"Tell me which word does not belong in this group: *card*, *cap*, *sell*, or *come*."
"Tell me which word does not belong in this group: *came*, *tape*, *taste*, or *rope*."

Phonemic Segmentation Tasks

The student must break a word apart into its constituent phonemes. For example:

"How many letter sounds are in the word *sad*?"

"Please tap on the table once for every letter sound you hear in the word *crime*." (Note: Consonant blends, such as *cr*, present more of a challenge for students in segmentation tasks because the two phonemes are closely blended.)

"Take markers from the pile in front of you and put out one for each of the letter sounds you hear in the word *tall*." (Game markers or cubes are sometimes used.)

"What are the letter sounds in the word *shape*?" (There are three: the /sh/, which is a consonant digraph—two letters making one sound—the /a/, and the /p/.)

Ehri and Nunes (2002) surveyed research on phonemic awareness training and concluded that segmentation tasks (and blending tasks) are more effective than the other types of tasks. The following segmentation activity can be used to help develop phonemic awareness:

1. Slowly pronounce a word in the student's vocabulary. Pronounce the word again and tap out the number of sounds heard. For example, *cat* has three sounds and would get three taps; *cake* also has three sounds and would get three taps.
2. Model this activity several times, with different words, gradually inviting the student to join in tapping the number of phonemes heard.
3. Ask the student to think of words to tap out. Continue this practice over a period of days or weeks, until the student is successful at hearing the number of phonemes in a spoken word and is able to tap for each sound heard.

Phonemic Deletion Tasks

The student must say the word that remains when a single phoneme is removed from another word. For example:

"What word would you have if the /s/ is removed from the word *cats*?"

"What is *slam* without the /l/?"

Phonemic Blending Tasks

Ehri and Nunes (2002) surveyed research on phonemic awareness and concluded that blending tasks (and segmentation tasks) are the most effective. In a blending task, the student must form a word from a series of separately spoken phonemic sounds. For example:

"What word would you have if you combined /m/, /oo/, and /v/?"

"What word is /s/, /o/, and /p/?"

Phonological Awareness

As noted in Sidebar 3.2 phonological awareness is a more general term than phonemic awareness because it includes an ability to focus on and manipulate larger units of spoken language. Phonological awareness tasks include all those listed under phonemic awareness, as well as those suggested in the following material:

Rhyme Generation Tasks

The student must list words that rhyme. For example:

> "Tell me some words that rhyme with *pad*."
> "Does *call* rhyme with *ball*? What other words rhyme with *ball*?"

Syllable Deletion Tasks

The student must delete a syllable from a word to form a new word sound. For example:

> "What word do you have if you take the *fel* out of *fellow*?"
> "What word would be left if you take the *mis* out of *mismatch*?"

Onset Identification Tasks

The student must identify the onset (initial letter or letters) in a word. For example:

> "What is the first sound in *cap*?"
> "What are the first sounds in *straight*?"

Rime Identification Tasks

The student must identify the rime (ending letters) in a word. For example:

> "What is the ending sound in *cap*?" (Answer: /ap/)
> "What is the ending sound in *straight*?" (Answer: /aight/)

Syllabication Tasks

The student must divide a multisyllabic word into its syllables. The teacher may first need to explain the concept of syllables, perhaps by using the word *beat* or *clap*, accompanied by a tap of the pencil on the desk or a clap of hands: "There is one beat [or clap] in the word *cap* and two beats in the word *father*."

> "How many beats are in the word *catapult*?"
> "Divide up the word *perfect* into its beats."

Phonemic/Phonological Awareness of Printed Letters

Pure phonemic and phonological awareness tasks involve only the sounds of language; they do not involve the use of printed letters. Catch-On Readers need a solid foundation in both types of tasks in order to succeed in reading. Leaving out the letters during instruction helps them to focus on sounds, rather than potentially confusing them.

There comes a point in instruction, however, when incorporating printed letters with the phonemic and phonological awareness tasks will enhance learning (Ehri & Nunes, 2002). As this point approaches, teachers may begin to demonstrate use of letters after a sound-based task is finished. They would start by demonstrating themselves, then move on to asking students to make the sound–symbol associations. For example:

TEACHER: Carlos, could you please tell me what sound the word *cap* begins with? [This is an onset identification task.]

CARLOS: Sure. It begins with a /k/ sound.

TEACHER: Great. Now, what is the word family ending in the word *cap*? [This is a rime identification task.]

CARLOS: That is /ap/.

TEACHER: Good. Let's look for a moment at these letter tiles. (*She displays the three letter tiles with* c, a, *and* p *printed on them.*) Which one of these would you think makes the first sound in the word *cap*? Which one makes the final sound? Which one would go in the middle?

Separate the phonological/phonemic instructional tasks from the sound–symbol tasks by allowing students to concentrate on each aspect. As learning progresses, the instruction begins to look more like phonics instruction as sounds and symbols are introduced into the tasks.

Rhyme

Another way to help students develop this auditory/visual match is to help them develop the auditory concept of rhyme in relation to the similarity among word endings. Simple word endings (called "rimes" or "phonograms"), such as *-at, -ot, -an, -am,* can be used to develop both the concept of rhyme and the sound–symbol relationships in the words (see Letter Clusters and Rimes in the appendix).

1. Tell the student that the day's lesson involves rhyming words ending with /an/. Start by saying, "I can make a rhyme with /an/. Listen carefully: *Dan.* Now you think of a word that rhymes with /an/ and *Dan.*"

2. Get the student involved in developing a list of rhyming words. For example, to elicit *pan* from the child, the teacher might say, "I'm thinking of a word that starts with *p* and is something you use for cooking." To elicit *man,* the teacher might say, "Your father is a m-m-m . . . " Say the words aloud as they are written and point out that parts of each word look alike. The look-alikes are what make the words sound alike.

3. A final list of words used with the child might include the following: *Dan, man, tan, fan, pan, can.*

Rhyme should also be practiced in an auditory mode, because students need opportunities to manipulate individual sounds and word parts. Students can be asked to think of words that rhyme with *fun, cat,* or *quack.* These can be real or nonsense words, as long as they rhyme. Later in your lesson you and the students can identify which of the words were nonsense.

Songs and poems offer many opportunities for rhyming words to be used. One popular song, "A Hunting We Will Go," has many opportunities for rhyme to be practiced, again and again, depending on what is "caught."

WRITING TO READING APPROACHES

Writing and reading are interrelated processes that should be taught as integrated rather than separate skills. In a sense, when students write they recognize the need to read, and when they read, they recognize the need to write. Chapter 5 provides more details on how to tailor writing and reading integration instruction for Catch-On Readers.

Engaging Catch-On Readers in writing activities helps them understand the role of written language in communication. Although writing activities may require more structure for the Catch-On Reader than for the student who is naturally making the links between reading and writing, these activities can be modified for use in small group and tutorial sessions. The degree of modification will depend on the level at which the student is successful.

Traditionally in American literacy instruction, reading was taught first and writing followed. The Whole Language movement of the 1980s brought about a major reevaluation of this policy, so that in today's classrooms reading and writing are introduced at the same time. Writing is encouraged by allowing children to use temporary spelling (sometimes called invented spelling) in their writing. The children sound out words, then write the corresponding letters as best they can. Note, in Figure 3.1, that David spelled *armies* as "anomies," *baseball* as "basball," *birds* as "berids," and so forth.

It often goes unrecognized by teachers attempting to use whole language approaches in kindergarten and first grade that writing is the major whole language method of teaching phonemic awareness and phonics in this approach (Gentry, 2000). As children sound out the words and print the corresponding letters, they are getting practice in letter–sound relationships. Writing slows down the process of phoneme/grapheme correspondence, so that children are able to see the relationships between sound and printed symbol. The key to success here is the teacher's involvement during the writing activity (Sipe, 2001). The teacher should be available at the writing center, giving feedback and drawing student attention to letter–sound correspondences. Classroom aides and parent volunteers can also play an important role in supervising classroom writing or writing centers. For Catch-On Readers especially, close monitoring and steady feedback are critical.

USING MANIPULATIVES

Making Words

"Making words" (Cunningham & Cunningham, 1992, 2002) is a guided activity for helping students understand sound–symbol relationships and letter–sound sequences for accurate spelling. Cunningham and Cunningham note that teaching sound–symbol correspondences and spelling is important for students who are having difficulty understanding the use of the alphabetic principle as a reading/spelling strategy. Catch-On Readers often evince this lack of understanding.

In the making words activity, teachers first develop a list of words that they want to teach. These words should include words that:

1. Can be sorted into patterns to be emphasized (see section on word sorting, below).
2. Are both little and big, so that the lesson is multilevel.
3. Can be reassembled with the letters in different places, to remind children that when spelling words, the order of letters is crucial.
4. Might include a proper name or two to remind children when we use capital letters.
5. Most of the students have in their listening vocabularies.

Making words can be carried out with individuals, small groups, or a whole class. Planning the lesson begins with the first word you want to teach. We might choose the word *flower.* Write the word on a large card. Print the consonant letters (*f*, *l*, *w*, and *r*) and vowels (*o* and *e*) on large cards, for the class pocket chart and small cards for individual student use. Print uppercase letters on one side of each card and lowercase letters on the other side. Give each child the letters he/she will need for the lesson. A photocopied sheet with the needed letters printed inside square boxes can be distributed to each child, who can then cut them apart with scissors for use in the activity.

Start with a two-letter word composed of letters from the target word, such as *we*. The teacher writes the number 2 on the chalkboard to indicate a two-letter word, tells the students to make the word *we*, and presents the word in a sentence. Students construct the word from their letters cards. A student who was able to put the letters in the correct sequence is called to use the large cards and make the word for the pocket chart.

The lesson progresses in the same way for three-, four-, and five-letter words, or until the word for the day has been constructed. For example, three-letter words that can be constructed from *flower* include *low*, *row*, and *woe*; four-letter words include *flow*, *wore*, *lore*, *flew*, and *fore*. These words can be sorted for rhyme, phonogram patterns, vowel combinations, or word endings.

In Clay's (1985, 2001), "making and breaking" activity, on which Cunningham and Cunningham's making words procedure was based, she supplied magnetic letter kits and cookie sheets for children to use in forming words and adding, subtracting, changing letters from the original word to make new words. *Red* might become *rid*, then *rids*, then *ride*, then *pride*, and so forth.

We suggest that the teacher proceed slowly with Catch-On Readers. Be sure each Catch-On student understands the task at each step and demonstrates adequate auditory discrimination (i.e., the ability to distinguish similar letter and word sounds).

Word Sorting

The advantage of hands-on activities such as making words is that students actively participate in the learning process in a more effective way than, for instance, simply circling items on a phonics worksheet. The letter cards serve the same function as manipulatives in early mathematics instruction. Word sorting also allows for this active involvement.

The manipulatives involved in word sorting are word cards. These can be large cards used in a pocket chart at the front of a classroom, or the words can be printed in boxes on a sheet of paper and distributed to the children to be cut into separate cards. Although the manipulatives involve the use of whole words, the actual purpose of a word sort is not so much to teach whole word identification as to draw the child's attention to the print and sound components of each word.

Choose words that can be sorted in a variety of ways, especially those ways to which you want to draw attention. For example, if you are studying onset (at the beginning of words) blends, include several words that begin with each of your blends: *str*, *sl*, and *pr*.

Then have the children look at the words to find categories of similarity and difference, or identify such categories yourself. Have one child at the front of the room sort the large word cards into the categories, while the others use their smaller word cards to sort at their desks.

SUMMARY

The Catch-On Reader's difficulties with recognizing words in print are associated with the challenge of understanding the functions of printed language. Teaching strategies for these students, therefore, should function primarily to help them successfully understand the purpose and process of learning to recognize words for reading and writing. Building the size of their sight-word vocabulary or the repertoire of their phonics strategies has an important, but secondary, purpose for Catch-On Readers. Teachers use a variety of approaches to help improve Catch-On Readers' word recognition, aiming to provide them with the flexible ability to apply sight-word recognition, decoding strategies, phonemic and phonological awareness, and strategies learned from writing as they read. Making words and sorting words are methods that have recently gained in popularity among teachers because of their high student engagement.

Chapters 4 and 5 present approaches to teaching reading that can be very effective in working with Catch-On Readers: the language experience approach and reading–writing integration. Many teachers of young children use both, but some go beyond occasional use to choose one approach or the other to form the central part of the classroom reading and writing curriculum.

CHAPTER 4

Helping Catch-On Readers Using Language Experience Approaches

The "language experience approach" (LEA) is a powerful and natural way to introduce young children to reading. This approach makes a direct link between the students' oral and written language. It is also an effective way to help Catch-On Readers bridge the gap between their oral language and another author's written language.

Allen (1976) developed the concept of the LEA to help students learn to read. Children can easily read stories that they themselves have created, especially if these stories are short in length and focused in content. The basic procedure is to ask the student to dictate a sentence or story based on some past experience. The teacher prints the student's dictation and reads it back to the student. The student then repeatedly rereads the LEA story with the teacher's help, until he/she can read it independently. Teachers carry out minilessons on such concepts as word boundaries, left–right print direction, or punctuation during the writing and rereadings.

When working with a Catch-On Reader, the teacher should clearly define the purpose of each LEA lesson. For example, is the purpose of a given lesson to develop sight words, to successfully read what has been dictated, or to further develop the student's oral language? Identifying focused objectives based on the student's needs is critical to the learning process.

Students who are more verbal will dictate long stories. However, if they cannot learn to reread the stories with approximately 95% word accuracy, the stories are too long. If a student consistently dictates stories that are too long for him/her to learn to reread, the teacher should explain the purpose of the LEA lesson to the student. Stories that are long negate the purpose of developing accurate word recognition because students find it too difficult to recall the exact words used. Stories that are three to five short sentences in length are usually appropriate for Catch-On Readers.

Allen (1976) warned that teachers must be careful to use the students' own language, not lead them in word choice. If the word choices are those of the teacher rather than the student, the dictated language experience stories will probably not be read with precision. Most teachers, though, do some amount of editing as they print the students' dictation. Allen's (1976) LEA method follows these steps:

1. The teacher and student decide on a past experience about which to write. Often this experience involves a recent activity in school or at home.
2. The teacher neatly prints the student's story. If the activity is conducted with a small group or class, the story is usually printed on chart paper (called a language experience chart).
3. The teacher reads each sentence after it is printed and points to the words as they are read (i.e., she tracks the reading).
4. The teacher asks the student to read each sentence after it is printed.
5. The teacher and student reread the whole story, and the student provides a title for the story.
6. Supported readings continue until the student is able to read the title and the entire story.
7. During the writing and rereadings of the story, the teacher introduces relevant print and word recognition concepts or asks questions about them.
8. Several words are selected from the dictated story to be learned as sight words. These words are usually selected by the student, written on index cards, and filed for practice in a word bank.

The teacher should make several copies of the language experience story so that it can be used for games and activities such as the following:

• Cut sentences from the story and arrange them in random order; the student then reconstructs his/her story by putting the sentences in the correct order.

• Cut sentences into words; the student then reconstructs individual sentences by placing the words in the correct order.

• Create a memory game by writing pairs of several key words from the story on index cards. The game is played by placing the cards face down on a table. The student starts the game by turning over two cards and reading the words. If the two cards have the same word, it is a match and the student collects the cards. If the cards have different words, they are replaced face down on the table and the next player takes a turn.

WORDLESS PICTURE BOOKS

Another form of LEA is to have students "read" wordless picture books from the classroom library and write their version of the story. This activity is a step toward bridging the gap between a student's language and that of another author. The students "read" the pictures in a book and tell their story about the pictures. Basic language experience steps are then followed, with the teacher writing the stories the students dictate about the picture book. Students then reread their own stories and often supply their own illustrations. The teacher also may write each sentence of the student's story on separate sheets of paper and ask the student to draw a picture of each story segment, thereby turning a wordless picture book into an authored story.

Wordless picture books range in levels of interest from early primary to young adult. Older Catch-On Readers often find that wordless picture books provide the stimulation and motivation for dictating story events and rereading them successfully. An engaging alternative is to use comic books with older readers. Use whiteout to cover the words and ask the students to develop their own interpretation of the pictures.

INITIAL LANGUAGE EXPERIENCE (ILE)

In her work with children experiencing difficulties in learning to read, Sally Lipa (Lipa & Penney, 1989) developed a program called "initial language experience" (ILE). It is intended as a short-term activity to help students get started in reading by providing them with initial experiences in translating oral language into written language. This method is based on the notion that the sentence, rather than the word, conveys the initial unit of meaning. As students discover that they can read their dictated sentences, they learn to identify the words comprising those sentences as separate and distinct units. Reading is modeled as a purposeful communication activity. The steps follow:

1. The teacher asks, "What word(s) would you like to learn today?" or "What would you like to write about today?"

2. The teacher says, "Tell me about the word. Why do you want to learn to read that word? Let's write a sentence using the word." The teacher may orally supply a sentence stem. For example, "I like _____"; "My name is _____"; "My teacher's name is _____."

3. The teacher writes and reads the student's sentence; the student reads the sentence. At this step the teacher also may help students develop the notion of mapping speech to print. Directions such as, "Put your finger on the first word" or "Put your finger under each word as you read" usually help the student understand this relationship. Giving these directions is also a diagnostic teaching strategy, since the teacher then can observe whether the student has acquired speech/print correspondence.

4. Recognition of individual words. In this part of the lesson, the student learns to recognize and identify words as units comprising different letters and sequences of letters. Many young children do not know how to attend to the features of a word. Therefore, their recall of particular words is very poor. Activities for helping students recall special features of words include these:

   a. Ask the student to reread the sentence.
   b. Ask the student to find specific words: "Find the word _____."
   c. List the words that comprise the sentence in a column. For example, the sentence "My name is Dan" would be written:

My

name

is

Dan

Ask the student to read the words in the column. At this point the student usually recognizes that the words in the list are the same as those in the sentence. After reading the words from top to bottom, ask the student to read the words from bottom to top. Keep the sentence visible so that the student can refer to it as a self-check on accuracy. Usually students refer back to the sentence to recall the word. This behavior should be encouraged because the student is employing a strategy to identify words. The sentence has been dictated as a unit of meaning; now this unit can be used to learn individual words.

5. Identifying special auditory and visual characteristics of words. More practice may be needed in identifying the special features of individual words. Activities that foster this ability include the following:

"Word match" is a practice activity in which the words in the student's sentence are randomly listed in two columns. Ask the student to draw a line to connect the words that match.

My	is
Jack	name
is	Jack
name	My

Another word-match activity requires the student to locate the word that looks just like the one on the left.

My	Jack	is	name	My
name	is	name	my	Jack

"Finish the sentence" is an activity that presents a series of the same sentence in which different words have been deleted, as shown below; the student fills in the blanks. One complete sentence is used as a model for the student.

My name is Matt.   _____ name is Matt.

My _____ is Matt.   My name is _____.

"Part to whole sentence reading" is another activity that can be used to further develop students' sight-word vocabulary. Print each word of the student's sentence on an index card, slip of paper, or Post-it note. Mix up the words so that they are not in the order in which the sentence was dictated. Ask the students to reorder the words so that they make a complete sentence. Students who are just learning to acquire a sight-word vocabulary should have their dictated sentence in clear view so that they can match the cut-out words to those in their sentence. Students decide how the sentence starts, what word comes next, and so forth.

For example: Using the sentence, "My name is Dan," the student is presented with the word cards in the following order: "Dan name My is." Ask the student to read the correctly printed target sentence and then look for the word card that starts the sentence. When the student selects "My," the word is placed as the first word in the sentence. The student locates the next word, reads it, and places it after the first word. This procedure continues until all the words are used. Then ask the student to read the sentence aloud and point to the words as they are read.

This game-like activity can be continued by asking the student to locate and pick up words in the sentence. For example, you might say, "Pick up *Dan*." "Pick up *name*." "Pick up *My*." Cut-up stories have regained popularity through the use of this activity in Clay's Reading Recovery program (1993).

Additional games can be played with the word cards. Teacher-made Concentration, Old Maid, and Crazy Eights are highly motivating for the student. Be sure to keep the full sentence available for the child's reference.

LANGUAGE EXTENSION LESSONS (LELs)

Lipa and Penney (1989) developed a lesson scenario that incorporates language skills with reading and writing for use with Catch-On Readers. The purposes of "language extension lessons" (LELs) is to (1) guide students in focusing on salient features of a picture, (2) generate language about those features, and (3) provide the student with a structure for developing a stock of basic sight words. Pictures obtained from magazines or catalogs can be pasted onto card stock and laminated. The specific steps in the activity follow:

Step 1. Identification of Labels

1. The picture is shown with the query, "What is it?" or "What would you call it?"
2. The most common labels are written on the chalkboard by the teacher (e.g., *horse, truck, banana*).
3. The children read the words with the teacher, while the teacher points to each word, thus matching an oral label to a written label.

Step 2. Metacognitive Probe

The teacher probes for further discussion by asking, for example, "What else can you tell us about this?" "What does it do?" "What is it used for?" "Where would you find it?" During this discussion, the teacher writes words or phrases on the chalkboard that she selects as being understood by most or all of the children in the class.

Step 3. Generating Oral Sentences Based on Discussion

The teacher elicits a sentence about the picture from each child and writes it on the chalkboard. The teacher reads each sentence (word by word) as she writes it. When all sentences are completed, the teacher rereads each sentence, pointing to the beginning of the sentence and each subsequent word. Through class discussion, vote, or teacher's choice, one sentence is selected as the target sentence of the day for the children to write. Now the teacher erases all the sentences from the chalkboard and rewrites the target sentence on it.

Step 4. Mapping Oral Language to Print (Written Language)

1. The teacher models reading the sentence while pointing to, and sweeping the hand under, each word.
2. The children read the sentence in chorus with the teacher.
3. Each child then reads the sentence alone at the chalkboard, while pointing to each word as the teacher has modeled.

Optional: At this point in the presentation the teacher might ask individual students to locate, identify, and read specific words in the target sentence.

Step 5. Mapping Written Language to Reading

1. Depending on their ability, children now copy the sentence from the chalkboard, copy the teacher's model that has been written on their paper, or trace over the teacher's model. As the children acquire skill, they will gradually do their own writing.
2. Children reread the sentence from their paper while pointing to each word. As in Step 4, the children can be asked to locate and identify specific words.

Step 6. Reinforcement

1. Students' sentences (preferably in sets of five) are bound into storybooks for rereading.
2. Students practice reading and writing the sentences and identifying individual words.
3. Students or the teacher rewrite the stories as strips, cut apart the words, or make word cards and reconstruct the sentences. Always reread the individual words.
4. Games can be played using word cards and a game board.

Several variations of the above steps can be used, depending on the competence levels of the students. Initially, some of the younger children might find it difficult to copy the sentence from the chalkboard; the teacher or aide can write the sentence on the paper for those students, and then they can trace the sentence and reread it.

TECHNOLOGY-BASED ACTIVITIES

Word-processing computer programs can be used as another way to publish language experience stories. Students can do the typing, which helps them focus on the sequence of individual letters within words and locate specific letters on the keyboard (see Sidebar 4.1). The procedure reinforces the concept of word boundaries and punctuation.

Students can type their stories and bind them into a book. Space is often left at the top or bottom of the story for illustrations. A drawing program can be used to create pictures, as

---

Sidebar 4.1. Principles for Technology Instruction

When organizing instruction that involves the use of computers, the following key principles should be kept in mind.

1. *Technology does not replace the teacher.* The key to effective technology use in literacy education is the human element. Teachers plan and implement the curriculum. Technology is simply a teacher aid in curriculum implementation. Claims by hardware and software publishers that use of their materials will save schools salary costs should be examined critically, given that past practice has virtually never substantiated the contention.

2. *Technology does not make life easier for teachers.* Especially in initial years of students' computer use, teachers have to work harder to plan and implement technology in their classrooms. Yet the end results for the students are worthwhile: improved learning and preparation for their future adult lives in which electronics will play a key role.

3. *Children should become familiar with the process of using computers as tools in literacy tasks simply for its own sake.* Some teachers ask the question, "Why should I use computers when research indicates that use of more traditional methods—children's literature circles, journaling, cooperative learning, and others—is just as effective?" Children whose schools fail to encourage use of technology are disadvantaged in terms of their understanding of a device that is now critical in our society and in most vocations. Literacy teachers should make use of technology in their classroom because of its inherent importance outside the classroom in reading and writing tasks.

4. *The literacy curriculum should benefit from, and offer benefits to, the technology curriculum.* Many schools have a strong technology curriculum that helps students learn such skills as proficient keyboarding, principles of disk operating systems, and operation of standard application software, such as word processors, databases, and spreadsheets. This computer knowledge makes use of computers in the literacy curriculum much more efficient. In turn, extensive use of computers in the literacy curriculum demonstrates to students the importance of technological awareness and gives students practice in implementing meaningful technology skills.

5. *Careful curricular planning is necessary for effective computer use in maintaining a balanced literacy curriculum.* There is little doubt that, just as drill and practice worksheets are often overused in public schools, so is drill and practice software. Simply transferring worksheet drills to computers may increase student motivation, but that increased motivation does not justify overuse of impoverished teaching methods. A student who would rebel at doing an irrelevant or inappropriate worksheet may eagerly carry out the same activity when it means using a joystick to specify answers on the computer screen. The differences in the student's motivation in these two instances does not, however, necessarily validate the content or purpose of the instructional activity.

---

in the programs KidPix and KidWorks 2. Plastic book binders can be used to hold the stories together in a professional looking book. For an alternative form of classroom publication, use KidPix's subprogram titled "Slide Show," which provides a timed display of the children's works on the computer monitor. Other LEA activities for Catch-On Readers that make use of computer and telecommunications technologies are described in Chapter 7.

There is no doubt that the most important contribution of the computer to the classroom is the range of experience it offers in the area of writing. In terms of practical implementation of the principles of writing process, computers offer ease of revision—a benefit when teaching the principle of revision. The interest value of computer-based writing also makes a significant contribution to the teaching and learning of writing, especially with Catch-On Readers who may need special motivation to overcome their frustration with their slow achievement.

In addition to the now-familiar standard word-processing operation, computer writing software provides guidance for writers in terms of topic and structure by supplying a framework to support writing. The software also provides feedback, especially in terms of the mechanics of writing, such as spelling and simple grammar. Colorful software, used in creative and stimulating ways, can be employed to maintain student interest. Newer multimedia software allows children to go beyond simple text to add illustrations and pictures, sound and voice, and even video segments to their writings.

The word-processing and graphics functions of KidPix were used to create the story in Figure 4.1. Sara, in the spring of her first-grade year, wrote in a journal about a classroom catastrophe, using pencil and paper, and with the help of her teacher. She also used word cards from the egg unit that the class was studying, which were posted at the classroom writing center.

Figure 4.1 displays the final draft. The first draft was printed by hand on three pages and read as follows:

I had chick egg's.
They are in a incubator.
I was happy when they
came. I like chicks. do
you? They are on a
counter. they are brow
and white. it tacs
21 days to have chicks
and it is the frst day
that we have the eggs.

———

Then sumthing taribul
hapend! the inculoator
brok and the eggs
gract! I fet awful.
the cstotnse came.
Then the necst day
mrs. marion got one egg
from eech clasroom.

I was happy now. and
mrs. marion got a
estu incubator from
mrs. grinnel. I was
excited. now we had
anuther inculoator.

———

the chicks hacht!
the are so cyoot. I love
them. one gumt into
mrs. Marions hand. I
hooled one chick to
I pikt it up. I like
chicks vary, vary,
vary much. do you?

Mrs. Marion's Class Had Chicks

by Sara

I had chick eggs. They are in an incubator. I like chicks. Do you? They are on a counter. They are brown and white. It takes 21 days to have chicks.

The first day I was happy that we had the eggs. Then something terrible happened! The incubator broke and the eggs cracked! I felt awful. Then custodians came. The next day Mrs. Marion got one egg from each classroom. I was happy now. Mrs. Marion got an extra incubator from Mrs. Grinell. I was excited. Then we had another incubator.

After 21 days the chicks hatched! They're so cute. I love them. One jumped into Mrs. Marion's hand. I held one chick too! I picked the chick up. I like chicks very, very, very, much. Do you?

FIGURE 4.1. *"Mrs. Marion's Class Had Chicks."*

The teacher helped with editing, then Sara typed the story herself. Parent volunteers and the teacher provided help during the typing sessions. During class reading and writing periods, the computers in Sara's class were almost constantly in use as students typed their stories for publication. After the stories were typed, pictures were pasted into the text.

SUMMARY

Language experience approaches teach children to read using their own words and stories. Children learn that their oral language can be transformed into print, which can in turn be read by themselves and by others. At the same time, children learn other basic print concepts as well as word-recognition strategies. Teachers can customize instruction to the needs of individual Catch-On Readers using initial language experience and language extension lessons. Computers provide creative, motivating opportunities for application of language experience principles in instruction.

Language experience can be one tool in the teacher's arsenal, or it can be the central feature of instruction for Catch-On Readers. Similarly, the role of reading–writing integration described in Chapter 5 can vary from one of many teaching strategies or it can be the major form of instruction.

Helping Catch-On Readers by Integrating Reading and Writing

Historically in literacy instruction, the teaching of reading and writing has typically been kept distinct in the classroom curriculum. Within the past 20 years, however, educators have increasingly come to realize that integration of reading and writing instruction builds on a language foundation that is common to both processes. The constructive processes involved in integrated reading/writing activities communicate a clear sense of the purpose of written language to all emerging readers, including Catch-On Readers.

In addition, careful observation of Catch-On Readers' writing can provide useful insights into how best to guide instruction. As previously noted, Clay (1985) described teaching as a "conversation in which you listen to the speaker carefully before you reply" (p. 6). Close analysis of students' writing plays an important role in helping understand their language processes.

In recent years, the teaching of writing has undergone a revolution in which emphasis on the final product has been replaced by recognition of the importance of the writing *process* (prewriting and planning, draft writing, revising, editing, and publication or sharing). The final steps of this process—publication in finished form and/or sharing of results with an audience in a presentation—are always critical. They provide writers with a sense of purpose, a goal of reaching out to a specific audience, and a feeling that writing is a social act carried out in a community of authors, not an isolated, individual event. Sharing can also provide an opportunity for the teacher to assess progress and make plans for future instruction (Wagner, Nott, & Agnew, 2001).

SELF-WRITTEN BOOKS

The activities used in the language experience approach (LEA) (see Chapter 4) are among the most useful methods of integrating reading and writing for Catch-On Readers. Self-written books are the product of an LEA activity in which writing and reading provide a natural way for Catch-On Readers to (1) learn about the reading process, (2) develop a sight-word vocabulary, and (3) promote a healthy attitude toward literacy activities.

Themes for self-written books can be chosen by the teacher or they can be creative works generated entirely by students. For example, during the fall of his second-grade year, David used invented spelling to write and illustrate an eight-page book about his favorite animal, the eagle. It was made from a single sheet of paper, cut in half horizontally, assembled one sheet on top of the other, folded in half vertically and taped together to form an eight-page booklet:

Eagles

eagles can fly out of sight

eagals can fly lorge dsdnis [distances] with out flaping there wings.

eagls are reptors [raptors].   reptors mean they eat meat.

there are many kinds of eagles   bold eagle, golden eagle, fish eagle

reptors have a beak that hoks [hooks] at the end

eagles have big wings.

some eagls are big.

"I" BOOKS

"I" books are intended to model reading and writing processes and help students learn basic sight words. They can also serve as an interest inventory—a device used early in the instructional sequence to ascertain students' background and interest (see the Interest Inventory in the appendix). Because "I" books are centered around student interests and background experiences, they provide motivation for reading. The teacher usually suggests the type of book that is to be developed: *I Like, I Want, I Have, I Need, I Love, I Work, I Am,* and *I Play.*

Basic materials for the "I" books include magazines, paper, scissors, markers, and tape. First the teacher selects the title that will be used for the book; for example, *I Like.* Students are asked to look through magazines and tell the teacher when they locate a picture of an item they like. For example, Stacey looked through a magazine and came across a picture of a book. She said, "I like this. I like books." The teacher told Stacey to cut out the picture and paste it on a sheet of blank paper. Under the picture the teacher wrote, "I like books." (Another possibility is to have the student do the writing by copying the teacher's model.) Next, Stacey was asked to read the sentence, and then she continued with the task of finding other pictures that she liked and wanted to include in her book.

This procedure is continued until the students have a booklet of "I like" pictures and sentences. Then they reread their entire books. If the teacher uses the procedure with groups of students, individuals can read their books to others in the group. The books can be stored in a classroom library for other students to read.

This procedure provides students with a simple but meaningful experience in which the reading process can be practiced and focus placed on word recognition. Repeating the same sentence stem throughout the entire book provides consistency. Sight words are read within a meaningful context, and the pictures provide visual clues to the content words. In sum, basic print concepts are modeled during the writing and reading of the sentences.

CONTENT AND THEMED BOOKS

Content and themed books are created as study aids in learning science, social studies, arithmetic, or health concepts (or to review concepts that have been taught). Sentence stems are supplied to students to help them (1) learn the basic content, (2) develop basic sight words, and (3) as a guide in their writing and reading.

For example, in a science unit about animals that live in the jungle, the student's book might include one page for every animal that is studied. One page of the *Animals That Live in the Jungle* book might display a lion and the following sentence stems provided by the teacher:

>   A lion is _____.
>   A lion has _____.
>   A lion lives _____.
>   A lion eats _____.

Pictures drawn by students should be included on separate pages. Be sure to ask the students to read their stories and to talk about their pictures.

JOURNALS

Writing in journals encourages students to express themselves in a personal way. The teacher invites students to write about topics and events that are important to them, using invented spelling whenever necessary to convey their thoughts (see Chapter 8 for more information about invented, or temporary, spelling). Journal writing helps students learn to (1) form individual letters, (2) translate individual sounds to letters, and (3) segment whole words into their component sounds.

Teachers usually model how to write journal entries so that students understand their purpose and format. The greater the individual attention given by teachers or aides, the more valuable the experience can be in helping Catch-On Readers develop their knowledge of sound–symbol relationships and sight words. In whole language approaches to reading, daily journal entries and other forms of writing are the primary vehicle by which children learn about sound–symbol relationships (Dahl, Scharer, Lawson, & Grogan, 1999).

In David's kindergarten class's daily "learning center" hour, for example, his teacher would spend most of her time sitting at the writing table, providing support to children writing in their journals. The support would include suggesting ideas and sometimes specific assignments for writing. Also, the teacher helped in sounding out words as the children employed their invented spelling abilities, simultaneously developing their knowledge of sound–symbol relations. Three or four students at a time would be encouraged to use the writing table while other children played at the puppet center, climbed on the jungle gym, or read along with books on tape at the listening center. The teacher made sure that all children cycled over to the writing table on a frequent basis.

After modeling the process, the teacher should ask students to write in their journals. Circulating among the students, the teacher asks what they are writing. Sometimes the teacher asks permission to write the student's message in conventional print, especially if conventional print will be necessary to interpret the writing at a later date. Although writing students' entries in conventional spelling is not necessary for all students, it may be helpful for Catch-On Readers who become frustrated by their attempts to write a message. The teacher's transcription can provide a record of the students' communication as well as his/her growth toward conventional spelling abilities.

Be aware that journal writing can be emotional and stressful for some children. Regardless of the procedures and guidelines followed, therefore, teachers should maintain flexible and nonintrusive behavior as they guide students to gain control of their written messages.

Several modifications of journal writing are often necessary for Catch-On Readers. Although they typically have lots of thoughts to contribute to oral discussions, Catch-On Readers may "clam up" when faced with journal writing, finding it tedious to think of what to say and then decide how to write it. The teacher may want to help these students narrow their topics until one with sufficient interest for writing is selected.

Many Catch-On Readers do not understand the match between oral and written language sufficiently to write in journals. They bog down right from the start and cannot seem to think of anything to write. These students often benefit when teachers ask them to orally state their sentence(s) prior to writing.

Sentence stems can be provided for Catch-On Readers who have difficulty speaking and writing in full sentences. The teacher can support these students by providing sentence stems such as "I like _____," "I did _____," and "I went _____."

In response journals—a variation on journals that can evoke strong motivation—the teacher writes responses to students' entries. This personal communication between teacher and students conveys the message that each person's thoughts are worthwhile. Wollman-Bonilla (2000) investigated "family message journals," a variation on response journals in which children write journal entries and family members respond. These serve the same purpose as standard response journals but save teachers the time needed to respond to class sets of journal entries.

WRITING IN RESPONSE TO READING

Writing in response to reading helps students reflect consciously on interesting parts of stories and provides a structure for activating the processes involved in comprehending.

Students are asked to think about a story that has been read and write one or more sentences in response. The sentence may refer to the main idea, the part the student liked best, the favorite character, or a favorite plot event. With any writing activity it is important to talk to students prior to writing to help them clarify their intended statements. Teachers can help students reflect on what they have written by asking questions that help them focus on the main idea, the main character, or descriptive words. This segment of writing can be influential in helping students convey their ideas and read for meaning.

TECHNOLOGY AND STORY CREATION

Many computer software programs are now available that present students with computer pictures, in response to which they write their own stories. These programs provide Catch-On Readers with high interest materials that allow for creativity and success. Some programs allow students to make their own pictures and write their own stories, as discussed earlier in this chapter. Other programs provide prepared pictures that can be customized by the child and stories written on the computer screen and then printed in color.

Sara's visit to Sea World stimulated in her a love for dolphins. She used *Imagination Express: Destination Ocean* (Edmark) to create pictures and stories about life under the sea. Sara first chose a background, an underwater coral reef. She then used the mouse to select and place prepared pictures of fish, dolphin, boats, and scuba divers (called "stick-ons" or "paste-ons") in the background. Finally, she used her own invented spelling and novice keyboarding abilities to type a story about her picture. A series of such pictures can be printed to form a book-like adventure story.

REWRITING FAMILIAR, PATTERNED STORIES

Rewriting familiar, patterned stories is an activity in which students compose a new story within the structure of a patterned or predictable story they have heard or read. To change the story, students must comprehend the original story and use their thinking skills to create a new story.

Teacher modeling and guidance is necessary to help the students choose a theme for the new story and to modify the predictable phrases. Examples of possible changes include a character with a new name and a different problem or altered events, utilizing a predictable language format similar to the original story.

Activities such as these involve not only Catch-On Readers but also others in the class; indeed, the whole class can engage in rewriting and illustrating a familiar story. Catch-On Readers learn reading and writing from their peers as they all sequence the events in the story, draw pictures to represent the events, and make a cover page and title page together.

Even books with low predictability can be used as patterns for young children (McElveen & Dierking, 2001). As they listen to the stories, for example, in Cynthia Rylant's *When I Was Young in the Mountains* (1982), they might recall personal experiences and write about them. Alternative endings might be provided for some trade books. Laura Numeroff's extensions of her popular *If You Give a Mouse a Cookie* (1994) into books with similar structures, *If You Give a Moose a Muffin* (1996) and *If You Give a Pig a Pancake* (1998), can serve as models for the children's creations.

SUMMARY

Introducing both reading and writing simultaneously to emergent readers has proven to build the language foundation that both processes share. This integration clearly demonstrates the purpose of written language to Catch-On Readers. Use of self-written books, highly structured writings such as "I" books, journaling, and writing in response to reading communicate the basic functions of language. They also provide the vehicle whereby teachers help Catch-On Readers develop their word-recognition abilities. Computers provide many innovative opportunities for helping students express themselves in print. For some teachers, integrated reading and writing methods form the centerpiece of instruction for Catch-On Readers.

Chapter 1 introduced Catch-On Readers, discussing the varying challenges faced by these students and instructional principles appropriate for helping them overcome their literacy struggles. We also provided case studies for two specific Catch-On Readers. Chapters 2 through 5 provided details about possible instructional interventions. Next, in Chapter 6, we will consider additional case studies representing the broad range of Catch-On Readers. Chapter 7 will complete our study of Catch-On Readers with suggestions for additional resources.

Thinking through Case Studies of Catch-On Readers

THINKING THROUGH KWESI'S STORY

In Chapter 1, we read about Kwesi's difficulties as he approached the end of second grade. Assessment on a formal reading test indicated that he was reading at the preprimer level, a kindergarten or early first-grade level. In response to significant failures in his attempts to acquire the basics of reading and literacy, Kwesi began to experience emotional problems. His mother asked that the school intervene in some way. The principal decided to move Kwesi into another classroom, one in which Mrs. Suarez, the teacher, used lessons based on the language experience approach with her lower achieving students. The school's reading specialist also was asked to conduct assessments of Kwesi's reading and literacy abilities.

Kwesi is a Catch-On Reader. His teacher had chosen to center the reading instruction for such students on the language experience approach. What does this choice mean in terms of the teacher's philosophy for best acquiring a foundation for future literacy development?

In their initial work with Kwesi, Mrs. Suarez and the reading specialist administered inventories on interest and attitude (see the Interest Inventory and Attitude Inventory in the appendix for examples). They found that Kwesi enjoyed having stories and books read to him. Anything associated with dinosaurs interested him, as did card games associated with TV shows, basketball, and the Candyland game. How might Mrs. Suarez capitalize on these interests in planning for Kwesi's language experience instruction? What activities might she use with Kwesi and her other struggling readers? Refer to the chapter on LEA (Chapter 4) as you consider these questions.

Mr. O'Connell, the school's reading specialist, administered an early literacy observational assessment. In the subtest on letter recognition (see Letter Name/Sound Test in the appendix as an example), Kwesi was able to identify all the uppercase letters, but he could not identify the following lowercase letters: *j* (as an *i*); *l* (identified as an *i*); *q* (identified as a *p*); *f* and *z* (did not attempt to guess these). In addition, he misidentified the *g* as a *p* but immediately self-corrected. Twenty-one of the lowercase letters were identified correctly.

On a writing sample, Kwesi was able to print his first and last names, but he used only the initial letter for all other words he attempted. On a test of his basic understandings about print (see the Print Awareness Checklist in the appendix as an example), he was not able to point to a period when asked, nor could he explain its purpose. He could not identify the title in a passage, nor was he able to identify a sentence.

When given a short list of one-syllable words (see High-Frequency Words in the appendix for examples) and asked to break them into their component parts (i.e., a phonemic segmentation task), Kwesi was unable to get a single word correct. On most of the words, he was able to isolate the first letter's sound. For example, he said "/r/" for "red." He was not able to isolate any medial or final phonemes, and he found this task very frustrating.

A final subtest measured sight-word recognition. He was presented with a list of several of the most commonly used words in English. He correctly identified the words *the* and *a*, but he was unable to identify such words as *to*, *did*, *it*, or *you*.

Mrs. Suarez made use of her small group lessons to continue to observe and assess Kwesi's reading and literacy level. His oral language ability was strong in some areas. In one lesson that involved a wordless picture book, Kwesi was able to make up an imaginative story that corresponded well to the pictures. However, he seemed to be unaware of the concept of rhymes. When asked to give a rhyme for the word *met*, he was unable to respond. Only when given more examples, such as *let* and *set*, was he able to give an answer: *Pet*.

His ability with printed text, of course, was low. He often confused similar letter sounds, such as /m/ and /n/. When doing a "making words" activity (see Chapter 3), he would create nonsense words but not recognize that they were not real words.

Paying attention was also difficult for him. During reading sessions, his eyes and mind would wander, and would start to discuss matters unrelated to the studies at hand. It became clear that fast-paced and varied activities would be needed to hold his attention.

As you consider the possibilities of using language experience approach activities with Kwesi, how might your instruction be informed by the assessment findings described above? What specific objectives might inform your choices as you engage him in language experiences?

In-depth consideration of a student such as Kwesi often involves assembling a large amount of information, including test scores, family and community background information, observational conclusions, and school performance data. The Master Cover Sheet for Cumulative Record (see Appendix) can be adapted by individual teachers and schools to meet their specific needs in organizing that information.

THINKING THROUGH SABRINA'S STORY

Sabrina had just completed first grade in a large city school. Her mother referred her to a university reading clinic because the school wanted to retain her in first grade. They reported that her reading level was below first grade, that she tended to be socially aloof, and that she had a poor attitude toward reading. Sabrina also was reported to have several physical difficulties, including poor vision that was corrected with glasses, and a gastrointestinal problem that had required corrective surgery.

Sabrina's school used a phonic basal reader program with decodable text, in which learning letter names and sounds was a prerequisite to learning words. Sabrina's teacher invited the school psychologist to observe Sabrina during a phonics lesson. The psychologist wrote the following report of the observation:

> All the children came to the front of the room and sat around Ms. Hill. The purpose of today's lesson was to learn the letter v and the sound associated with it. Sabrina wouldn't leave her desk in spite of repeated requests from Ms. Hill. She shook her head and put it down on the desk, covering her ears to block out the noise of the v sounds and words.

The school psychologist reported that Sabrina had poor memory for unrelated information such as random numbers and words but excellent recall of meaningful information. She noted that Sabrina was quite attentive during the psychologist's test and enjoyed the motor activities, the arithmetic, and determining how items were alike and different. This test did not provide the psychologist with information that would account for Sabrina's unusual behavior in class.

Speculate about the causes of Sabrina's reading difficulty. What would you do to help her become an active participant in reading class and to overcome her reading difficulty?

THINKING THROUGH DESHAWN'S STORY

Many teachers today encourage children to make daily journal entries. This activity helps students organize their thoughts for communicating with others, encourages personal expression, and provides opportunities for discovering the speech/print match as they engage in various levels of invented spelling. As noted, some teachers respond to their students' journal entries in an effort to create a personal, ongoing dialogue with their students.

DeShawn was reading at a preprimer level, whereas most of his classmates were reading at a second-grade level. He had a very limited sight-word vocabulary. He knew some sound–symbol associations, but he was not able to apply them as a decoding strategy. DeShawn was very discouraged about his slow progress in reading and writing.

How could the teacher determine why DeShawn is having so much difficulty making journal entries?

During a conference with DeShawn, Ms. Hill learned that DeShawn did not like writing in his journal because he did not know what to say, so he kept writing the same sentence over and over. He was also embarrassed because he could not spell.

His school records indicated that he had a language delay in the areas of semantic retrieval and naming. That is, he had trouble finding the words to express himself because he often forgot what something was called (e.g., *apple pie, bike, salt,* or *sugar*). He also had difficulty organizing his thoughts to express himself. The speech/language therapist had worked with him the previous year but was not able to include him in the program this year. Although DeShawn's reading was developing very slowly, he had not been referred to the psychologist for evaluation for a learning disability. His other teachers had not alerted the principal to his reading and writing difficulties.

How would you help DeShawn?

THINKING THROUGH HILARY'S STORY

Hilary, a first grader, was having trouble developing a sight-word vocabulary; in fact she had not learned any words. She did not know most of the letters and their sounds, and she did not maintain a one-to-one speech/print match. She had difficulty reading her own language experience stories that had been transcribed by the teacher. She was far behind her classmates in understanding the reading process. Most of Hilary's classmates were ready to read their first book in a basal reader series. Her teacher, Mrs. Carter, was certain that Hilary would have difficulty and ultimately fail if she was asked to learn to read using the basal.

What activities would you use to help Hilary acquire the basic sight words?

THINKING THROUGH MARGIE'S STORY

Margie, a first grader, loved listening to stories and reading big books with the teacher and her classmates. However, the teacher noticed that Margie could not identify separate words. When asked to point to each word as she read, it was apparent that she was tracking randomly. Margie also did not know many of the alphabet letters or the sounds that are commonly associated with those letters.

The teacher was concerned that Margie was not focusing on the correct print elements when a big book was read. For example, one day Margie was assigned to a group that was asked to read a poem that had been read aloud by the teacher and then read by the group several times. The teacher observed that Margie was not reading the printed words but substituting her own words. She also lost her place in the print and generally neglected to focus on the words.

How would you help Margie acquire the concept of word boundaries?

SUMMARY

Case studies of Catch-On Readers provide teachers the opportunity to think through the issues involved both in causes of reading and literacy struggles and in instructional interventions. In all cases, Catch-On Readers struggle with acquiring the foundational concepts of what reading and writing are all about. Their literacy functioning is at the very lowest levels, as they are hindered from moving on in achievement by the lack of this foundation. The reasons for their difficulties, however, can vary greatly. Teachers can make use of a broad variety of potential interventions. With some Catch-On Readers, any of the interventions will be effective, but with others teachers must carefully explore a variety of options to choose the one that seems to match the students' needs best.

Chapter 7 provides a collection of resources that teachers may use to learn more about Catch-On Readers and to provide them with effective instruction.

Additional Resources for Helping Catch-On Readers

REVIEW OF PART ONE: THE CATCH-ON READER

We described the Catch-On Reader as one who has difficulty understanding what readers do. This child often has not acquired the basic concepts of print, such as word boundaries, left–right progression of reading, the presence of a message in print, and the units of letters and words. Strategies and teaching techniques to help the child get started in reading include reading predictable text, shared reading, lap reading, partner reading, several types of language experience approaches, and writing to reading approaches. A variety of commercial programs, including Reading Recovery and Early Success (discussed below), provide models of instruction for Catch-On Readers.

KEY RESEARCH, THEORY, AND METHODS RELATED TO CATCH-ON READERS

Clay, M. (2001). *Change over time in children's literacy development*. Portsmouth, NH: Heinemann.

Clay, as the developer of the first-grade intervention program Reading Recovery, has played a key role in informing the teaching profession about teaching reading to children at the emergent level. This text is a summation of her years of study in the field of emergent literacy. Clay presents a series of benchmarks that describe the proficient reader at 8 years of age, then works backward to trace his/her development as a reader through the earlier years. A general overview of the Reading Recovery program also is presented.

Garcia, G. E. (2001). A theoretical discussion of young bilingual children's reading (preschool to grade 3). In J. V. Hoffman, D. L. Schallert, C. M. Fairbanks, J. Worthy, & B. Maloch (Eds.), *The 50th yearbook of the National Reading Conference* (pp. 228–237). Chicago: National Reading Conference.

Georgia Ernest Garcia is one of the leading authorities on the application of reading and literacy instruction for children from the ten million homes in the United States in which English is not the first language. Garcia surveys research to support the key assumption of bilingual education that children transfer knowledge in skills from reading in one language to reading in a second language. In fact, she notes, only the less successful bilingual readers "shut off" their knowledge of the first language when reading in the second.

Garcia warns against considering the bilingual child as having completely distinct needs from the monolingual child: "Many of the same underlying processes that characterize the reading of monolingual children also appear to characterize the reading of bilingual children" (p. 228). Teachers of reading can apply their understandings of what constitutes effective instruction, whether the children are from English-speaking homes or homes in which a language other than English is spoken.

Extended discussions of this article's topic are available (Garcia, 2000).

Hiebert, E. H., & Taylor, B. M. (2000). Beginning reading instruction: Research on early interventions. In M. Kamil, P. B. Mosenthal, P. D. Pearson, & R. Barr (Eds.), *The handbook of reading research* (Vol. 3, pp. 455–482). Mahwah, NJ: Erlbaum.

This extensive review of research surveyed a variety of early intervention programs, including seminal research from the 1970s by Dolores Durkin (1974–1975) and more contemporary approaches such as Marie Clay's Reading Recovery program and Gay Su Pinnell's guided reading approach. Findings suggested that programs consistently made gains in achievement, but that these gains were not sustained once the program ended. The authors suggest that research and development be carried out on programs designed to sustain the gains made in early intervention.

MATERIALS AND CURRICULA FOR CATCH-ON READERS

Reading Recovery Program

Reading Recovery was developed by Marie Clay as an intervention for first-grade children who are struggling to acquire reading and literacy. The program pairs a tutor with a child for 30 minutes a day over a 20-week period. Although official Reading Recovery tutors are trained and certified by licensed training centers, the methods used are widely known. Activities emphasized include making words, writing with the use of invented spelling, and daily introduction of a new book through a shared book experience lesson. . The tutor carries out a daily "running record" assessment (see the appendix) during the shared book experience activities. Published resources include:

Clay, M. M. (2000). *Concepts about print: What have children learned about the way we print language?* Portsmouth, NH: Heinemann. An introductory guide to administering Clay's popular Concepts about Print test.

Clay, M. M. (2000). *Running records for classroom teachers.* Portsmouth, NH: Heinemann. An introductory guide to administering running records.

Clay, M. M. (1993). *An observation survey of early literacy instruction.* Portsmouth, NH: Heinemann. The administration and scoring guide to the popular observation survey. Many authors and publishers have used this survey as a model for creating their own versions.

Clay, M. M. (1982). *Reading Recovery: A guidebook for teachers in training.* Portsmouth, NH: Heinemann. Clay's comprehensive guide to organizing and teaching a Reading Recovery program.

Early Success

This 30-week curriculum is based heavily on the approach to first-grade intervention popularized by Reading Recovery. Houghton Mifflin has adapted the curriculum to make it amenable to small group instruction, and the publisher has added a level that provides for second-grade instruction. Lesson plans and materials make the Early Success curriculum easy to understand and apply. Lessons are designed for daily instructional periods of 30 minutes. The first half of each lesson involves shared book experience lessons, using the leveled readers provided in the curriculum package. The second half of the lesson involves word-level and writing activities. The curriculum is accompanied by an observation survey assessment instrument similar to that originated by Marie Clay.

The Houghton Mifflin website is *www.hmco.com*, and the specific Early Success website is *www.eduplace.com/lds/inter/esuccess*.

TECHNOLOGY RESOURCES FOR CATCH-ON READERS

Computer-Mediated Word Recognition

Mike (2001) described the impact of computer software that matches text and speech, thereby allowing struggling readers to interact with material that otherwise would be impossible for them. Catch-On Readers are typically "word bound" in that their reading is so slow and halting that they have forgotten what was at the beginning of a sentence by the time they reach the end. Computer-mediated word recognition allows the child to click on an unfamiliar word and hear it pronounced. This technology is available in electronic storybooks for primary-grade youngsters (Balajthy, 1996). By using scanners, optical character recognition (OCR) software, and talking word processor programs, teachers can create similar opportunities to help struggling readers with the materials read in class.

Popular series of electronic books include:

Living Books. Novato, CA: Broderbund/The Learning Company. Online: *www.broderbund. com.* This series includes storybooks by Mercer Mayer (*Just Grandma and Me*) and Mark Brown (*Arthur's Teacher Trouble*).

Disney Storybooks. Los Angeles, CA: Disney Interactive Software. Online: *www.disney.com.*

Wiggleworks. New York: Scholastic. Online: *www.scholastic.com.*

Language Experience Activities

Many LEA activities can be carried out using computers, which allow greater freedom for revision and may provide greater motivation for students. A popular program for such LEA activities is KidPix (Broderbund Software, Novato, CA; *www.broderbund.com*). KidPix allows children or adults to type in stories, then illustrate them with an imaginative and involving drawing program. KidPix is simple enough to be used by very young children.

Direct Instruction

DaisyQuest and *Daisy's Castle.* Waldoboro, ME: Great Wave Software/McGraw Hill. Online: *www.greatwave.com.*

These two programs are designed for children at the emergent level; they require no reading ability or letter recognition skills. They include phonological awareness activities such as rhyming, segmenting of sounds within words, and blending of sounds.

SUMMARY

Catch-On Readers' literacy development has reached a plateau at the earliest levels, the emergent levels of literacy. Their struggles may be due to any of a wide range of problems that affect their understanding of the purposes and functions of print. Instruction will provide an individualized balance between direct, guided instruction and rich and creative experiences in reading and writing.

In Part One, we studied the causes and characteristics of the struggles facing Catch-On Readers. We examined two issues of primary concern, that of the Catch-On Reader's need to first understand the basic functions of print language and then to understand the basics of how to recognize words in print. Two major approaches to helping Catch-On Readers acquire literacy were described in detail: language experience and reading–writing integration. Finally, we examined additional case studies of Catch-On Readers and resources for their instruction.

In Part Two, we introduce another important group of struggling readers, the Catch-Up Readers. These students are no longer experiencing the struggles typical of Catch-On Readers. They understand the basic functions of print and are beginning to establish a foundational understanding of reading and literacy. Something has happened to stymie their efforts to continue achieving, however. These Catch-Up Readers have begun to fall further and further behind their peers in reading and literacy achievement.

PART TWO

Catch-Up Readers

Who Are the Catch-Up Readers in Your Classroom?

SARA'S STORY

Sara knew she was in trouble.

She loved school. She adored her second-grade teacher. She was quite popular, and children flocked to be her friend. She was not outgoing—in fact, in new situations she could be quite shy. At those times, her voice was barely audible and she looked down at her lap, finding it hard to meet anyone's eyes.

But as she warmed up to the situation, she would come alive. Other students wanted to be with her. And she was a good friend, too. She cared for others. She took her Sunday School lessons very seriously indeed, and the "love others as you love yourself" guidelines were a firm rule by which she tried to live.

Of course, there was another side to her. Her mom and dad would nod appreciatively to the teachers for their comments on Sara's work at school and her popularity and upbeat personality, then they would look at one another in bewilderment. "I wonder what brings out 'the dark side of the Force' at home," her father once muttered as the couple left the teacher conferences.

Dr. James Dobson, the founder of the Colorado family advocacy group Focus on the Family, wrote a book called *The Strong-Willed Child*. Sara's parents kept it on their bookshelf because Sara's home behaviors seemed to fit the characteristics of such children to a "T." She could be imperious and demanding or worse: When she decided she wanted something, or didn't want something, she could be unrelenting. It was almost as if Sara's ability to be even-tempered and kind was exhausted at school, and her frustrations were let out at home.

Now, in the middle of her second-grade year, those frustrations centered on reading. "I can't read. I can't read. All the other children read better than me," she sobbed into her pillow during bedtime prayers, her parents reported. "They are all reading chapter books. They are reading *Little House on the Prairie* and I can't even read the baby books in the class." In fact, only one child in the class was reading that series, which was on a fourth-grade readability level and far too difficult for the others. But a good number of the children were reading chapter books written on a second- or third-grade level, such as the *Polk Street School* series and the *Berenstain Bears* chapter book series.

Her teacher assigned 15 minutes of recreational reading a night. Children could choose their own material for these sessions, and they could either read themselves or have their parents read to them. As the year progressed, however, the teacher began to encourage the children to read silently themselves or aloud to their parents. Sara self-consciously refused to read aloud. She insisted either that her parents read to her, or that she be allowed to read silently. But her mom and dad had noticed that she was actually doing little more than looking at pictures in the books during the silent reading. When they encouraged her to read aloud from the books she had chosen, she shouted "No!" and stomped off to cry.

Sara was in the third reading group in class, the lowest. Her teacher was not very concerned, because she believed that Sara was still within the average range of abilities, but her parents were worried about her attitude and lack of achievement. They had her assessed by a reading specialist, whose findings corroborated the teacher's. Sara was reading at a late first-grade level, which was not so far below the average that a classroom teacher would be very concerned. A typical class of mid-year second graders would be comprised of children ranging from early first grade (preprimer or primer) through third or fourth grade in reading ability. Sara's mastery of one-syllable sight words was encouraging, as was her understanding of phonics relationships. However, she was not up to par in applying phonics rules in actual reading situations, and she did not even attempt to decode multisyllabic words.

Two or three children in Sara's class, classified as needing special education, were functioning well below Sara's level. They were receiving tutorial reading instruction at the early- or mid-first-grade level. Sara's reading group was working with materials at the early-second-grade level.

Sara was never one to hide her emotions at home. Her mom called her "Sarah Bernhardt" privately. It became more and more evident that Sara was very upset, and she even began to express a reluctance to attend school. She complained of stomachaches in the morning, and she missed two or three days of school. She refused to read at home.

Sara's mom and dad visited the school to discuss their concerns. The teacher agreed that she could give Sara closer attention and some limited individualized work in reading. The parents and teacher decided on a two-pronged effort. The instruction in her small group was appropriate for development of sight words, phonics and context analysis skills. Her teacher used a whole language approach, which centered on children's literature units, but she was quite direct in teaching strategies and skills as they were needed in reading the literature. The teacher agreed to inform Sara's parents about which strategies and skills were focused on each week. The parents were advised to begin using much easier books for recreational reading than Sara had been choosing. This change, in combination with the strategy of the parent reading one page, then Sara reading one page, overcame much of Sara's reluctance to put in her at-home reading time. The parents managed to get Sara to spend almost 30 minutes a day in reading, given that they (child and parent) alternated the reading.

The parents also reinforced the teacher's step-by-step word-recognition procedure during the home reading sessions. Because of the home–school contacts, they were aware of what words Sara should be able to recognize and what words were simply too difficult for her. In their reading together, they stopped the oral reading and guided Sara to use her word-recognition strategies when she miscued a word that she should have recognized. For example, they might cover the second syllable of a word with a finger, ask Sara to phonetically analyze the first syllable, then move on to the second in like fashion. Or they might ask, "Did the word you said just now make sense in the sentence?" to encourage context analysis.

Within several weeks, Sara began to tire of the first-grade-level picture books she was bringing home from her classroom. She began to read more challenging picture books written at a second-grade level, such as the *Arthur* and *Berenstain Bears* picture books. Two months later, as the end of the school year was approaching, her parents tried out a series of chapter books, including the *Berenstain Bears* and *Arthur* chapter books designed for older students than the picture books. After several more weeks, Sara chose a *Babysitter's Club Little Sister* book, about a young girl named Karen who was both adventurous and a trifle troublesome. Sara struggled through it, alternating pages with her mom or dad, but by the end she was hooked on Karen's adventures. She bought every book in the series that she could find at garage sales that summer. By the end of the summer, she was reading completely on her own, well above grade level, even enjoying *Little House on the Prairie* during her third-grade year. By the end of third grade, she had read all the *Harry Potter* books, written far above her actual grade level—twice.

In retrospect, Sara's parents felt that the two-pronged approach to helping Sara catch up with her peers was crucial. First, both they and the teacher made a concerted effort to help Sara develop effective word-recognition strategies. The teacher taught the strategies and skills in class, and through newsletters sent home, she helped the parents become aware of them as well. Second, the parents made use of the teacher's recreational reading requirements to motivate Sara to spend extensive time reading, and they reinforced the word-recognition strategies she was learning in school. Their efforts supplemented the classroom reading and literacy program that was already rich in children's literature, discussion, and writing.

DESCRIPTION OF THE CATCH-UP READER

Sara was a Catch-Up Reader. Catch-Up Readers lag behind their classmates in the level of literacy that they have acquired. These students have difficulty meeting the demands of reading and writing that are expected at their age and grade levels.

The difficulties faced by these children may not always seem serious. In Sara's case, for example, the teacher and parents' efforts were quickly and dramatically rewarded by improvement in her reading achievement. Unfortunately, the reading and literacy difficulties faced by Catch-Up Readers often go unrecognized for extended periods. These difficulties create a roadblock to further reading and literacy development and they generalize to aspects of the literacy processes that were at first unaffected. For example, a comprehension difficulty might impede writing achievement.

Finally children become emotionally upset, miss days of school because of the illnesses such disturbances promote, and battle their parents about recreational reading and other homework assignments. The scene is set for extended academic failure and the personal and social failures that accompany it.

REASONS FOR READING DIFFICULTY

Sara is intellectually capable, responsive to adult interventions, and blessed by parents and teachers who are caring, committed, and competent. Catch-Up Readers, in general, do not necessarily have all these benefits at work on their behalf. However, all are distinguished from Catch-On Readers in that they have mastered the basic concepts of print and were successful in learning the early print processing and meaning processing aspects of reading and literacy. They are distinguished from Stalled Readers largely in terms of the severity of their reading and learning problems. A Checklist of Reading Behaviors (see Appendix) can be used to evaluate reading performance across the grade and ability levels. Catch-Up Readers respond to well-planned, creative reading and literacy instruction that is individually tailored to their needs, though it may be implemented in small group settings with other children who face the same challenges.

Instruction of Catch-Up Readers can be carried out in the classroom but may need to be supplemented in a tutorial or small group setting outside the regular classroom. A frequent failing of school programs designed to help Catch-Up Readers is that they replace regular classroom instruction with reading and literacy instruction in another setting. The students' time-on-task in learning reading and literacy, a vitally critical prerequisite to their academic growth, does not increase.

Instruction that is carried out at a slower pace than the developmental classroom program is called adaptive (or adapted) instruction. Such instruction is geared toward students whose intellectual potential is limited. Classroom teachers attempt to set reasonable expectations and attend to the needs and interests of such students. However, when expectations are so low that instruction is slowed down, the lack of progress almost guarantees that struggling students will never achieve reading proficiency. Today, adaptive instruction has come to be known as one type of compensatory instruction—instruction that is designed to compensate for difficulties faced by Catch-Up Readers and bring them up to grade-level achievement standards. Students whose intellectual abilities are limited can achieve reading and literacy growth by additional time-on-task in instructional settings, not simply by moving at a slower pace.

Corrective instruction is carried out in the classroom by the teacher, an aide, or a specialist. In Sara's case, the parents also participated. This instruction addresses the individual needs of the Catch-Up Reader. Careful monitoring of student achievement, recognition of potential difficulties, and a competent and thorough instructional response are the responsibilities of every classroom teacher. Effective classroom teachers play the key role in identifying and providing instruction for Catch-Up Readers. In fact, such prompt and effective corrective instruction keeps many potential and incipient Catch-Up Readers from further problems and puts them back on track in regular developmental instruction. In our case study of Sara, concerned parents and intervention by the classroom teacher was sufficient to alleviate the difficulty.

Remedial instruction is provided outside the regular classroom by a teacher with specialized reading and literacy skills for assessment and instruction. Such a teacher is often called a reading specialist and the location of instruction is often called a reading clinic. Specialists remain in close communication with the child's classroom teacher, and both cooperate to provide instruction that is as seamless as possible in the classroom and clinic.

Obviously, there is a wide variety of reasons that students read at lower levels than their peers. Nevertheless, reading difficulties usually result from (1) word-identification problems, (2) vocabulary problems, (3) comprehension problems, or (4) a combination of the three (Barr, Blachowicz, & Wogman-Sadow, 1995). In Sara's case, for example, word identification was the problem.

We briefly examine five broad categories in an effort to offer ideas as to why some children become Catch-Up Readers:

- Limited literacy experiences prior to school entrance
- Delayed maturation and physical development of auditory, visual, cognitive, or motor systems
- Cultural and environmental differences
- Cognitive makeup
- Inappropriate school experiences

Limited Literacy Experiences

Limited literacy experiences prior to starting school may place students at a disadvantage for formal instruction in reading and writing. That is, they may not enter school with a well-developed oral language base. They might have had limited literacy experiences in their home environments, with less than average time spent listening to stories or participating in conversations with adults and other children. They might have had limited experiences outside their homes, with few family outings and lack of instruction in the meaning of signs and symbols in their neighborhood.

Catch-Up Readers often lag behind their peers in developing literacy behaviors before school literacy instruction begins. Their problems typically surface in kindergarten, where it becomes apparent that their emergent literacy behaviors are not as developed as those of their peers. Allington (1994) warned that the poorer performance of these children is often mistaken as a poorer capacity to learn.

While other kindergarten and first-grade students are acquiring skills and reading abilities specifically associated with word identification and comprehension, Catch-Up Readers are still acquiring an understanding of the reader's role in processing print. That is, they are still learning abstract concepts about print conventions and language communication, such as phoneme segmentation and word boundaries. Lack of prior experiences within the home environment coupled with school instructional policies may affect the progress of students throughout their elementary school years (Allington, 1983, 1994, 2002).

Delayed Maturation and Development

Maturation and physical development of auditory and visual processes, neurological and cognitive systems, and language may not have developed to the level at which formal classroom instruction is beneficial. The ways in which reading and literacy are taught in the classroom, including the commercial reading programs involved, can have a negative impact on the Catch-Up Reader's abilities to successfully engage in reading activities.

For example, slower maturation and physical development in the auditory system make it difficult for a student to learn sound–symbol associations, auditory discrimination, and sound blending. Students with such delays will lag behind their peers. Phonics-based programs, which depend heavily on these abilities, may be especially problematic. Learning skills that are taught out of context, such as occurs in the synthetic phonics approaches that require a sophisticated grasp of grapheme–phoneme relationships, demands a high level of abstraction. This puts unrealistic demands on students whose processing systems are not well developed.

Cultural and Environmental Differences

Children whose home and community environments are outside the cultural mainstream may find themselves at risk for learning delays in acquiring the literacy behaviors associated with schooling. Au (1993, 2002) pointed out the need for teachers to be aware of students' cultural backgrounds and to provide opportunities that demonstrate respect for them.

Part of demonstrating this awareness and respect involves teaching in a manner that makes a comfortable match with the teaching and learning carried out in the home. The possibly conflicting roles involved in home and school literacy need to be resolved so that the student can successfully engage in literacy experiences (Cook-Gomperez, 1986). Students whose home environments are in conflict with the school environment may lag behind their peers in their ability to participate in, and benefit from, school literacy programs. Au and Kawakami's (1994) review of research, for example, found that teachers had positive results when they accepted students' home languages, respected family values, and adapted their discussion and questioning to the patterns used in the culture of the local community.

Cognitive Makeup

Cognitive makeup can influence the rate at which literacy is acquired and the level that is achieved. Low aptitude or intelligence may have a negative influence on school achievement. That is, a child with below normal intelligence may learn to read and write at a slower rate than classmates of average intelligence. Teachers should bear in mind, however, that the relationship between intelligence level and reading achievement is complex. Most children who are below average in intelligence learn to read without difficulty.

Teachers should use caution in using IQ, aptitude, or other intellectual factors as barometers for determining expected rate of reading acquisition and for determining expected reading levels. Special care must be taken not to overemphasize the results of group IQ or aptitude tests. Such tests may be used as screening devices, but teachers should be aware of their limited statistical reliability. In addition, if the test involved reading, the IQ score may not reflect a valid intelligence measure for children who have reading and literacy difficulties.

As noted earlier in this chapter, children with low-normal and below-normal IQs usually learn to recognize words and comprehend text without difficulty. Their achievement can be at a level far beyond that which might be expected when IQ measures are given inappropriate weight by educators.

Inappropriate School Experiences

The schooling received by a child may result in poor reading achievement. Absenteeism may be high during critical instructional periods. High mobility, especially characteristic of disadvantaged families, may lead to poorly connected instruction. Teacher inexperience can present problems. The match between schooling and home learning may be poor. The child's formal reading program may not engage him/her, or it may not capitalize on the child's strengths in learning. There may be a lack of willingness and determination on the part of the school system to succeed with struggling readers (Neal & Kelly, 2002).

We recognize that schools are limited in their ability to provide optimal instruction for all their students. Some of these limitations may lie beyond the power of individual teachers, schools, and districts to rectify. Nonetheless, the teaching profession and public school systems are committed to striving toward this goal. Modifications and improvements of school-based learning experiences play the most important roles, both in intervening to prevent children from becoming Catch-Up Readers and in remedying the difficulties faced by children who are already Catch-Up Readers.

INSTRUCTING THE CATCH-UP READER

Materials and Strategies

As noted, Catch-Up Readers have attained a certain measure of reading and writing skills and abilities—significantly more than the Catch-On Readers discussed in the first section of this book—but these skills and abilities are below those of their average achieving peers. Teachers can use the same materials as used with average achievers, but they should be written at a less complex level. Teachers should be aware that Catch-Up Readers might have considerable difficulty with abstract comprehension activities. Teacher questions such as "What is the main idea of this paragraph?" are a challenge for any reader, but Catch-Up Readers may face particular difficulty in dealing with the abstract concept of *main idea*. Instruction of Catch-Up Readers should provide sufficient focus on the child's specific needs through the use of word identification, oral reading fluency, or comprehension activities.

Materials should be self-selected ones that elicit high interest, as much as possible. To overcome motivational difficulties caused by lack of progress, it is important for readers to have an opportunity to choose the type of book they would like to read. Classroom grouping patterns should include heterogeneous groups composed of both good and poor readers, so that Catch-Up Readers can choose a group whose reading interests are similar to their own.

Catch-Up Readers benefit from direct instruction in the strategies they can use in order to gain higher-level concepts from their reading material. They may not know how to use the strategies that a good reader uses, such as how to identify main ideas or how to make reasonable predictions. Teachers should keep in mind that strategy instruction is different from drill instruction. Overuse of dull, repetitive, and time-wasting drills has been an unfortunate characteristic of some reading classrooms. Strategy instruction, on the other hand, engages children by offering relevant concepts on how to overcome the reading challenges they are experiencing.

For example, Catch-Up Readers benefit from teacher modeling of how to recognize organizational patterns in text or how to apply sources of prior knowledge to the text they are reading (Block, Oakar, & Hurt, 2002). It is important to clearly demonstrate strategies and not assume that students can or will use a strategy simply because it has been introduced in a lecture. Modeling and practicing strategies with several different types of reading material are essential. Unless a strategy has been internalized by modeling and practice, it is likely that the student will revert back to nonstrategic reading when he/she is reading independently.

Instructional Goals

The Catch-Up Reader needs to become a strategic, comprehending reader. This reader should use the most efficient and effective cue systems (such as graphophonemic, syntactic, or semantic) to gain meaning from text (see Sidebar 8.1). Because word recognition difficulties often interfere with comprehension, this reader needs to learn to use the context in a very efficient manner. Word recognition, vocabulary, and comprehension should be stressed during teacher modeling activities.

Sidebar 8.1. Cue Systems

Kenneth Goodman, a scholar at the University of Arizona and past president of the International Reading Association, has helped educators recognize that readers bring a variety of kinds of knowledge to the reading task. His cognitive model of reading (Goodman, 1967, 1976) is called a top-down model, because it emphasizes the information readers bring to reading. (Models that instead emphasize the effect of the printed material itself are called bottom-up models.)

One important outgrowth of this model is the study of children's miscues—situations in which a child's oral reading does not match the printed text. Goodman convincingly demonstrated that miscues during oral reading often give some indication of the reading processes occurring in the child's mind.

Three kinds of knowledge brought to the reading task by readers are:

1. *Graphophonemic.* knowledge about graphemes (printed letters) and phonemes (letter sounds). A child who miscues the word *breath* as *broth* is demonstrating graphophonemic knowledge, despite the error.

2. *Syntactic.* knowledge about grammar. Tommy was reading a sentence from one of the Berenstain Bears: "The Too-Tall gang began to dance around the Bear Scouts, pretending to paddle." Instead of *paddle*, he read *point*. His ability to recognize that a verb was needed to make a grammatical sentence (even if he did not have the explicit grammatical knowledge to know the term *verb*) is an example of syntactic knowledge. We also see that the graphophonemic similarity of his miscue to the target word was limited to the initial letter.

3. *Semantic.* knowledge about meaning. In the example above, Tommy had seen a picture of the Too-Tall gang dancing around the Bear Scouts. It seemed that they were pointing at the Scouts. He used his knowledge of the plot situation and the picture to help identify the printed word *paddle.*

Sidebar 8.2. Avoidance Behavior

Children often exhibit behaviors designed, consciously or unconsciously, to avoid unpleasant events. Disruptive behavior in class can be the result of a child's negative attitude toward reading or other subject matter. This negative attitude is often fueled by the frustration and failure experienced in attempts to master the subject matter. Teachers try to determine what factors underlie disruptive behaviors.

Children often do not know the root cause of their avoidance, or even that they *are* avoiding anything. They can be very subtle in their use of avoidance behavior. "Tuning out"—not paying close attention and disengaging from class activities—might not be readily noticed by the teacher. The quiet student might easily "fall through the cracks," unless the classroom teacher remains alert.

JIMMY'S STORY

Mrs. Jerome was in the process of getting to know the students in her third-grade class. It was September of the school year, and she took this month to closely observe the students in her care. She wanted to know their likes and dislikes, their work habits, and their personal relationships with other children. She observed the children during independent reading and writing activities. She took note of their discussions with each other and their contributions to class discussions.

Mrs. Jerome was puzzled about Jimmy. He was always leaving his desk to sharpen a pencil, talk to a neighbor, go to the bathroom, or find an item in his book bag (see Sidebar 8.2). As a result, his written work was seldom completed when he finally handed it in. Sometimes his work was not handed in at all, and she would find a half completed paper crumpled up inside his desk. However, he contributed to class discussions and was well liked by his classmates.

Her observations of his reading behavior suggested that he read at a slower rate than his peers. He preferred to listen to his classmates read aloud rather than taking a turn himself. Examining the work he turned in, she noted that he continued to make extensive use of invented spelling (see Sidebar 8.3). Few words were spelled correctly.

Mrs. Jerome wondered if Jimmy might have a word-recognition problem that was interfering with his reading development. His slow reading might be the result of difficulty in decoding and recognizing words on sight. His avoidance behaviors toward independent work might be the result of his poor reading ability. She decided to have him read aloud while she took a running record of his oral reading from the book currently being read by the class, a chapter book that was rated at the third-grade level. Running records are informal assessment devices used by teachers of young children. As a child reads a passage aloud, the teacher follows along with a piece of blank paper to record results. The teacher puts a checkmark for each word pronounced correctly and writes down any miscues in each line of the target passage.

Results of the running record confirmed Mrs. Jerome's hypothesis that Jimmy had a word-recognition problem that was interfering with his ability to complete third-grade work on par with his classmates. She referred Jimmy to the reading specialist to determine

Sidebar 8.3. Invented Spelling

In order to encourage writing in the early years, kindergarten and first-grade teachers usually allow children to spell as best they can, rather than requiring standard spelling. Many teachers find that young children learn to enjoy writing. It even becomes an important part of their life when it can be done without the cognitive burden of producing precise spelling and the time-consuming exercise of looking words up in a pictionary or dictionary.

When properly taught and applied, invented spelling can be used for reinforcement and practice of grapheme–phoneme correspondences. A first-grade child might want to use the word *careful*, for example. The invented spelling approach does not allow the child to simply jot down whatever comes to mind. Instead, the child sounds out the word, phoneme by phoneme, which might come out like *k-a-r-r-f-l*. Feedback given by teachers, aides, volunteers, or parents gradually reinforces knowledge of letter–sound correspondences.

Invented spelling is sometimes called temporary spelling. Teachers' goals include a transition to traditional spelling starting slowly in first grade, gradually strengthening in second and third grades, so that by fourth grade, children are well on track to becoming knowledgeable spellers.

the extent of his word-recognition difficulty and to determine if there were any other reading-related problems. Mrs. Jerome had perused his file by this time, so she knew that Jimmy's aptitude scores (see Sidebar 8.4) were above average.

The reading teacher reported the results of her assessments and confirmed that Jimmy read very slowly. He tried to sound out every word but had little success with this method because he had not mastered letter–sound correspondences and had difficulty blending sounds to form words. The reading teacher noticed that Jimmy had particular difficulty with double vowels (such as the *ai* in *bait*—a vowel digraph in which two vowels make one

Sidebar 8.4. Intelligence and Aptitude Tests

Intelligence and aptitude tests are designed to inform teachers about a child's potential for performance in school. Intelligence (or IQ) tests are based on the assumption that there is a single global factor (i.e., IQ) associated with success in school-related learning. Aptitude tests attempt to assess a variety of such factors.

Children should be encouraged to actualize their fullest potential, no matter what their IQ or aptitudes may be. These tests can be helpful in trying to determine whether a child who is experiencing difficulties face global challenges to succeeding in school, or whether there are simply deficiencies in specific skills.

sound corresponding to the well-known phonics rule "When two vowels go walking, the first does the talking"—or the *ou* in *house*—a diphthong in which the tongue glides from one vowel sound to another vowel sound) and r-controlled vowels (such as the *er* sound in *her* or the *ar* sound in *car*).

Mrs. Jerome discussed Jimmy's case further with the reading teacher. They talked about the strategies and activities Mrs. Jerome could use with Jimmy to improve his word recognition and speed of reading. Mrs. Jerome needed guidance in determining the strategies she should model and how she would plan the time to work with Jimmy.

We continue our analysis of Jimmy's story in Chapter 13.

KEVIN'S STORY

Kevin, also a third-grader, had a comprehension problem. His teachers were concerned about his poor understanding of basal reader stories and his difficulty recalling and organizing information from text.

Kevin's standardized test scores for first grade indicated that he had been in the 15th percentile for comprehension and the 75th percentile for word recognition. His second-grade standardized test scores in reading were 12th percentile for comprehension and 70th percentile for word recognition. (See Chapter 13 for information on interpreting standardized test scores.) There was a clear disparity between his performance on the comprehension and word-recognition measures.

Mrs. Swanson, his teacher, wanted to help him improve his ability to comprehend information. She studied his file and found that his IQ, at 112, was within the normal range. Puzzled about his comprehension difficulties, Mrs. Swanson asked the reading teacher to help her plan strategies to which Kevin might respond.

The reading teacher, Mr. Hammond, decided first to assess Kevin's reading using an informal reading inventory (IRI; see Sidebar 8.5). He found that Kevin was reading at the third-grade level for word recognition but the early second-grade level for comprehension. Analysis of Kevin's responses to comprehension questions on the IRI suggested that he had difficulty with all types of questions: literal, inferential, evaluative, and vocabulary. He often responded with "I don't know" to the questions. Facts eluded him, and he could not remember the specific details of particular situations. Even more often, he had difficulty making inferences and judgments about information in the text. He was not reading "between the lines."

In order to obtain additional information about Kevin, Mr. Hammond and Mrs. Swanson planned several diagnostic teaching experiences. These activities would be carried out during the normal course of classroom instruction, and the results would be closely studied in their efforts to obtain a clearer diagnostic picture.

When Mrs. Swanson scaffolded the reading experience by first modeling the processes and procedures that Kevin should use as he read a selection, the teachers were attempting to identify at what level Kevin could understand text. Although the IRI suggested that Kevin was reading at a second-grade instructional level, he might be able to improve his comprehension to deal with his third-grade classroom materials with the help of direct modeling .

We continue our analysis of Kevin's Story in Chapter 13.

Sidebar 8.5. Informal Reading Inventories

The informal reading inventory (IRI) is a commonly used informal assessment device that is individually administered. Some teachers create their own IRIs, but the great majority purchase one of the many commercially published versions. Administration and scoring procedures are explained in each test. For each of the IRI sections, teachers obtain three scores: (1) an Instructional Level score, indicating the grade level or levels at which the child can best be instructed; (2) a Frustration Level score, indicating the grade level at which instruction would be prohibitively difficult for the child; and (3) an Independent Level score, indicating the grade level at which instruction would be very easy for the child.

Once the entire test has been administered, the combined scores are used to determine overall Instructional, Frustration, and Independent reading levels for the child.

The accuracy of IRI scores has been called into question. Despite this potentially serious flaw, teachers find these assessments to be quite useful for obtaining insights into individual students' reading processes and strategies (Paris, 2002).

An IRI typically has four parts:

- *Graded Word Lists*. The child reads lists of words aloud. The words in each list reflect a specific reading grade level. From this subtest, teachers determine a Word Recognition Out-of-Context score.
- *Graded Oral Reading Passages*. The child reads short passages aloud, each at a succeedingly more challenging grade level. After each passage, the teacher asks 10 questions. The teacher records the miscues during oral reading and the results of the comprehension test. From this subtest, teachers determine a Word-Recognition-in-Context score and an Oral Reading Comprehension score.
- *Graded Silent Reading Passages*. The child reads short passages silently, each at a succeedingly more challenging grade level. After each passage, the teacher asks about 10 questions. From this subtest, teachers determine a Silent Reading Comprehension score.
- *Listening Comprehension Passages*. The teacher reads short passages to the child, each at a succeedingly more challenging grade level. After each passage, the teacher asks about 10 questions. From this subtest, teachers determine a Listening Comprehension score.

CLARA'S STORY

Clara was reading below her peers in her fourth-grade classroom. Her teacher, Mrs. Prescott, was concerned. She decided to observe Clara as she interacted with her peers, worked within reading groups, read independently, and completed written work. Mrs. Prescott also contacted the reading teacher to find out if Clara had a history of reading difficulties and what had been done about them in the past.

The reading teacher, Mrs. Dee, reported that Clara had received remedial reading services in second and third grades but had achieved a standardized test score above the cut-off level for children who would receive services for this school year. As a result, she was not eligible for remedial services in fourth grade. Mrs. Dee told the classroom teacher that Clara had been taught grapheme–phoneme correspondences and word-recognition skills. She also had received lessons in comprehension development involving listening to stories and answering questions.

Mrs. Dee recommended additional assessment to determine Clara's reading level, her approaches to word recognition, the processes she used to comprehend, and her spelling and writing abilities. Mrs. Dee offered to administer an IRI to Clara and share the results with Mrs. Prescott.

In the meantime, Mrs. Prescott began observing Clara during reading and writing activities. Sitting with Clara's reading group, Mrs. Prescott asked Clara to read a page of a basal reader story out loud. Clara's reading was halting as she frequently corrected her many miscues, but her miscues often made sense syntactically and semantically. Then she would realize that something was wrong, and she would self-correct. The frequency of these miscues and self-corrections made reading aloud very difficult for Clara. However, when Mrs. Prescott asked Clara to retell what she had read, much to her surprise Clara retold the events and their sequence.

The IRI results revealed that Clara's overall reading level was at grade 4, with word recognition her major difficulty. Clara read the word lists on the IRI at a second-grade instructional level, but her oral reading within the paragraphs and her comprehension were at grade four. Mrs. Dee found that Clara did not have a well-developed sight-word vocabulary and did not use decoding skills to identify words. Clara had difficulty with both one- and two-syllable words. There did not seem to be a pattern to her miscues, given that some of the miscued words were basic sight words and others were not. Some miscued words contained double vowels but other words with double vowels were correctly identified. Mrs. Dee reported that Clara could listen and respond to comprehension questions at the sixth-grade level on this IRI.

Mrs. Dee concluded that Clara's word-recognition difficulty was inhibiting her overall reading growth.

Mrs. Dee's assessment and Mrs. Prescott's observation of Clara during reading were consistent. Clara overused the context, taking guesses at words she did not recognize.

We continue our analysis of Clara's story in Chapter 13.

MARTIN'S STORY

Martin, a fifth-grade student, entered Mr. Zink's class in September of the school year. He had been receiving Title I services (see Sidebar 8.6) on and off since third grade due to low scores on standardized tests. His scores across the years are reported in Figure 8.1.

Mr. Zink observed that Martin was a quiet boy who seldom volunteered information during class discussions. When Mr. Zink called on him unexpectedly, he often would not or could not respond to his questions.

Martin was working with a small group of students who were reading several books from the *Goosebumps* series by R. L. Stine (1993). Although Martin read at the same rate as his peers, observation of the group dynamics indicated that he did not offer much in discussion.

Sidebar 8.6. Title I

Title I (once called Chapter I) is a federally funded program that provides compensatory education to children who are at risk of poor school performance. Title I funding was instituted to aid disadvantaged school districts. Those districts receive more funding from the Title I program than districts comprised of higher socioeconomic neighborhoods. Many programs titled Reading Lab, Reading Clinic, Reading Program, and so forth, are actually funded, in large part, by Title I.

A review of Martin's written work suggested to Mr. Zink that his spelling ability was average. His responses in comprehension activities revealed that he could answer literal-level questions but was not able to answer interpretive-level questions that involved integrating the information from several places. Mr. Zink examined a book report that Martin had completed after reading *Be Careful What You Wish For* (Stine, 1993):

> This was a story. A girl wanted to get at her friends who didn't like her.
> She made a wish but it wasn't what she wanted. She made anuther.
> She ate worms And was like a bird.

In looking at the report, he was concerned about Martin's recall of information and his ability to organize it in a written composition. He wondered if Martin had difficulty comprehending what he read.

Mr. Zink asked the reading teacher to conduct further assessment of Martin's comprehension abilities. He also asked for suggestions for working with Martin in the classroom.

We continue our analysis of Martin's story in Chapter 13.

EMANUEL'S STORY

Emanuel, a third grader, appeared to be a very slow reader. He used his finger to keep his place as he read, and Mr. Stevens, his teacher, observed him mouthing each word as well. In reading groups, other members of the group would become very impatient with him as Mr.

Grade	Word identification	Vocabulary	Comprehension
2	59 (5)*	41 (5)	16 (3)
3	63 (6)	38 (4)	23 (4)
4	70 (6)	39 (4)	8 (2)

*Percentiles (stanines).

FIGURE 8.1. *Martin's Stanford Achievement Test scores.*

Stevens waited for Emanuel to finish reading. Mr. Stevens considered taking him out of the group and giving him individualized instruction, but he was reluctant to make Emanuel feel different from the other students.

Mr. Stevens decided to carry out diagnostic teaching in order to gain insight into the root of Emanuel's slow reading. The reading teacher conferred with Mr. Stevens about Emanuel and helped with suggestions.

First, Mr. Stevens listened to Emanuel read aloud and took a running record of this reading while timing a 100-word segment. He found that Emanuel decoded most of the words, recognizing very few on sight. Thus he was not surprised that it took Emanuel 4 minutes to read the 100-word segment—far longer than normal. Mr. Stevens also noted that Emanuel read with little expression or enthusiasm. In fact, his reading of the passage sounded as if he were reading a list of words. Mr. Stevens concluded that Emanuel was so intent on decoding the words that he ignored other requirements of oral reading. Interestingly, when Emanuel was asked questions about what he has read or to retell the story, his comprehension and recall were very accurate.

We continue our analysis of Emanuel's story in Chapter 13.

SUMMARY

Catch-Up Readers understand the basic concepts of print and have been successful in the earliest stages of reading acquisition, but they are falling behind their peers in achievement. They are failing to meet the task demands in reading and writing that teachers expect at their age and grade level. Imperatives of instruction for Catch-Up Readers revolve around a program that is individually tailored to their needs. Teachers must determine whether reading difficulties arise from word recognition, vocabulary, comprehension problems, or from some combination of the three. Appropriate instruction must then be supplied, combined with an emphasis on motivation and engagement.

Reasons for the problems faced by Catch-Up Readers often fall into one or more of five broad categories: limited literacy experiences, delayed maturation, cultural and environmental differences, cognitive makeup, or inappropriate school experiences. The teacher's goal is to study the students' strengths and weaknesses in order to provide the Catch-Up Readers with strong and flexible word-recognition capacities, a growing vocabulary, and strategic approaches to both narrative and expository comprehension. Chapters 9 to 12 will deal with each of these four curricular objectives in turn.

CHAPTER 9

Helping Catch-Up Readers with Word Recognition

The problems faced by Catch-On Readers who are struggling with the very beginning concepts of word recognition are discussed in Chapter 3. Such students are challenged in acquiring basic print concepts, such as the meaning conveyed by print, the word or sentence as a unit, or the constituent parts comprising a spoken or printed word.

Catch-Up Readers, on the other hand, understand the fundamental principles on which literacy is built. They have developed a basic sight-word vocabulary and have learned some or (occasionally) all of the major phonics skills. At the least, they understand the concepts underlying the learning of such literacy skills. Their problem tends to be quantitative rather than qualitative, in that they have not kept up with their peers in level of achievement. One key reason for this lag is that Catch-Up Readers are not able to identify a sufficient number of words as they read (Carver, 2000).

Some of the methods used with Catch-On Readers are equally appropriate for the Catch-Up Reader. Word banks, for instance, can be used in a variety of creative, game-like activities to increase sight-word vocabulary. Word sorts are useful in helping children to think actively about the print features that characterize similar and different words.

VISUAL/MEANING EMPHASIS

Sight Words

Sight words are basic high-frequency words that are recognized instantly without applying any word-attack strategies. These words are encountered in print so often that they should be recalled without any analysis of the component parts (see Chapter 3).

Children's sight-word vocabularies have two categories: function words and content words. Catch-Up Readers often have difficulty recognizing function words—basic, high-utility words. The abstract qualities of these words do not allow the reader to easily access them from memory. For example, words like *have, come, now, how,* and *this* cannot be pictured mentally. They are not like the content sight words that produce vivid visual images, such as *elephant, monkey, chair,* and *house.*

In addition to the challenges posed by their abstract nature, function words are often orthographically similar; that is, they look alike. Consider the following words for their similar visual features:

> now/how
>
> come/came
>
> what/went/want
>
> no/on
>
> were/where
>
> saw/was

In many instances, just one letter distinguishes the two words. Readers who have difficulty distinguishing the distinctive features of both letters and words tend to confuse these words when they are encountered in print. Typically, readers resort to guessing, often substituting one of the lookalikes for the printed word.

However difficult to recognize these words may be, function words form the glue of sentences. Incorrectly identifying these words can change the intended meaning of a sentence, paragraph, or selection, leading to comprehension difficulties. Some students are so intimidated by their difficulty in recognizing function sight words that they will not try to correct their miscues during oral reading even when the sentences do not make sense.

Sammy, for example, was reading the following target passage aloud:

> Jack wanted to go fishing with his father. He wanted to catch a big fish.
>
> Father said, "We have to get a fishing rod, and some bait. Then we will go
>
> to the pond.

Sammy actually read:

> Jack went to get fishing when his father. He went to get a big fish.
>
> Father said, "We like to go a fishing rob, and so—. When we get at a the
>
> pond."

Note how Sammy's miscues of basic function sight words distorted the meaning of the sentence. Yet despite those distortions, Sammy made no self-corrections at all. He was so intimidated by his inability to identify these function words that he did not even try to derive meaning from text.

For any particular child, the second category of sight words, the content word, will be determined by the basal reader program, the literature selected for classroom reading, and the stories and books read independently. A student who reads at home for recreation will have a larger sight-word vocabulary than a student who does not read outside of the school setting. Thus size of sight-word vocabulary varies from child to child, depending on what and how much is read.

Lists of high-frequency sight words are readily available for teachers' use in knowing which words appear most frequently in text (see High-Frequency Words and Grouped High-Frequency Words in the appendix). An informal assessment instrument can be constructed easily from such lists to determine which words the Catch-Up Reader still needs to learn.

The Dolch Sight Word list of 220 high-frequency words, categorized by reading level, is a popular instrument (Dolch, 1939) that is based on words commonly found in published basal readers. The list is useful as a general guide to the words students will read as they progress through primary grade readers. The Fry Instant Word Lists (1999) of the 1,000 most common words can also be used as a guide to the words students acquire through the grades. In addition, Fry offers the *Instant Word Comprehensive Test* (2001a), in which students read the lists of words and the teacher records which words are identified and which are not. An accompanying book, *The Instant Word Practice Book* (2001b), provides extensive worksheets for reinforcement exercises on the words.

Research studies are equivocal regarding the best way to teach sight words. Some studies have indicated that sight words taught in isolation are better recalled, whereas other studies have reported that words learned within sentence contexts are recalled better (Breznitz, 1997; Singer, Samuels, & Spiroff, 1973–74; Tan & Nicholson, 1997).

Kibby (1989) taught words to disabled readers under one of two conditions: (1) context or (2) minimal context. The context method included reading the target word within a sentence context and focusing on meaning usage and visual characteristics. The minimal context method included the teacher presenting the printed word in isolation, then saying the word in a sentence, while drawing the students' attention to the distinctive visual features of the word. The results of this study indicated that subjects in the minimal context group learned at twice the rate of those in the context group.

Before translating research into practice, teachers should keep in mind that much research has been based on children's short-term learning of sight words. Long-term retention of words and the transfer of words learned in one context to another are two of the problems common to Catch-Up Readers. If our goal is to help students recognize printed words in lists, teaching in isolation is acceptable. However, a major goal of reading instruction is successful interaction with, and comprehension of, text. Helping children transfer their knowledge learned from the study of isolated lists or word banks to text is a critical feature of successful reading instruction.

Historically within the field of reading, the directed reading activity (DRA) has been a dominant lesson plan pattern. Until the whole language movement of the 1980s, which introduced a variety of additional lesson plan patterns, almost all basal series lesson plans were DRAs. The DRA included the teaching of several new sight words prior to the reading of each new story. The words were introduced in isolation, but then the children would encounter the words in text, usually more than once in the story. After reading the story, there were often additional reinforcement exercises that dealt with the new words and reviewed sight words introduced in earlier lessons.

As in the DRA, teachers can use prereading work to introduce new sight words to Catch-Up Readers. As he/she prereads the lesson materials, the teacher identifies a few words the student is likely to have trouble recognizing. The words are presented on the chalkboard or on index cards. Distinctive features such as spelling and phonics rules, roots and affixes, or special meanings can be discussed.

The student is told to look for these words as he/she reads. Teachers often alert the student to the fact that one of the words is located on the page he/she is about to read. Giving clues makes locating the word more interesting and eliminates some of the anxiety that a student may have in attempting to read a previously unknown word.

After the selection is read, the student can write the new words on individual index cards, including a sentence containing the word on the back of each card. Each word is added to the student's word bank and can be used for sight-word games or word-sort activities (see Chapter 3).

Students at the second-grade level or higher often keep their sight words in alphabet-type books, when their collection of cards becomes too large to be manageable. They can make a page for each letter of the alphabet and bind the book with a ring binder or with a multipronged plastic clip. As the student encounters new words, he/she writes them in the appropriate page with an accompanying sentence or definition. The sentence helps the student recall the word, especially if the sentence was his/her own composition.

To help children learn to recognize words, the teacher can directly model how to locate the identifying features within words. For example, if the student is having difficulty identifying the word *have*, instruct him/her to examine it carefully then respond to the following questions:

- What looks special about this word?
- What sounds do you hear in the word?
- What sound is prominent?
- What letter is associated with that sound?
- How do you think you can best remember this word?

Sight words become automatically recognizable through repeated exposure. Average readers might learn a new sight word with 5–15 exposures. Catch-Up Readers may need many more exposures. Providing easy reading material helps students internalize sight words and provides opportunities for them to use surrounding context clues and pictures for word recognition.

Predictable Language

Predictable language books, poems, and stories are an excellent way to increase a student's sight vocabulary. We noted that predictable language books are commonly used with the Catch-On Reader (see Chapter 2); however, they maintain their learning value throughout the primary and intermediate grades. Publishers now offer many series that provide repetitive and predictable language, graded in difficulty to meet the word-recognition and comprehension needs of both younger and older elementary children.

Pictures

The use of pictures for word recognition is often discouraged because the student's attention goes to the picture, not to the features of the word to be read. However, pictures that accompany a story or selection are often quite helpful as cues to certain words on the page. In the case of Catch-Up Readers, instruction should include teaching the reader to use and integrate all available cues.

AUDITORY/MEANING EMPHASIS

In the previous section, we discussed strategies in which visual information is the primary tool for recalling words. In this section, we discuss strategies in which auditory information is primary. Phonics, the teaching of grapheme–phoneme (i.e., letter–sound) relationships is usually associated with an auditory emphasis for word learning. In a typical beginning reading curriculum, the phonics component would target between 50 and 90 rules for instruction. Reading in English, however, involves over 500 such rules (Juel, 1994).

There is no debate among educators over the issue of the importance of a child coming to know letter–sound correspondences as a prerequisite for further reading development. There is, however, considerable discussion of just how this knowledge can be developed in children. Goswami and Bryant (1992), for example, provided findings that emphasized the importance of phonogram instruction. Ehri and Robbins's (1992) findings suggested that knowledge of individual graphemes and their corresponding phonemes (as in synthetic phonics instruction) is more central to early reading. In fact, the whole issue may depend on students' early reading abilities. Poorer readers, such as Catch-Up Readers, may benefit more from direct instructional approaches. Better readers may do very well with less sequenced and directed whole language approaches (Juel & Minden-Cupp, 2000).

Phonogram Approach

One common approach to word-recognition instruction is a focus on phonograms. Phonograms are units of speech that include a vowel followed by at least one consonant. For example, *an*, *ane*, *ap*, *ene*, *ed*, *ip*, *ite*, *ick*, *on*, *ope*, *up*, *ut*, and *un* are phonograms (see Letter Clusters and Rimes in the appendix). Phonogram-based instruction goes by many different names, including linguistic phonics, key words, word endings, word families, orthographic analogies, and onset-rime instruction.

These word endings are recalled easily by students, and they can be used as the basis for identifying unfamiliar printed words that are already in the students' oral vocabularies. Processing these letter chunks when reading is more efficient than letter-by-letter synthetic phonics (Johnston, 1999). An advantage of using phonograms is that the complex sound systems of vowels are more stable and regular within word families (Adams, 1990).

We suggest using one pattern per lesson and reviewing previously taught patterns and words with each subsequent lesson. For example, we might start with the pattern *an*. The teacher says and writes, *This is the word part an*. I can think of a word that rhymes with *an*— *pan*. Can you think of a word that rhymes with *pan*?

The teacher can provide clues if the student cannot think of a rhyming word. For example, "I'm thinking of a word that rhymes with *pan* but it starts with the sound m-m-m. Pan—M-m-m-man." Once the student grasps the idea that changing the initial consonant creates a rhyme, he/she usually can think of many rhyming words. The teacher should write these words in a list:

an

man

pan

can

fan

Dan

Nan

After the list is complete, ask the student to reread it. If the child has problems recalling the words, tell him/her to draw pictures next to the words as clues. For example, a picture of a can could be drawn next to *can*. After the first reading, however, a new list should be created without the pictures and in a different word order, so that the child is led to concentrate on the print characteristics of each word.

The first reading should proceed from top to bottom, the second reading from bottom to top. The third reading should include words that are randomly pointed out by the teacher or student.

We suggest that the student use one or more of the words in a sentence or sentences after generating and reading the list. Some of the sentences can be silly (e.g., "Nan ate Dan's socks" or "Nan sat on the fan"). Sometimes students try to use many words in nonsense sentences (e.g., "The man with the pan can fan Dan"). Remember that your purpose is to show the student letter patterns that have the same sound and that can be used for auditory analysis when decoding an unknown word. Be sure to tell the student that the sentences are "silly" and do not make much sense, but that the analysis will help them recall patterns for word identification.

Instruct the student to place the listed words on index cards or in his/her word book for continued practice. Once the student learns the pattern, he/she will be able to read many words. In fact, we have motivated many reluctant and discouraged readers in our clinic with this technique:

TEACHER: I bet you'll learn 10 new words by the time you leave here today!

STUDENT: No, I don't even know 10 words.

At the end of the session, the student is asked to read his/her 10 new words. Of course, you do not have to promise 10 words. Try five words if the child is very reluctant to engage in reading. Much also depends on the pattern you choose: It is easy to generate 10 words with the *an* pattern but not as easy with the *id* pattern.

Analytic Phonics

Analytic phonics is another method that helps a student focus his/her auditory processes to decode a word. Several examples of words that begin or end with the same letter–sound are presented for analysis and the child is led to recognize the pattern for future use in decoding. In basal series printed prior to the whole language movement, analytic phonics was widely used in teachers' manuals in conjunction with what was once called the "whole word method."

Give the student a list of words that have the same initial or final phoneme/grapheme correspondence, such as:

duck

dime

David

deer

Ask "What do you see that is the same about each word?" to elicit the fact that all the words start with the letter *d* and with the sound /d/. Say the words several times with the children, emphasizing the beginning sound. Cover the word list and ask them to write the beginning letter of the words you are going to say, then say the words on the list in random order. Uncover the list and ask the children to match their beginning letters with those of the words on the board.

Next, write a sentence on the chalkboard (or introduce chart paper prepared ahead of time) that contains a word that starts with the letter *d*. For example: "The doll has a red hat." (It helps if you include a picture to support the context, but cover the picture initially.) Read aloud with the children, "The _____ has a red hat."

Ask the children what they think the unknown word will be and if they have any clues they can use to help them figure it out. Point out that the word starts with the letter sound they have been learning—*d* and /d/. "What word could it be? The dog has a red dress? The duck has a red dress? What could have a red dress?"

"A girl."

"Yes, but *girl* doesn't start the same way as our word."

"A mother."

"Yes, but *mother* doesn't start the same way as our word." Continue in this manner, until the children run out of clues or guess the word. Then show the picture of the doll and confirm that this is the word.

It is important to model how to use phonic cues for word recognition in this way. The same procedure can be done for final letters and sounds within words. It is necessary to model this process repeatedly, because it is a difficult concept for Catch-Up Readers to grasp. Some younger children might not be able to discriminate the subtle differences in the sounds of the consonants and vowels; that is, they have poor auditory discrimination skills. If so, this approach becomes an exercise in futility and should not be used.

Synthetic Phonics

The term *synthetic* denotes the process of synthesis, in which parts are blended. Sound blending experiences are very helpful to Catch-Up Readers if they have gained enough cognitive ability to be able to generalize across sounds and form words from these gross approximations. That is, taking the individual sounds in the word *dip* (/d/, /i/, /p/) and pronouncing them one by one, then trying to determine what word is composed of those individual sounds, is a cognitively challenging task. Most Catch-Up Readers, however, do have enough sophistication to be successful in this blending task, though it may take instruction and modeling.

Sound blending ability is essential to effectively use phonics as a word decoding strategy. It is the pivotal skill that lies between applying individual sounds to letters and forming a word from the sounds. Blending is particularly emphasized in phonics basal series (sometimes called decodable text basals) and supplemental phonics materials, available from many publishers.

As noted in this chapter and in Chapter 3, most of the research related to beginning reading and phonemic awareness suggests that phonemic awareness of several auditory tasks (e.g., phonemic segmentation and letter–sound relationships) is important for successful reading (McBride-Chang, 1995; Snider, 1995; Stahl & Murray, 1994; Yopp, 1992). Although this chapter is about the Catch-Up Reader (i.e., one who has already acquired some reading ability), the issue of learning and using knowledge of letter–sound relationships is still relevant. Students who acquire word recognition in a natural way, by discovering the use of phonics through reading and writing, do not require a significant amount of direct instruction. Catch-Up Readers, who have not come to understand the relationship of sounds to symbols, certainly do require direct instruction. The teacher needs to decide when this instruction will be most effective—before or after a basic stock of sight words has been established.

If the Catch-Up Reader is unsure of letter–sound correspondences, use a direct procedure to teach these correspondences. The area of letter–sound correspondences that is most difficult for the Catch-Up Reader is that of discriminating and applying vowel sounds to decode words. A strategy for teaching follows

1. Select the letter–sound relationship that will be taught. For example, a teacher might select from among short vowels, long vowels with an *e* at the end of the word, *r*-controlled vowels, or vowel digraphs in which the first letter takes the vowel sound (*ai*, *ea*, *oa*). Short vowel sounds are often difficult for students to discriminate, so plan for additional teaching and practice.

2. Locate and list words that contain the vowel sound you want to teach.

3. Begin the lesson by showing the student the letter(s) of the selected vowel. Model the name of the letter(s) and the sound the letter(s) makes. Select about five words from your list and present them to the child, saying them slowly and emphasizing the vowel sound.

4. Show the student how to sound blend the letter–sounds in this word by (a) blending each phoneme (p-a-n), (b) blending the initial consonant and the vowel (pa-n), or (c) by using a phonogram approach (p-an). Ask the student to blend the sounds within the words, using your modeling techniques.

5. Dictate the words to the student, asking him/her to spell them using the sounds he/she hears. Compare the student's spelling of the words with the traditional spelling. Examine any differences and talk about them with the student.

6. Select three or so other words that contain the same vowel pattern. Dictate these words aloud and have the child spell them. Again, compare the student's spelling with the traditional spelling.

7. Prior to this direct teaching lesson, locate a reading selection containing words that represent the sound patterns you have been teaching. After each page is read, ask the student to "be a detective" and find the words that have the same pattern.

Writing and Spelling Techniques

Writing stories, messages, journal entries, and reports helps Catch-On Readers develop a sense of the auditory processes involved in reading and spelling. Children progress from scribble writing through various stages of invented spelling to traditional spelling (Gentry, 2000; Richgels, 1995; Sipe, 2001). In whole language instruction, writing is the major strategy for developing knowledge of grapheme–phoneme relationships. Children sound out words they are writing and receive feedback from peers and teachers on accuracy (Dahl & Scharer, 2000).

Writing is an important part of literacy development and should receive attention and instruction throughout the school years. Students should have the opportunity to practice extensive writing in which varying types of written communication are used (e.g., narrative and expository forms and several voices). Writing helps students gain knowledge of traditional spellings, use different types of grammatical constructions, and increase their knowledge of word meanings.

LANGUAGE/MEANING EMPHASIS

All too often, focus on the word recognition abilities (or lack of them) of struggling readers is limited to the word level. Catch-On Readers benefit from instructional development of a flexible repertoire of word-recognition strategies that goes beyond the word level to the sentence level. Readers learn that the words and meanings surrounding an unrecognized word can help them identify it.

Context

Using context is a major word-identification strategy for Catch-Up Readers. Several research studies have pointed out that poor readers use context more than good readers, presumably because good readers have a large "storehouse" of sight words and phonics skills which they access for word identification (Carver, 2000; Stanovich, 2000). Instruction in the use of context clues along with strategic application activities is necessary to develop this skill in Catch-Up Readers.

Context provides both semantic and syntactic cues within a sentence or paragraph. At the sentence level, syntactic cues are often dominant. At the paragraph, or longer, discourse level, semantic cues are used more dominantly. In instruction on context skills, readers are taught to use one or more of the following strategies when they come to a word they cannot identify immediately:

1. Skip the word, read to the end of the sentence, and think of a word that would make sense.
2. Reread the sentence up to the point where the unfamiliar word occurs and think of a word that would follow and make sense.
3. Read to the point of the unknown word, look carefully at the beginning, middle, and ending letters, and think of a word that would fit. Read to the end of the sentence. Always verify that the resulting guess makes sense.

Catch-Up Readers have difficulty effectively using context when there are too many unknown words in the sentence. Using texts that are above the instructional levels of students impairs their reading, because their ability to use context breaks down when the text is too difficult.

Syntactic Cues

Cues used by readers within a given sentence are primarily syntactic ones. *Syntax* refers to the grammatical arrangement of words within a sentence. Native speakers of the language being read implicitly understand the grammar of that language. This implicit understanding contains indirect cues to the unknown word. For example, "Walked dog his the man" is not a grammatically correct English sentence. If the words are rearranged, "The man walked his dog," the sentence becomes grammatically understandable and acceptable. Most readers expect to encounter conventional grammar when reading.

Catch-Up Readers who are overly involved in efforts to decode every word, relying too heavily on auditory strategies in their word-recognition repertoire, do not attend to the grammatical constraints of sentences. When assessing a child's oral reading, a clue that such a problem has developed is revealed when the student substitutes words that do not make sense within the sentences being read. This type of reader needs direct instruction in attending to the unfolding structure and meaning of a sentence.

When attempting to determine an unknown word by using syntactic cues, the Catch-On Reader needs to learn to (1) anticipate the part of speech that is appropriate, and (2) think of a number of words that would make sense. Few Catch-On Readers have an explicit knowledge of formal grammar—that is, the terms identifying the actual parts of speech, such as *noun*, *verb*, *pronoun*, and so forth. However, an implicit understanding of grammar— that is, knowing what kind of a word would make sense—is sufficient.

In an instructional lesson targeted to the sentence level of context analysis, ask students to do the following:

1. Read to the end of the sentence (see examples below).
2. Say the sentence out loud, leaving a blank for the unknown word.
3. Make several possible choices.
4. Test the choices to see if they fit in terms of grammar and meaning.
5. Look at the first and last letters of the word and match these letters against the anticipated word(s).

1. Jack _____ his dog. (**called**—verb)
2. The _____ called on Susie to read. (**teacher**—noun)
3. The teacher said, "Sit _____." (**down**—adverb)
4. _____ big dog growled at the child. (**The**—article)
5. Go _____ the principal's office. (**to**—preposition)

Semantic Cues

Semantics refers to the meaning of words, sentences, and longer units of discourse. Drawing upon background knowledge and the surrounding context, proficient readers are able to make predictions about unrecognized words. Examples of sentences in which the reader will use primarily semantic cues are given below:

1. The _____ on the bike is flat.

2. There is not an elevator, so you'll have to walk up the _____.

3. My plants are dry; they need _____.

4. The American flag is red, white, and _____.

Note that the reader has to have background knowledge to use the semantic cues. For example, if the reader did not know the colors of the American flag, the word *blue* would not come to mind automatically, based on the other words in the sentence.

Dahl and Samuels (1977) developed a hypothesis-based test strategy for using syntactic or semantic cues for word identification. The following basic steps are included in their strategy:

1. Use information from the passage.
2. Make a prediction about what the word could be.
3. Compare the printed and predicted words (test the hypothesis).
4. Accept or reject the prediction.

Language cues (syntactic and semantic) can be combined with graphophonemic clues to give the reader further help in identifying words. Aulls (1982) suggested the use of a successive cloze measure for helping readers successfully learn to predict words. If the reader has difficulty with the initial task, various clues to word identification are provided in successive readings of the sentence.

1. The dog chewed his _____.

2. The dog chewed his b_____.

3. The dog chewed his b____ e.

4. The dog chewed his b___ne.

Discourse Cues and Cloze Instruction

Sometimes the syntactic and semantic cues within a sentence do not give the reader enough information to make a hypothesis about the unknown word. Sometimes the reader cannot recognize enough words within a sentence to make a hypothesis about still yet another un-identified word.

During assessment of oral reading, this reader may frequently miscue by substituting incorrect words. He/she may understand the gist of the content but will miss the specifics. This reader needs to be taught to think about the selection and go back to words that he/she miscued to understand the meaning of the passage. Fluent readers typically comment on a word they have misread, perhaps saying, "That doesn't make sense." When they finish the sentence, they go back to the miscued word, noting "Oh, that word was *snow* and I said *show.*"

Examine the miscues in the paragraph in Figure 9.1, taken from the administration of an informal reading inventory.

The examiner began by telling the student the name of the selection, "The Circus Train." During reading, however, the student had so much difficulty identifying key words

The Circus Train

Mark was ~~excited~~ *extra*. It didn't ~~matter~~ *much* that it was only five

o'clock on Tuesday morning. He was ready to get out of bed, get

dressed, and catch *geT* the school bus to [Centerport] *P*. Today, the ~~circus~~ *curos*

was coming to town. Mark's teacher, Mr. Wade, had arranged for

the whole fifth grade class to help set up the ~~circus~~ *kirks* tents on the

~~fair~~grounds in Centerport. This was going to be the best day ever,

Mark ~~thought~~ *said* to himself. It didn't take him long to ~~throw~~ *PUT* on his

old clothes. He was almost out the ~~front~~ door when he heard his

mother say, "Have a good time. I'll be at the ~~fair~~grounds ~~soon~~ *so*."

The school bus and the ~~circus~~ *kiTes* ~~train~~ *Try* [arrived] *P* in Centerport at

the same time. The ~~noise~~ *nose* and the ~~smell~~ *small* of the animals told ~~the~~ *a*

children that the [circus] *P* [train] *P* had arrived. [Confusion] *P* seemed to be

everywhere, but Mark's teacher told everyone ~~to~~ *who* watch the

workers carefully. They each ~~had~~ *have* a [special] *P* job to do. Yes! Mr.

Wade ~~was~~ *saw* right. ~~Pairs~~ *Parts to* ~~of~~ workers went ~~to~~ *on* each car of ~~the~~ *a* train,

along with ~~the~~ *a* animal trainers. Mark ~~wondered~~ *was* ~~what~~ *That* would

happen when ~~they~~ *he* opened the car doors.

FIGURE 9.1. *"The Circus Train."*

(Omitted words or part words are signified by circles. Words marked with a *p* indicate that the examiner had to pronounce the word for the child. Substitutions are written above the target words.)

that she did not use the cue in the title word *circus*. As she struggled to read the paragraph, small words that she usually recognized on sight (e.g., *this, it, at, on*) presented difficulties and were miscued. Towards the end of the reading the examiner provided the student with the word *circus*. When asked what the story was about, the student replied, "The kids go see a circus train," indicating that she had understood the gist of the passage. However, she made so many miscues that answers to detail-level questions were incorrect.

Direct instruction using cloze passages helps students learn to use the context for word-identification cues. A cloze passage is created by substituting underlined blank slots for words in a passage. Sometimes the deleted words are chosen by the teacher, and sometimes they are random deletions, such as every fifth or tenth word. The student's task is to guess what word would go in the slot. In assessments that use cloze to determine a student's reading level, exact matches between the guessed word and the deleted word are usually required (see Appendix for Sample Cloze Assessment). In the instructional use of cloze that we are suggesting here, semantically and syntactically appropriate words would be acceptable.

An overhead projector is often used when working with a group of students, as they use different sets of syntax and semantic cues to determine an unknown word. Typically, the teacher starts the lesson by reading up to the blank space in a cloze passage. Students then brainstorm for words that would fit in the blank, and teacher and students read the rest of the sentence. Given this new information, some of the suggested words would no longer fit the blank space, but new words can be brainstormed.

The teacher then supplies the beginning letter of the target word. Again, some of the brainstormed words are removed and new words generated. Next, the teacher supplies the ending letter of the target word. Words that do not fit the blank are removed and new ones brainstormed. Finally, the teacher supplies the word, and the students discuss their thinking processes.

DEVELOPING AUTOMATICITY AND FLUENCY

Many Catch-Up Readers are constrained from reading fluently by the stress of employing word-by-word recognition strategies. They read connected text as if they were decoding lists of words. Fluent reading requires the ability to decode words with automaticity (Richards, 2000; Zutell & Rasinski, 1991)to recognize words instantly and without significant cognitive effort. Automaticity is developed through large amounts of time-on-task in reading and through forms of practice that emphasize accuracy, expression, and smoothness of reading, such as those that involve the modeling of fluent reading and practice with repeated oral readings (Gerdes, 2001).

Gerdes (2001) surveyed existing research to identify four possible causes of dysfluency in reading:

1. Spending too much time reading text at the child's frustration level
2. Failure to apply various word-recognition strategies flexibly.
3. Lack of time in classroom and recreational reading.
4. Overemphasis on subskill work and isolated drills in reading instruction.

Chunking

Chunking is an oral reading procedure designed to help the student read phrases and sentences in a meaningful way. This technique is intended for the student whose reading is word-by-word and whose comprehension may therefore suffer.

To implement this procedure, the teacher selects a passage from a text or story at the child's instructional level. If there is sufficient time for preparation, the passage may be retyped with one chunk unit per line for use when reading together. The teacher reads the first phrase or thought unit, using the appropriate intonation, phrasing, and pace. Then the student reads the same phrase or unit. They proceed in this manner, alternating back and forth, through the entire passage.

Finally, the teacher tapes the student reading the passage one more time. Together, they listen to and discuss the difference in the second reading in terms of fluency, intonation, phrasing, and pace.

Matching Words and Word Parts

Helping students identify word parts and familiar words as a technique for decoding unknown words is another word-attack strategy in which Catch-Up Readers often need direct instruction. They overlook the distinctive features of words and word parts, or they fail to recognize the same patterns or features in other words (Nagy, Winsor, Osborn, & O'Flahavan, 1994).

After reading and discussing a story, words can be selected from a student's word bank (e.g., the words *can*, *help*, *from*, *cold*, and *get*) and targeted for another lesson unit, perhaps locating the same words in the reading selection or the language experience story. As the student reads his/her story or textbook, he/she is asked to look for these words or words with similar word parts.

For example, Jenny found the word *can* on the first page of her story. Later she found the words *ran*, *hold*, and *pet*. Her teacher was pleased with her *looking* skills and asked her to look further for similar word parts. This time Jenny found the words, *mom*, *develop*, *sandal*, and *settle*. These word searches help the student focus on specific word parts. Games can be played with classmates and/or the teacher in which the students try to see who can find the most lookalike words and who can find the most word-part words.

Paired Reading

In choosing strategies that provide Catch-Up Readers with effective exposures to new words, teachers may be tempted to rely on methods that emphasize "repetition and replication" rather than "transaction and transformation" (Griffin, 2002, p. 766). Learning methods based on social interaction, such as paired reading strategies, can be powerful tools in helping Catch-Up Readers gain the multiple exposures to new words that they need, while simultaneously developing a broader, more engaged view of what reading is all about. Generally, two readers are paired together for the purpose of oral reading; the students may be in the same classroom, in the same grade level but in different classrooms, or in different grade levels.

One of the most popular implementations of paired reading is that of peer tutoring, in which a more able reader helps a less able reader. This application has relevance for the Catch-Up Reader who requires practice reading stories and expository selections. Teachers carefully match the tutor and the tutee, so that optimal gains in reading will be achieved for both students. Usually there is no more than 2 years of grade difference between the two students. If the more able reader is too far superior to the less able reader, boredom and minimum reading growth may characterize the former's experience.

Another approach to paired reading involves students of the same reading ability, paired together for the purpose of guiding each other through particular stories in a reciprocal tutoring arrangement. In practice, the words one student does not know are often known by the other.

Teachers must allot time to organize, monitor, and evaluate this type of instruction. Teacher organization is essential to the effectiveness of the program, in that the teacher must be careful to pair students who will work well together, whose reading levels are not extremely different, and who do not need the teacher's constant attention. Careful monitoring is important so that book choices are appropriate and the peer relationships are amicable. Pairs should keep a record of the books read as well as make journal entries regarding their feelings about participating in the activity.

In a research study that concluded with a positive evaluation of the effects of paired reading, Griffin (2002) found that successful use of the method depends on the implementation of four guidelines:

1. Actively observe the pairs and regroup as necessary. Paired readers should use the time collaboratively.

2. Use minilessons that model the use of effective methods. One simple method that worked well, for example, was alternate page reading. Simply providing verbal instructions does not work as well for children as providing a modeled demonstration of the method.

3. Provide a range of student settings for paired reading—from couches to a rug on the floor to desks. Different pairs prefer different settings.

4. Know when to intervene even as you step back from the process, trusting students to organize their own sessions. Students are often able to set up their learning sessions more creatively without adult intervention.

SUMMARY

Unlike the Catch-On Reader (Part One) who is struggling to understand the basic principles involved in word recognition, the Catch-Up Reader has developed a basic sight word vocabulary and has learned some phonics skills. Many Catch-Up Readers, however, must expand the size of their sight-word vocabulary, the accuracy and fluency of their phonics skills, and other abilities related to a skilled and flexible word-recognition strategy. Teachers can choose from a range of approaches, a visual/meaning emphasis, an auditory/meaning emphasis, and a language/meaning emphasis. Once a solid foundation is in place, Catch-Up Readers begin to master their newly learned word-recognition strategies to achieve automaticity and fluency.

In all this, teachers play the central role. It is by close observation and targeted assessment that teachers identify the specific areas of difficulty faced by individual Catch-Up Readers. While many Catch-Up Readers struggle with word recognition, the lack of achievement in others arises from poor vocabulary, which we discuss in the next chapter, or from poor comprehension, which we discuss in Chapters 11 and 12.

CHAPTER 10

Helping Catch-Up Readers with Vocabulary

DEVELOPING VOCABULARY STRATEGIES

Whereas some Catch-Up Readers exhibit the difficulties in word recognition discussed in Chapter 9, many others experience severe reading limitations due to lack of vocabulary knowledge. Researchers and curriculum designers have long recognized that vocabulary plays a key role in successful reading. Methodologies arising from schema theory research in the 1970s helped teachers recognize that vocabulary growth comes from helping students make connections between words used to describe their world, rather than simply from memorizing lists.

The cognitive model of reading offered by Carver (2000) posits that verbal knowledge level is one of the two major aspects of reading development that can most effectively be improved through instruction. (The other major aspect amenable to instruction is word identification—increasing the number of words students are able to identify while reading—see Chapters 3 and 9.) Carver calls his approach the "rauding model," combining the words *reading* and *auding* (i.e., listening). Carver's construct of verbal knowledge refers to children's general knowledge of the world, of which vocabulary knowledge is an important aspect. The more Catch-Up Readers learn about their world, the larger will be their vocabulary and the greater will be their improvement in reading ability.

Disadvantaged children are disproportionately represented among the population of Catch-Up Readers, as they are among Catch-On and Stalled Readers. Of all the most insidious effects of poverty on children's educational growth, one of the worst may be the paucity in vocabulary development. Disadvantaged children are likely to have much smaller vocabularies than children from more privileged backgrounds. Their preschool experiences do not facilitate their acquisition of a sufficient oral vocabulary to experience success in school (Graves & Watts-Taffe, 2002).

Concerns about Traditional Vocabulary Instruction

William Nagy's research (Nagy & Scott, 2000) has made a significant contribution to the reading field's understanding of the role vocabulary knowledge plays in the reading process, as well as to identifying effective teaching methods. He is an opponent of traditional vocabulary instruction that emphasizes drill work, looking up definitions in a dictionary, and weekly testing of vocabulary words. These methods fail to improve reading comprehension for several reasons:

1. In-depth word knowledge is not produced by the instruction.
2. The comprehensibility of some texts does not require that a reader know the meanings of all words.
3. Teaching the meanings of words that can be derived from the redundancy of the text will not improve comprehension.

Nagy suggested that traditional approaches to vocabulary instruction be modified in three ways:

1. Integration of instructed words with other knowledge.
2. Provide sufficient repetition so that readers know what the word means and have had practice using it so that its meaning can be accessed quickly (see Sidebar 10.1).
3. Actively involve students in a meaningful process of learning the word.

Wide Reading

Teacher-directed vocabulary instruction alone cannot provide sufficient vocabulary growth for adequate achievement in reading (Pressley, 2000). Much of each student's vocabulary growth will come only through wide reading. Yet the processes of learning vocabulary from context or learning morphemes so that word parts can function as clues to vocabulary meaning are limited in their effectiveness, especially for poorer readers, even when they are taught how to do both (Blachowicz & Fisher, 2000). A reader's success in using context to infer meaning of an unknown word is often limited by the lack of repetition of the target word in the text and by the insufficiency of the context clues (Rhoder & Huerster, 2002). When morphemic analysis (i.e., the use of meaningful word parts as clues to word meanings) and

Sidebar 10.1. Drill and Practice Computer Software

Computers can serve as particularly effective learning tools for struggling readers. Both research and teacher experience indicate that many such students are motivated by technology. In turn, technology gives teachers new and innovative ways of teaching students concepts for which they may have developed negative attitudes due to continued failure. The very newness of the technology can entice such students, which helps teachers circumvent those negative attitudes.

In addition, computers confer status to the users, suggesting that they are engaged in cutting-edge learning. That status can work to overcome the negative image often associated with receiving instruction as a struggling reader.

Computer technology is used to supplement, not supplant, the teacher. As with any educational tool, computers are only effective when used appropriately. Only individual teachers, in direct contact with their students, can determine what is appropriate in any given instructional situation.

Drill and practice software provides students with additional practice on skills or concepts already taught by teachers. One type of drill and practice software is designed to reinforce skill acquisition, such as vocabulary development, or conceptual expertise, such as identifying the main idea in a passage. Reinforcement software provides detailed, response-specific feedback on student input. Explanations and guidance are provided for incorrect responses. For example, if a student incorrectly identifies the main idea of a passage, the software then offers an explanation of how the main idea could have been correctly identified.

Most drill and practice software lacks such detailed feedback for reinforcement, however. A second type of drill and practice software is best used for development of automaticity. That is, once a skill or concept has been learned, automaticity software helps students overlearn or review the concepts for long-term retention and fluency and speed of performance.

Drill and practice software is just one of many kinds of software, but it is the most widely available. In a survey of the availability of commercial software, Balajthy (1996) reported that, of 1,086 titles available for reading and literacy instruction, 504 (46%) were drill and practice.

context analysis are taught, students are able to use those strategies. But these abilities are quickly lost unless the strategies are reviewed on a regular basis (Baumann et al., 2002).

Each teacher must understand the dual roles of direct instruction and wide reading in vocabulary development. Conceptually difficult words or technical terms that are not explicitly explained in the text require direct teacher instruction.

In developing vocabulary for Catch-Up Readers, special attention should be given to expository text that presents new material to readers about their world, and especially about the aspects of learning most relevant to content area subjects in school. Catch-Up Readers with language differences—English language learners—can benefit from extensive exposure to children's books that focus on content area concepts, such as those from the sciences and social studies, in an effort to develop their English vocabularies (Matanzo, 2001). Low-level readers from disadvantaged backgrounds are sometimes deprived of such experiences by schools that focus almost entirely on phonics instruction and fictional stories (Neuman, 2001).

Direct Experience and Disadvantaged Children

Vocabulary development can play an especially important role when working with Catch-Up Readers from disadvantaged or culturally different backgrounds. Much vocabulary knowledge is gained through wide world experiences. Trips to museums and historical sites, tours of factories, offices, and laboratories, and vacations are valuable learning experiences where middle-class children learn about nature, their world, vocations, history, and other societies. Disadvantaged children simply do not have these opportunities, unless they are provided by the school and other social institutions (such as faith-based and community organizations).

An example from a college-level experience makes this point most effectively. Several African-American students from Manhattan were being driven from their college to a religious retreat in western New Jersey. It was a unique experience for them to be outside the city. They passed a field, and one of the students said, "Wow! Look at all the horses in that field." Another student retorted, "What's the matter with you? Those are cows, not horses!" None of the three had ever actually seen a field full of cows. The concepts and vocabulary involved with dairy farming and production and distribution of milk products were nothing more than abstractions for them. Middle-class children whose families had toured farms on weekend trips would have more concrete and vivid associations. Of course, the college students' urban experiences would have enriched their lives—and vocabularies—in ways that suburban and rural children would lack, but the reality remains that disadvantaged families are often economically unable to take advantage of much that city life and society offer.

Five-year-old David and 3-year-old Sara, two middle-class suburban children, were visiting a museum's American Indian exhibits. One diorama showed an Indian male running while holding a war club. They both shouted, "Look! He has a *rungu*!" They had spent several months in East Africa while their parents worked on professional projects. They had often seen Kikuyu men carrying such wooden clubs, called *rungu* in Swahili, on hikes in the forest. That initial connection led to a pattern of such connections as they studied the museum exhibits on the early American Indian cultures and discussed the possible relationship with Kikuyu tribal culture.

Concrete world experiences are of utmost value when children are attempting to incorporate learning new concepts and their related vocabulary. As disadvantaged children are exposed to more of these "wide world" experiences, they are able to make their own connections to new experiences and readings, and their vocabulary increases. Enriching the life experiences of such Catch-Up Readers has a marked payback in terms of reading development.

All too often, however, school-based field trips and other types of direct experience are so unfocused that little meaningful learning occurs. The benefit of these experiences can be maximized by careful planning that facilitates and focuses student learning and engagement. Teachers can circumscribe attention during a field trip to museum, for example, by creating a treasure hunt handout that poses questions about exhibits in the museum. The students fill out the answers as they find them in their explorations. The treasure hunts can be used back at school as the basis for discussion and elaboration of the concepts and vocabulary learned.

SEMANTIC MAPPING

Semantic maps are visual arrays that depict a concept or term and the words related to it. These arrays are alternately called maps, semantic maps, or webs. A semantic map contains nodes, drawn as circles, squares, or triangles, each of which contains a key word. Lines or arrows connect the nodes. Most types of semantic maps are used to develop vocabulary by helping students organize information, generalize about related terms, and draw relationships across the terms that are important for understanding text. The purpose of semantic maps is to show how a set of concepts, examples, and attributes of a target concept are related (see Figures 10.1 and 10.2).

In creating a semantic map, a key word or concept from the upcoming text is placed on the chalkboard or on a large sheet of chart paper. The teacher leads a discussion about the word, in which students are asked to think of terms to describe the word. Students might think in terms of *description* ("... is a ..."), *function* ("... is used for ..."), and *relationship* ("... is like a ...").

In developing the semantic map, words are listed on the board as they are brainstormed. Then they are grouped within related categories and given a category name. For example, categories for a semantic map about spiders might include *descriptions, habitats, types,* and *hunting methods*. Discussion should be active and engaging, as students brainstorm and categorize words. The final diagram can be created in a variety of formats. Semantic maps offer a valuable alternative to traditional vocabulary instruction using word

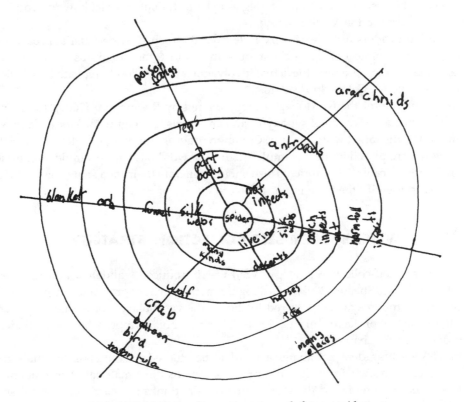

FIGURE 10.1. *Semantic map, web form—spiders.*

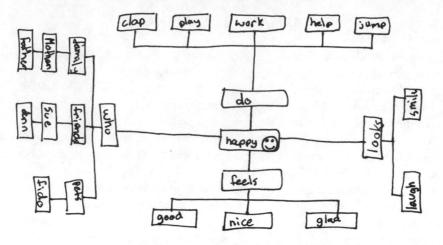

FIGURE 10.2. *Semantic map*—happy.

lists, because the visual diagram provides organization, structure, and purpose for working with particular terms and concepts.

When first introducing this technique, teacher modeling is important for the ensuing discussion and for helping students learn to use the strategy on their own. Once the strategy is learned, students can work in small groups to generate categories and maps on their own. The maps can be used as prereading strategies to help students predict how the vocabulary terms will be used in the reading selection.

Catch-Up Readers often learn very little from the rushed, superficial approach to vocabulary learning typical of many classrooms. In contrast, the numerous variations of the general semantic map promote the active involvement and in-depth, repeated analysis that is most desirable for Catch-Up Readers.

An adaptation of the word-map strategy offered by Rosenbaum (2001), for example, emphasizes the identification of synonyms and antonyms (see Figure 10.3 for a blank word-map model), if the target word has any. Common usages, examples, or related associations of new words are placed in the "Example" node. The word *cable*, for example, is commonly used in the term "cable TV." Students also should generate their own sentences that clearly use context to identify the meaning of the word.

VOCABULARY SELF-COLLECTION STRATEGY

The vocabulary self-collection strategy (VSS) was introduced, validated, and updated by Ruddell (Ruddell & Shearer, 2002). It is a highly motivational approach to learning vocabulary, in which students are empowered to choose the vocabulary words that they want to learn. It is a variant of the organic reading and key vocabulary approaches to word identification described in Chapter 3.

In VSS, each student nominates a word to be studied by the class or small group. Words are often drawn from the current classroom reading material. The student tells the class where he/she found the word, what he/she thinks it means, and why it should be on the class list. Class discussion about the word ensues, in which the word's defini-

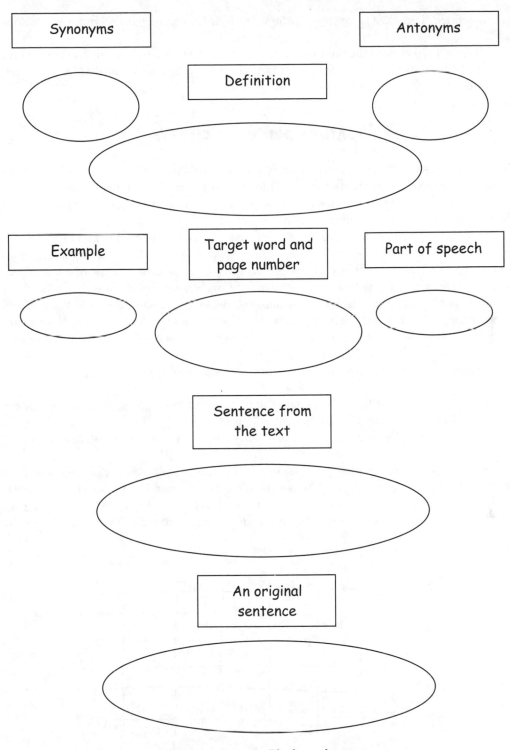

FIGURE 10.3. *Blank word map.*

tion is refined. Periodically, reviews of the word lists are conducted and quizzes administered.

Students can present the class with new words to learn by creating semantic maps on a poster. The maps help organize the students' presentations and can be posted for future reference by the class.

FEATURE ANALYSIS CHARTS

Feature analysis charts were popularized by Johnson and Pearson (1984). Sometimes called semantic feature analysis charts, they provide another approach to understanding the relationships among vocabulary terms and concepts. Feature analysis charts can be used as either a prereading or postreading vocabulary strategy.

One aspect of comprehending written material involves categorizing and organizing it for easy recall. Semantic feature charts are constructed so that students can organize the information about the terms they encountered within a given selection. Some of the information on a feature chart may be known prior to reading, whereas other information is added to the chart after reading. Feature charts allow students to compare similarities and differences among concepts that are being studied. Given that no two terms, concepts, or memberships within categories are exactly alike, feature charts are handy ways to visually portray the similarities and differences (see Figure 10.4).

Follow these steps in preparing a feature analysis chart:

• Select a group of terms that share differences and similarities, as described in the reading selection. List the terms in the left column.

• In the row across the top, list features shared by the words and those differentiating them.

• As a prereading activity with the class, put pluses or minuses beside each word beneath each feature, depending on whether the word is characterized by the feature. A notation of *n/a* (i.e., *not applicable*) can be placed in those cells that do not relate to the terms. Some columns might use symbols that more clearly differentiate characteristics than the

Metal	Hardness	Brightness	Value	Color		
gold	−	−	+	Y		
silver	−	+	+	G		
lead						
platinum						
aluminum						

Y = yellowish
G = silver gray

FIGURE 10.4. *Feature analysis chart.*

plus/minus signs. For example, in the "Color" column of Figure 10.4, a "Y" represents a yellowish color and a "G" represents a silver/gray color.

- Add additional words after the reading, if students have been exposed to more terms.
  - Add additional features, if useful.
  - Discuss the unique characteristics of each word.

Feature analysis charts are versatile learning tools, in that they can be used for teaching word meanings as well as organizing information from text. Catch-Up Readers can use them to increase their knowledge of word meanings and to improve their comprehension.

GIPES

The Gipes strategy is a motivational method that was introduced and validated by Gipe (1980). Although the method is less well known than either semantic mapping or feature analysis, we have successfully used it with both Catch-Up and normal-achieving readers and found the method to be very effective (see Figure 10.5).

First, a target word is selected for learning. (We suggest that this word be drawn from the story or content lesson that a student is preparing to read.) The small group or class then constructs a sentence that defines the word. This sentence can be a dictionary definition or one that the teacher simplifies for student understanding.

Next, students construct a second sentence that contains the target word used in a clear contextual situation so that the meaning of the word can be derived from the context. Last, students construct a third sentence containing the target word in relation to prior knowledge or experience of the student or group.

Each child writes the final sentences individually. These sentences engage the students in using the word in a situation that is personally meaningful. Later the students share their sentences with the group or class.

Our experiences using Gipes with Catch-Up Readers have been very successful. We were initially surprised at the ease with which students could construct Gipes after the teacher had modeled the process. We found that children are highly motivated to share their word-related personal experiences with the other students who have read the story.

Gipes can be used as a prereading or a postreading strategy for learning vocabulary. As a prereading technique, we suggest planning the Gipes activity around the words he/she wants to preteach. The teacher can create the first four sentences for the students. As a postreading activity, we suggest that students compose their own Gipes based on words in the story that need further explanation and exploration. Once the teacher has modeled the Gipes procedure several times, small groups of students can work independently on the activity.

MORPHEMIC ANALYSIS AND CONTEXT

Baumann et al. (2002) found that instruction in word parts (i.e., morphemic analysis) and context provided students with some limited ability to improve their vocabulary during reading. The research also noted that this ability declined with time; periodic review of the strategies is clearly essential.

1. *Blabbed* refers to someone who talks too much and tells things he shouldn't.

2. Jon blabbed Beth's secret to the whole school.

3. Donna promised not to tell anyone that her mother was having a baby, but she blabbed the news to all the neighbors.

4. When have you blabbed something?

1. *Crouch* means to stoop or bend as if getting ready to spring.

2. John crouched to get ready for the start of the 50-meter run.

3. The whole class got out of their seats and crouched low to the floor when the siren blew to warn them of a tornado.

4. Describe the last time you crouched.

1. *Console* means to make someone feel better or cheer him/her up.

2. Mother consoled Robbie when he dropped his ice cream cone by telling him that she'd buy him another.

3. The boys were consoled by their coach after they lost their ninth straight baseball game, when he told them he had a new plan for winning.

4. How have you consoled someone?

1. *Wheedle* means to coax or flatter someone to get what you want.

2. Jack wheedled and begged his mother until she gave him an extra cookie.

3. The class wheedled their teacher until she gave in to their requests for a Halloween party.

4. What have you done to wheedle Mom or Dad?

1. *Stronghold* is a strongly fortified place, a fortress or a fort.

2. The kindergarten boys built a stronghold out of large wood blocks to keep others out.

3. A castle is a stronghold having water around it and a drawbridge that could be raised to keep enemies out.

4. What is your stronghold?

FIGURE 10.5. *Sample Gipes.*

In Baumann's study, teachers provided students with examples of specific types of context clues. Consider the sentence below:

> The climb up the hill was an *arduous* task—long and hard work—for the children.

In this sentence, the meaning of the word *arduous* is provided via an appositive context clue in the phrase that follows it. Appositives are typically set off from the rest of the sentence by commas or dashes.

In the day's lesson on appositive context clues, examples were provided as well as a definition of the type of clue. Key words that tend to signal that type of clue were discussed (e.g., the words *or* or *a* are sometimes used to signal that an appositive is in use). During modeling of the examples, the teacher underlined the target word in blue, the signal words or signal punctuation in red, and the actual clue itself in green. Finally, students copied the examples from the board into their learning logs and completed a worksheet with additional examples.

In the lessons dealing with morphemic analysis, the class began with a discussion of the root words to be used in the day's lesson. Then examples of those root words with the target morphemes were presented. In a lesson focusing on the prefix *sub*, for example, the sample words might be *subzero*, *subsoil*, and *subconscious*. Definitions were obtained from the students or provided by the teacher, and the impact of the prefix on the meaning of the root word was described.

At this stage, a chart was placed on the board that included real words in which the prefix was used (e.g., *submarine*), made-up words in which the prefix was used correctly (e.g., *subrunning*), and words in which the letters to the prefix appear but are not functioning as the prefix in a meaningful way (e.g., *subject*). Students were encouraged to contribute additional examples. Finally, students completed a worksheet that required them to identify the meanings of words that have the prefix.

SUMMARY

The size of a reader's vocabulary plays a key role in reading and literacy. As Catch-Up Readers learn about all aspects of their world-science, geography, history, mathematics, literature, the arts-the larger will be their vocabulary. Children from economically disadvantaged homes are especially at risk of suffering from a lack of world experiences that lead to vocabulary development that will result in school success.

Teachers and parents encourage students to develop vocabulary by extensive reading. Other research-based methods focus on helping students connect new knowledge with existing knowledge, such as semantic mapping and feature analysis charts. Teaching students to work with word parts and to figure out words' meanings from context are also important features of the vocabulary curriculum for Catch-Up Readers.

Catch-Up Readers usually suffer from difficulty with word recognition or vocabulary or comprehension, or some combination of the three. We have seen how teachers can address these first two instructional goals. Chapters 11 and 12 focus on comprehension.

CHAPTER 11

Helping Catch-Up Readers with Story Comprehension

Catch-Up Readers vary in terms of the reading and literacy difficulties they exhibit as well as the causes of those difficulties. Comprehension is almost always a difficulty—after all, comprehension is the heart of reading. If a child has no comprehension difficulty, odds are good that few teachers or parents would be concerned about his/her progress.

Teachers can often identify underlying factors in a given child's comprehension problems. Sometimes the problems are embedded in the comprehension processes themselves. Perhaps the child simply does not understand appropriate strategies for gaining information from text and for recalling that information after reading. In many other cases, word-identification problems or poor vocabulary seem to be creating the comprehension deficits. In the case of poor vocabulary knowledge, the child may be experiencing a general deficit in world knowledge, due to a disadvantaged background, cultural differences, or cognitive limitation.

With those Catch-Up Readers for whom word-identification or vocabulary limitations function as the underlying factor in comprehension difficulties, teachers may be tempted to address the impeding factors and let comprehension take care of itself. This would be a mistake. Comprehension of text gives meaning to reading and literacy efforts. If reading real stories that are meaningful to children becomes a mere by-product of a teacher's efforts, the heart is cut out of the reading program's purpose. In Pikulski's (1994) review of research on remedial programs, reading for meaning was the central focus of those programs deemed effective. Block et al. (2002) found that one important characteristic of excellence in teaching reading is the provision of a wide variety of reading materials "so that every student can find a specific book with which to fall in love" (p. 191).

In addition to providing meaning to the curriculum, comprehension activities based on salient, engaging material afford teachers many opportunities to develop Catch-Up Readers' word-identification abilities and vocabulary knowledge. These opportunities allow Catch-Up Readers to apply their newly learned skills in the context of authentic reading. When working with Catch-Up Readers on comprehension strategies, a considerable amount of time is spent developing word identification and vocabulary.

Teacher-directed comprehension activities are only one part of the overall holistic efforts of classroom, school, home, and community for dealing with the difficulties evidenced by the Catch-Up Reader. Encouragement of recreational reading at home is crucial, for example. Not surprisingly, Neuman and Celano (2001) found evidence that students from disadvantaged homes have far less access to printed materials than do students from middle and upper socioeconomic environments. A comprehensive program must include efforts to place books and other high-quality printed materials in the hands of all students. Bear in mind, however, that *access* involves more than simple availability. Worthy, Patterson, Salas, Prater, and Turner (2002) found that dramatic success in improving the amount of voluntary reading by struggling readers requires materials that are interesting to the individual students and that are on appropriate difficulty levels. Books purchased by parents and relatives often fail to meet this criteria.

The methods described in this chapter focus on how teachers can offer guidance and support of students as they engage them at higher levels of comprehension processing. Too often, instructing struggling readers in comprehension is limited to asking lower-level questions about their reading material—in short, to testing rather than teaching them. Instead, Catch-Up Readers should be actively engaged in (1) the meaningful endeavor of connecting story content to their own lives and knowledge, (2) making predictions based on the text, and in identifying structural elements of stories to improve recall (Scharer, Lehman, & Peters, 2001).

STORY RETELLINGS

A natural way to help students recall story content and draw inferences and conclusions about a story is to ask them to retell the story in their own words. Retellings play a dual role for the teacher who is working with Catch-Up Readers: (1) in an instructional mode, they promote comprehension, and (2) in a diagnostic mode, they reveal students' recall processes.

Story grammar (also called story structure) refers to the basic structure of stories that includes the setting, plot complications, and climax. Providing explicit instruction in the components of story grammar helps Catch-Up Readers develop the quality and quantity of their narrative comprehension (Gambrell & Chaser, 1991).

When working with students to improve their narrative recall, planning plays a key role.

Prior to instruction, the teacher should read the story and be familiar with its grammar—the major episodes, the characters, and the central theme. After the reading the story to the class or small group, students are asked to retell everything they can remember. Some Catch-Up Readers have limited unprompted recall of stories. In such cases the teacher should prepare several specific questions about the story to guide their recall. The teacher uses the story grammar that has previously been constructed as a guide to further questioning:

- "Tell me more about _____."
- "Why do you think that happened?"
- "What other characters are in the story?"
- "What overall message did you get from this story?"
- "Let's reread this part of the story. You listen and try to get a picture in your mind as I read."

During the retelling and the discussion, the teacher can analyze student performance in a variety of ways to provide immediate feedback and future guidance. The checklist in the appendix (Story Retelling—General Analysis Checklist) helps the teacher keep track of general story grammar elements and how well students use those elements in recall. For more detailed and specific assessments of student performance, teachers can create retelling checklists based on some of the stories read during instruction. The Sample Story Retelling—General Checklist and the Sample Story Retelling—Specific Checklist (both in the appendix) give examples of two such checklists.

DIRECTED READING–THINKING ACTIVITY (DR-TA)

Catch-Up Readers benefit from receiving strong guidance during reading. Such lessons are often called *teacher-directed*, but more recently the term *guided reading* has become popular. A guided reading lesson pattern—the "directed reading–thinking activity" (DR-TA)—was developed by Russell Stauffer (1975) as a more engaging alternative to the lesson plan pattern used in most basal series—the directed reading activity (DRA). Teacher questions in the traditional DRA focus on simple recall of story material. In the DR-TA, in contrast, students are taught how to understand information in the text by engaging in a series of predictions prior to reading specified segments.

Stories selected for DR-TA lessons should be highly interesting and the story lines should suggest several possible outcomes. In other words, the stories should lend themselves to the use of prediction questions. In a DR-TA lesson the students predict story events and then read or listen to part of the story to verify or discard the predictions. As the story unfolds, predictions become increasingly accurate as students have more and more information upon which to base their predictions.

Predicting what will happen in a story provides a purpose for reading. Experiencing a sense of purpose is especially important for Catch-Up Readers, because they often find it difficult to become interested in the outcome of the story. Additionally, the reader who makes a prediction and then reads purposefully to check the accuracy of the prediction is better able to use inferencing and other higher-level comprehension skills. Use of the DR-TA activity teaches students to become active, strategic readers.

The DR-TA lesson pattern follows four basic steps:

1. The teacher creates a readiness for reading in the students by telling them the title of the story and asking them to examine the pictures on the first page. Then the teacher asks the students to predict what will happen in the story. These first predictions are written on the chalkboard or on chart paper.

Bear in mind that accuracy of predictions is not the emphasis at this point. Rather, focus is placed on whether the predictions are reasonable, based on the information available.

2. The students read a predetermined section of the story silently (or aloud) to check their predictions. After this initial reading, they modify the earlier predictions in light of the information they have just gained. The students discuss what happened in the selection and why it happened. General discussion of the story content follows. Then the teacher asks the students to predict what will happen next in the story. Based on the information they now have, their predictions should begin moving from divergent to convergent, as they use information to make predictions that more closely match what will actually occur in the story.

This pattern of making predictions and checking them can continue until the story has been completed. The number of prediction–check cycles depends on the story and the needs of the students. Sometimes, especially with older students, teachers use this DR-TA format to get students started in reading a story, then allow them to finish the story independently.

3. After finishing the story, a general discussion ensues, in which the teacher poses questions such as: "Did you expect that to happen in this story? When did you figure out the ending? What was the best part about this story? Would you have done what _____ [the main character] did? How would you change the end of this story?"

4. Typically, skills teaching follows: vocabulary development, concept formation, specific comprehension activities, or study skills. The teacher should determine the specific skills that are needed by the group and include these in relevant text-based, contextualized activities.

Stauffer's DR-TA lesson pattern was originally designed as a whole class activity. Individualized DR-TAs can be a powerful teaching tool for Catch-Up Readers, however, with questioning and skills instruction designed to meet a specific child's needs. Although DR-TAs are usually used with narrative text, expository text that has sufficiently predictable elements can be used as well.

EXPERIENCE–TEXT RELATIONSHIP (ETR)

The "experience–text relationship" (ETR) instruction technique is a teacher-directed, guided reading activity closely related to the DR-TA. Developed by Au (1979) specifically for children from multicultural backgrounds, this technique can be used effectively with all students. The group teaching lesson pattern is based on two key principles:

1. The understanding that students' background experiences will help them understand what they read
2. The power of socially constructed knowledge

Prior to instruction the teacher reads the story, considers the relevant background experiences students are likely to have had, and develops several questions that will be included in the lesson to tap this background knowledge. Three steps follow:

- *The experience step.* At the beginning of the lesson, the teacher uses the previous pre-pared questions to elicit predictions from the children about what will happen in the story.
- *The text step.* The students read a section of the story to check the predictions. The story should be read in segments, so that new predictions and comprehension clarification can be included throughout the story.
- *The relationship step.* General discussion of the story follows completion of the reading. The relationship step connects the key ideas in the text to the students' experiences. A key goal in this step is to show students that they can use their background knowledge to help them interpret and understand stories. The teacher and children summarize the main relationships after the discussion is complete.

Au (1993) likens the ETR lesson to "talk story-like lessons," in which children talk among themselves to construct meaning. Lessons such as these are based more on collaborative conversation than recitation. The teacher's role includes providing a high comfort level and structuring participation so that students think about text at higher cognitive levels.

PROBABLE PASSAGES

The "Probable passages" instructional method was developed by Wood (1984) to teach reading through prediction, discussion, and writing. Prior to reading, several key words from the story are selected by the teacher. The words are presented to the students, who are directed to place the words within categories that are related to the elements of story grammar. After the words are placed in categories, the students are asked to create an "incomplete probable passage," by using the words they have categorized to form a story.

Next, students read the actual selection or listen to the reading by the teacher to check the accuracy of their original predictions. After reading, the students discuss what happened in the story and compare the author's version to their own predicted stories. Then they write a "revised probable passage" that tells what actually did occur in the story.

Wood (1984) developed this strategy to be used with stories from basal readers, but it can be used with almost any story. The one caveat: The story contents should not be readily evident from the title or the words the teacher selects for the probable passage.

There are four stages in this strategy: preparation, prereading, reading, and postreading. We have modified these stages to accommodate the needs of the Catch-Up Reader and have found that this modified strategy is an excellent way to help such readers comprehend stories and improve sight-word vocabulary.

The procedure is time consuming; each story takes about 5 days of work. However, the thoroughness of the strategy is beneficial to Catch-Up Readers because they have ample opportunity to learn new words, predict story content, determine actual story content, discuss story content, and write a summary of the story. As a result, Catch-Up Readers feel secure about their understanding of the story, their newly acquired reading vocabulary, and their writing skills by the time they have completed the final step.

Preparation

The teacher selects an appropriate story and chooses several key terms or words that will require extra study (see Figure 11.1). These words are placed in random order on the chalkboard, overhead projector, or chart paper. If working in small groups, each group might receive a copy of the words and follow along with the teacher as he/she reads.

The teacher selects the story grammar elements that relate to the story. She then prepares an incomplete probable passage frame (see Figure 11.2) with these elements.

Prereading

The teacher reads the list of words to the students. They are asked to think about how they could group them within the incomplete probable passage frame. When first using this method, the teacher guides the group until they are comfortable categorizing the words independently.

For example, say the first word and ask students to predict in which category it fits. Discuss why a word or phrase might fit better in a certain category by questioning students about the story predictions they are making. Students also can add their own words, if needed, to construct their stories.

When working with Catch-Up Readers, ask them to write the words in the incomplete probable passages frame. (We recommend that two children share the writing and reading activities to enrich the social aspects of learning.) Writing the words provides a tactile and kinesthetic experience as they identify all the letters and their sequence, which enhances overall recall of the words. In this section of the lesson, the students take turns (1) discussing the categories in which each word should be placed, and (2) writing the words in the appropriate columns.

Next, the students discuss what could have happened in the story and then they create the incomplete probable passage (see Figure 11.3). The incomplete probable passage can be modified to fit the particular story, either prior to the lesson by the teacher or by the students during discussion. Teacher guidance is needed in this section to help the children fit their story into the patterned incomplete probable passage. Helpful questions include:

"How can we say that so it will fit this sentence stem?"
"Should we change the sentence stem?"
"How can we say that so it will make sense with the last few words?"

Catch-Up Readers should continue to work in pairs, each taking a turn sentence-by-sentence, with the teacher sitting with them or moving from group to group, facilitating the students' efforts as they compose the probable passage. Keep the probable passage frame

crocodile

zoo

barnyard

tree

hides

duck

scared

Mr. & Mrs. Sweetpea

flowers

FIGURE 11.1. *Probable passage word list (from* Crocodile in the Tree, *by R. Duvoisin, 1973).*

Setting	Character(s)	Problem	Solution	Ending
barnyard zoo	Mr. & Mrs. Sweetpea	someone gets scared	tree hides	flowers

FIGURE 11.2. *Incomplete probable passage frame.*

The story takes place _____

_____

_____ is a character in the story who

_____ .

After that, _____

_____

_____ .

Next, _____

_____ .

The problem is solved when _____

_____

_____ .

The story ends _____

_____ .

FIGURE 11.3. *Incomplete probable passage.*

handy so that students can use it to copy words. Accept invented spellings for words that are not on the probable passage frame. Although this step is very time consuming, it fosters sight-word development and enhances students' sense of ownership regarding their predicted story. After completing the predicted story, the pairs of students take turns reading their sentences. They can reread their probable passage by choral reading, or each can take a turn reading the whole passage.

Reading

The students read the story to find out how the author told his/her story. The story can be read (by the students or teacher) up to the point of an action or event that provides the students with enough information to change their view of the story. It is important for some Catch-Up Readers to have an opportunity to change their predictions immediately, once incoming information provides them with a different schema. Catch-Up Readers should continue to work in pairs, with direct teacher guidance, if possible.

Postreading

The students discuss and compare their probable passage version of the story with the author's version. They create another probable passage with the information gained from

The story takes place *in a barnyard* .

Crocodile is a character in the story who *is hiding in a tree and meets a duck* . After that, *he makes friends with all the farm animals and they hide him in the barn* . Next, *Mrs. Sweetpea sees him and is scared* . The problem is solved when *the crocodile brings Mrs. Sweetpea flowers every morning* . The story ends *with the crocodile living on a farm and helping Mrs. Sweetpea in her flower garden.*

FIGURE 11.4. *Completed probable passage.*

reading or listening to the selection (see Figure 11.4). Discussion and comparison of the predicted story with the actual story is conducted with the teacher and the pairs of Catch-Up Readers. Sometimes it is a good idea for different pairs to present their probable passages to the whole group. In fact, small group discussion is best followed up by the students within the large group sharing their stories.

In addition, Catch-up Readers are often asked to draw a picture of their favorite part of the story. Although the writing and copying aspects of this lesson plan are often slow and tedious for Catch-Up Readers, the results are well worth the time and effort. Students are proud of their stories; they have committed several words to sight memory; they are active participants in writing a story when presented with several words; and they are active comprehenders.

STORY MAPPING

"Story mapping" is another comprehension strategy that uses the elements of story grammar to help students understand the plot events, the role of characters, and the theme of a story. Story mapping provides readers with a set of questions which they use to organize the major parts of the story. Story mapping helps students develop a general sense of story structure, and it enhances readers' comprehension of particular stories.

This procedure requires that the teacher review the story to be read and list its essential story grammar elements (see Figure 11.5). In creating this map, the teacher should consider major events, both explicit and implicit, and major links between the events.

A more structured story map based on story grammar can be created from the worksheet presented in Figure 11.6. The teacher develops questions based on the story grammar elements and creates the map with the students by asking questions and helping them formulate their answers to fill in the worksheet and then create the map.

Research supports the use of story mapping with students who have not developed an implicit understanding of story grammar, and with poor readers. If a Catch-Up Reader has difficulty recalling story elements and their sequence, the use of story maps is highly recommended as long as the teacher assists the students with the activity in a meaningful way and does not use it as a busy-work assignment.

STORY FRAMES

The concept of "story frames" was developed by Fowler (1982). Although similar in purpose to Story Maps, story frames offer a more comprehensive analysis of certain aspects of a particular story so that students' attention can remain on one aspect until it has been fully developed. Fowler suggested five types of story frames (1) story summary with one character, (2) an important idea or plot, (3) setting, (4) character analysis, and (5) character comparison.

Story frames provide structure for readers by presenting an organized way of responding to the components of specific stories.

Fowler suggested using the following steps when constructing story frames.

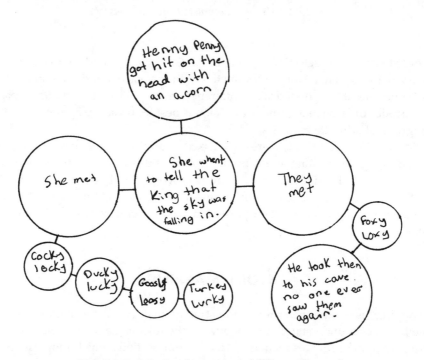

FIGURE 11.5. *Story map of "Henny Penny."*

Title: "The O'Learys and Friends"

Setting: The roof of the O'Learys house and their yard.

Characters: Susan the cat, the O'Learys, Susan the lady, neighbors

The Problem: Susan the cat can't get down from the roof of the O'Learys' house. The neighbors come by to offer suggestions for getting the cat off the roof.

The Goal: To get the cat off the roof and keep her safe from harm.

Event 1:   The O'Learys have moved to a new house. The children want to make friends. They see their cat on the roof and try to get her down. The neighbor, Susan, comes over to help.

Event 2:   Susan the neighbor brings milk for the cat. Mr. O'Leary puts a chair and a mop outside the window.

Event 3:   Other neighbors come to help. Lots of cats come to drink the milk. The neighbor goes on the roof.

Event 4:   The cat isn't on the roof. She is in the backyard drinking milk.

Event 5:   Mama gets lemonade for everyone. The O'Learys have friends. The other neighbors get to know each other.

Resolution: Susan the cat is off the roof. The O'Learys know their neighbors.

FIGURE 11.6. *Story map worksheet of* The O'Learys and Friends *(Berg, 1961).*

Part A: Teacher's Preparation

1. Read the story and identify the aspect on which you want to focus (e.g., concepts, plot, or facts).

2. Sketch out a paragraph that addresses the type of information on which you want to focus.

3. Take the completed paragraph and delete all words, phrases, and sentences except those needed to maintain the purpose of the paragraph. Do not remove too much information, especially when first introducing the concept of story frames.

4. For later lessons, try your frame with other stories that are similar to the one for which the frame was intended. Modify the frame so that it can be used flexibly in different situations. Figure 11.7 provides examples of story frames.

Part B: Instruction

1. The teacher and students read the story or content selection.
2. The teacher presents the story frame.
3. The teacher and students discuss possible responses to the first sentence of the story

Character Story Frame #1

This story is about a _____ named _____.

_____ tried to _____.

The story ends when _____.

Plot Story Frame

The problems start when _____. After that, _____.

Next, _____. Next, _____.

The problem is solved when _____.

Setting Story Frame

The story takes place in _____. The time setting of the

story is _____. I know this because the story shows

_____. Other clues that show when and where the story

takes place are _____.

Character Story Frame #2

_____ is an important character. _____ is

important because _____. One time she or he _____.

Another time, she or he _____. I think that _____

is _____ because _____.

Character Comparison Story Frame

_____ and _____ are two characters in

the story. _____ is _____.

_____ is _____. For example,

_____ tries to _____ and

_____ tries to _____.

FIGURE 11.7. *Examples of story frames.*

frame, then consider subsequent lines and discuss possible responses. The teacher directs students to determine if the information being added to the story frame is related to the previous information and if it makes sense. Discussion continues as teacher and students move back and forth in the story frame to make as many connections as possible.

4. The teacher rereads the completed sections of the story frame to the students at each stage, so that they can hear and use prior information.

5. After direct teaching and modeling has been conducted, students can begin to fill

out story frames independently. For Catch-Up Readers, directed teaching may be needed for a number of lessons before the students can do the task alone.

SEMANTIC WEBBING

"Semantic webbing" is a useful tool for (1) recalling or thinking through events in a story, (2) helping Catch-Up Readers develop specific purposes for reading, (3) tapping into their existing schemas for the story, and (4) tapping into their background information. It is most useful for stories about familiar topics or themes. The steps are as follows:

1. One important aspect of the story is identified by the teacher and written on the chalkboard or the overhead projector. It is usually written in the form of a question and placed within a circle. Figure 11.8 provides an example of the results of a class discussion in which students were predicting upcoming events in a story.
2. Students' hypotheses in answer to the question are written in circles as web strands around the question and dotted lines are used to connect strands related to each other. Supportive or elaborative hypotheses are placed in circles connected to the inner ring of circles.

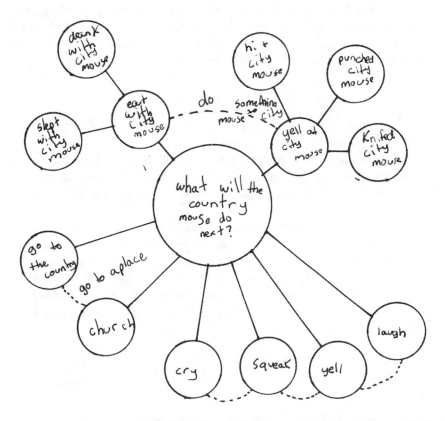

FIGURE 11.8. *Semantic web for* The Country Mouse and the City Mouse *(Fisher, 1994).*

This procedure can be repeated for major events throughout the story or for individual chapters in a book.

STORY PREVIEWS

A "story preview" is a summarizing statement about the content of the story to be read. It can be read by the teacher to the students or read by the students themselves. The story preview provides readers with background knowledge for the story, identifies key ideas, and shows how these ideas are related. It usually ends with a question that intrigues students and draws them into reading the story. Many basal readers include a story preview in the teacher's manual.

An example follows.

> Brad Cameron lived in New York City with his big brother Jake and his dad. His mom had died two years ago after a long illness. Life changed for all the Camerons when Mom died. Dad couldn't hold down a job anymore, and Jake got in with a bad gang in the neighborhood. Nobody had time for Brad.
>
> One day Brad came home from school to find that his whole life was about to change. There was Uncle John sitting on the steps outside their tenement house. Uncle John was there to take Brad on a wild adventure to Africa. Brad's heart pounded when he thought of leaving his home to go far away, but he didn't know how hard his heart would pound when he and Uncle John had to fight for their lives.

SUMMARY

Comprehension is the heart of reading, and it is almost always a difficulty for Catch-Up Readers. If the underlying factors involve word recognition or vocabulary, attention to those aspects of literacy is crucial, as discussed in Chapters 9 and 10. The student will also need support for comprehension in classroom reading, using methods such as those presented here.

When the teacher observes and assesses a Catch-Up Reader's presenting problem to be comprehension, methods such as those in this chapter focus on teacher guidance and support of student engagement in narrative text: Retellings, experience–text relationships, probable passages, story mapping, story frames, semantic webbing, and story previews.

Chapter 12 extends the emphasis on comprehension in the present chapter to deal with comprehension in the content areas. It focuses on reading of expository text in such topics as science and social studies.

Helping Catch-Up Readers with Content Area Reading

STRATEGIES FOR COMPREHENSION OF EXPOSITORY TEXT

Readers who have difficulty comprehending text, such as Catch-Up Readers, often do not select or apply appropriate comprehension strategies and are not as likely to regulate the use of these strategies as effectively as good readers. Part of the challenges faced in the classroom by Catch-Up Readers is the difficulty of the text. Textual material that is appropriate for the average students in a class is probably far too challenging for Catch-Up Readers. Both good and poor readers can be taught to effectively apply comprehension strategies (Pressley, 2000). When the text material becomes too difficult for poor readers, however, their ability to apply strategies quickly breaks down. Teachers need to be aware of the difficulty level of texts used for instruction and avoid putting Catch-Up Readers in situations where they are forced to deal with (or, more likely, fail to deal with) a text that is above their instructional level.

Since so much classroom reading material is expository in nature, strategy instruction in how to deal effectively with it is an important component of helping Catch-Up Readers (Smolkin & Donovan, 2002). Teachers can give instruction and practice on a variety of kinds of strategies:

1. Those in which students can use their background
2. Those that focus the reader's attention on major points in a selection
3. Those that use pictures and other graphic aids as cues to inferencing and retention

When planning instruction, however, bear in mind that simply throwing a host of strategies at Catch-Up Readers—no matter how creative or current those strategies may be—falls short of the basic requirements needed to facilitate successful achievement by Catch-Up Readers. Key factors in working effectively with students who are experiencing failure are (1) tailoring instruction to meet their needs and interests, and (2) persisting in efforts to find the right materials for each student. Worthy et al. (2002) found that success with struggling readers rested heavily on the time and effort expended by teachers to reach their students as individuals. After the death of the singer Selena and the release of a movie about her, for example, Mexican American students read and wrote with enthusiasm on that topic, which had touched them personally. Tying content area instruction to topics of high interest, even if those ties are a bit ambiguous (as, for example, in creating math word problems based on a recent current event), is a vital part of the creative teacher's role.

In recent years, attention in the field of reading has shifted from purely cognitive reading models, that focus solely on internal mental processes, to social constructivist models that pay attention to the effects of student and teacher belief systems on reading instruction and on the relationship between reading and discussion. The traditional viewpoint in content area instruction is represented by the phrase "learning from text," which emphasizes a linear causal relationship between reading and learning. Social constructivist viewpoints revise the phrase to "learning *with* text" in recognition that students have much to contribute as they construct their own knowledge through transactional learning situations that take place in the classroom community of learners (Vacca, 2002). Education of Catch-Up Readers is greatly advanced by an enriched understanding of the transactional complexities involved in text learning.

In this chapter we explore a variety of teaching strategies that can be used to help Catch-Up Readers enhance their comprehension of expository text. Bear in mind that these strategies are often useful with average and above-average readers as well, though these readers may already have effective strategies in place (Balajthy, 1986; Pressley, 2002). In addition, keep in mind that many of the strategies can be used with narrative as well as expository text.

STRATEGIES USING BACKGROUND KNOWLEDGE

Advanced Organizers

We learn new information by making connections with information we already know—by building bridges from the known to the unknown. David Ausubel, an important early cognitively oriented researcher of reading and study strategies, suggested that reading comprehension and recall would be helped by a prereading activity he called the "advanced organizer" (1968)—a short summary of important information in an expository text, written at a more general level than the actual text. For example, a student might read an advanced organizer that contains the highlights of a chemistry chapter and some of the key vocabulary. Then, when he/she reads the full chapter, he/she will be better able to make connections between the general, high-level information already learned and the new, more specific and detailed information in the chapter.

When Catch-Up Readers are faced with social studies or science readings beyond their instructional level, providing them with advanced organizers can be very helpful. Catch-Up Readers may not know how to use them effectively, however, so they may need both motivation and guidance. Explicit instruction and modeling in how to use advanced organizers will help these children in learning:

1. How to spot key ideas in the advanced organizer
2. How to learn new technical vocabulary
3. How to recognize the overall organization of the chapter that is reflected in the advanced organizer
4. How to make connections between what was learned from the advanced organizer and the new, more complete knowledge to be gained from the full chapter.

K-W-L

Early years of schooling often emphasize the importance of decoding and word identification rather than comprehension of text. With Catch-Up Readers, who often exhibit word-identification difficulties, the instructional stress on comprehension may have been especially weak. Therefore, it is important to emphasize comprehension development and to model strategies that students can use to understand text when they read independently.

The step-by-step procedures of K-W-L (Ogle, 1986) allow for ease in modeling this effective strategy to students. K-W-L is the acronym for three self-administered questions:

- K—what do I know?
- W—what do I want to learn?
- L—what did I learn?

K-W-L was not originally developed for struggling readers, but the strategy is effective with this group. Ultimately, a teacher's goal is to help students internalize the strategy and use it automatically to help them comprehend whatever they are reading. Modeling the strategy repeatedly in class is important in the early stages, as Catch-Up Readers are introduced to it.

K—What Do I Know?

First students create worksheets for this lesson by dividing a piece of paper into three vertical columns (or three horizontal rows) and writing K, W, and L at the top of the columns. The organization can be done individually, in groups, or by the whole class. In this explanation we use the whole class context.

Readers, guided by teacher questions, brainstorm what they already know about the topic to be read. Students think about their previous experiences and their firsthand knowledge of the topic. It is important to keep the topic specific rather than general so that the students will be able to brainstorm information that is closely related to the text to be read. For example, if the topic involves Mayan buildings and architecture, limit the brainstorming to that area rather than the more general issue of "What do we know about the Mayans?"

The teacher records results of the brainstorming on the chalkboard or chart paper. After the brainstorming, the students organize the information, grouping it into categories in the "K" section on their worksheets.

For example, in one class students were going to read about the topic of mosquitoes. In preparation, the teacher led them in a class brainstorming session, which resulted in a list on the chalkboard:

K
Bite
Ponds
Summer
Buzz
Itch
Stagnant water
Night time
Bug spray
Females bite
Swamps
Hot, humid

During the categorizing session, one of the student groups developed two categories: "Breeding Grounds for Mosquitoes" and "Characteristics of Mosquitoes." Small group work encourages a maximum of student engagement, analysis, and discussion.

W—What Do I Want to Learn?

The W step allows individuals to select their own purpose for reading. During the brainstorming, discussion, and general questioning, students begin to form their own interests and curiosities about the topic being studied. The teacher builds on these interests and curiosities by raising questions that have not been asked, by expanding on the students' ideas, and by piquing interest in ideas not previously considered.

The W section of the worksheet contains a list of questions to which the readers want to find answers.

In our "mosquitoes" example above, small groups developed questions such as:

"Do mosquitoes bite other animals, like cows and deer?"

"How do I protect myself from mosquitoes?"

"Why do mosquitoes bite some people more than others?"

L—What Did I Learn?

Finally, students read the expository text to find the answers to their specific questions. As they find the answers, they write them on their worksheets in the L column and record other important information there as well. After reading, the teacher asks individual students what they learned and which of their questions remain unanswered. Figure 12.1 illustrates a sample K-W-L chart.

K(now)

After you get a touchdown, you do a field goal.

If you don't get a couple of downs, you punt.

If you do well and get an interception, you can get a first down.

You can play good or bad, lose or win. You do your best.

Jim Kelly is a quarterback. He passes the ball.

The Bills can beat the Dolphins.

They wear helmets and pads so they won't get hurt.

W(ant)

How do you get to the Super Bowl?

How many games do you need to win?

How many players are on a football team?

Who teaches famous players to play football?

How do they run so fast? Who is the fastest?

How do coaches choose players?

Why do coaches get so mad at TV?

L(earn)

A football field is 100 yards.

There are 11 starting spots on most tackle football teams.

Coaches get mad because they are losing.

If you are running to a touchdown, don't look back.

FIGURE 12.1. *Completed K-W-L worksheet.*

Think-Alouds

A think-aloud involves readers in expressing their thoughts during reading. These self-reports include the mental images they develop from reading the text and the hypotheses about meaning they form as the text unfolds.

Think-alouds can be used as strategies for teaching children how to self-monitor their comprehension. Self-monitoring is a component of metacognitive processes—those conscious and unconscious executive control functions so central to skilled reading. Catch-Up Readers often exhibit poor metacognitive skills. Their reading exhibits:

1. Inability to form relevant hypotheses about a text's meaning prior to reading
2. Ineffective use of prior knowledge
3. Poor monitoring of reading
4. Failure to actively use "fix-up" strategies when confusions arise

Think-Alouds for Instruction

The think-aloud process is best introduced to Catch-Up Readers through modeling activities carried out by a teacher. First, the teacher reads aloud from a selected passage that will be difficult for students to comprehend. Difficulties can include contradictions, ambiguities, unknown words, unknown references or figures of speech, or difficult syntax. During the reading the teacher models her thought processes aloud by:

1. Making predictions ("I think . . . ")
2. Describing a mental picture ("I see . . . ")
3. Sharing an analogy ("This reminds me of the time . . . .")
4. Verbalizing a confusing point ("This doesn't make sense . . . ")
5. Demonstrating fix-up strategies ("I'd better reread . . . ")

After reading the selection, the teacher guides the students to verbalize their own thoughts:

> What did you think about as you read this selection?
>
> What picture did you get in your head?
>
> Could you see _____ or did you hear the _____?
>
> What do you think will happen next in this selection?
>
> Why do you think so?
>
> What do you know so far about this selection?
>
> Do you still think that _____? Why or why not?

When introducing a new strategy such as the think-aloud, a good rule of thumb is to provide several modeling sessions before pairing students to begin practicing on their own. Bear in mind that less able readers will need a great deal of support during think-alouds (Baker, 2002). At this stage, the listening partner should contribute his/her thoughts to the think-aloud, just as occurs in the teacher–student modeling.

Finally, students are encouraged to practice the think-aloud strategy independently. Teachers can encourage students to apply the strategy by frequently modeling it and by asking students questions about their line of thinking during class reading discussions.

One strategy for encouraging and monitoring Catch-Up Readers in their first independent attempts at think-alouds is their use of a checklist containing possible strategies, such as the one in the appendix (Student Guide for Independent Think-Alouds). As the children read, they use the checklist to recall think-aloud strategies that might help. Not all the strategies will be appropriate to use in most reading situations, but children should be encouraged to use as many as possible. After using a strategy, they check it off and describe in writing how they used it and whether it helped in comprehension.

Think-Alouds for Assessment

Wade (1990) suggested that think-alouds can also be used to diagnose how readers approach the comprehension process. She identified five diagnostic categories that can be revealed during think-alouds:

1. *Good Comprehender.* This student is an interactive reader who constructs meaning, monitors comprehension, and repeatedly makes and revises hypotheses.
2. *Non-Risk-Taker.* This is a bottom-up reader who does not go beyond the text. This reader often responds, "I don't know," or repeats words and phrases from the text without recognizing a connection to its meaning.
3. *Nonintegrator.* Although this student does use text clues and prior knowledge, he/she does not relate the information to the whole text. Each segment of reading includes a new hypothesis that is not related to what he/she previously read.
4. *Schema Imposer.* This student retains his/her original hypotheses about text meaning, even when the information that unfolds clearly calls for new hypotheses. The student makes the information fit his/her original hypothesis.
5. *Storyteller.* This student draws more on his/her personal experiences than on the information in the text. Some students identify with a character in the text and read into the text what they would do themselves in the text situation, not what the character really did.

We suggest that you apply these categories as you do your diagnostic teaching with Catch-Up Readers who are not monitoring their comprehension. If your students exhibit characteristics of one or more of these categories, center your questioning on areas that will allow the student to discover that he/she should (1) look back and use prior text information or (2) abandon an original prediction if more recent information does not support it.

Individual children can be monitored over a period of days or weeks with the Using Think-Alouds for Recognizing Patterns in Student Reading grid, located in the appendix. Observations of each type of behavior are written in the appropriate section until a pattern is determined. Think-alouds are useful assessment tools; teachers can monitor the children's oral summaries of their thinking for clues as to the processes being employed to make meaning from text.

Think-alouds can be powerful teacher modeling tools to help Catch-Up Readers become proactive comprehenders who focus on meaning instead passive word callers who focus on word-by-word reading (Duke & Pearson, 2002). Such students remain outside of the literacy environment of the text as they struggle with the language of literacy discourse. They benefit greatly from directed instruction with the use of think-aloud techniques to help them develop connections to the text.

SQ3R

SQ3R was the first and most widely known of the step-by-step study procedures known as "acronym techniques." It was developed in 1946 by Francis Robinson (1970) and popularized as a five-step procedure for reading expository text, such as textbook chapters.

S—Survey

Students examine the information-rich sections of the chapter by reading the title, the major headings, and the summary, and looking at the pictures. They think about the topic and what they need to learn about it.

Q—Question

Students consider the information they have learned about the chapter and compose general questions about what they think they will learn as they read. Looking at the major headings, they turn them into questions before they read each section.

R—Read

Students read to answer the questions they raised as they surveyed. Be sure to draw their attention to the tables, graphs, and captions.

R—Recite

At this point, students answer the questions they raised prior to reading the text. They give the answers verbally, write them in their notes, or discuss them with another student.

R—Review

Periodically, students review what they learned by rereading their notes or skimming the chapter headings.

Subsequent educators have proposed many adaptations of SQ3R, including additions of such steps as writing, outlining, or self-testing. Application of the procedure suffers from a failing common to study skill methods: that of personal preference. Students typically fall into one of two camps when using SQ3R—like it or hate it. There is seldom any middle ground, and Catch-Up Readers may well fall into the latter category.

Many of the students who need SQ3R the most lack the self-discipline and motivation to use it consistently—which is the case for all comprehension strategy instruction. Like other strategies discussed in this chapter, SQ3R requires teacher guidance and modeling before a Catch-Up Reader can use it independently and profit from the structure of the approach.

Figure 12.2 provides a worksheet students can use to structure their studying. The worksheet allows the students to refer to written material to guide them in their review. However, we found that several sessions of direct instruction were necessary for the students to feel comfortable using this approach.

STRATEGIES FOCUSING ON MAJOR POINTS

Prequestioning

A teacher-directed approach to building reading comprehension through prereading experiences is to present the students with a few written questions prior to reading. The questions help students develop a mental set or schema about the selection. Students are told to read all of the questions prior to reading the selection. The first question is then reread and students read until they find the answer to that question.

Some Catch-Up Readers will point to the line of print in which the answer is found but not be able to paraphrase the answer. If so, the teacher needs to model how to read the an-

1. What is the title of the chapter?
2. What are the major topics in the chapter?
3. Turn the first heading into a question.
4. Read the material following the first heading, looking for the answer to your question.
5. Answer the question without looking back. Check your answer.
6. Turn the second heading into a question.
7. Read the material following the second heading.
8. Answer the question without looking back. Check your answer.
9. Continue this process with each major section of the chapter, using the space below.

FIGURE 12.2. *SQ3R worksheet.*

swer and explain it by paraphrasing it. Some readers need additional support and modeling by the teacher to find the answers; some will read the whole selection but not find the answer to a question.

In such cases, after the question is read, the teacher models for the students what information they should be looking for as they read. For example, the first question in Figure 12.3 asks, "Where are mushrooms grown?" The teacher might hold up pictures of commercial mushroom growing operations in caves or sheds and ask, "What do these pictures tell you?" The teacher also might ask the students if they ever eat mushrooms at home. One student might answer something to the effect of, "Oh! My mom cuts them into pieces and fries them. We like to eat them with steak." If the answer is "no," explain that mushrooms are vegetables and ask how their mothers or fathers might cook vegetables.

CHILD: Well, Mom cooks peas in a pot with some water.

TEACHER: Yes, that is called boiling. Does your mom ever fry vegetables, like potatoes?

Catch-Up Readers who have difficulty finding the answers will need additional scaffolding. Figure 12.3 gives line numbers where the answers can be found.

Prequestioning is a restrictive procedure in that students will read only to locate the answers to specific questions. They may not recall much of the incidental text material. However, it is useful for Catch-Up Readers who are not reading for the purpose of comprehension to have a directed structure, such as these prequestions, as well as teacher modeling prior to reading.

Questioning Techniques

Questioning is an important way to help students (1) recall what they have read, (2) connect information gleaned from various parts of the text, (3) make judgments, and (4) think beyond the text to develop critical and creative thinking. Questioning helps students focus on the important information in the text. Questioning may take place after reading, but teach-

1. Where are mushrooms grown? (line 1)

2. What are three ways in which mushrooms can be prepared? (line 4)

3. What is the name of one kind of mushroom? (line 6)

4. What are poisonous mushrooms called? (line 2)

5. What do mushrooms add to a dinner? (line 8)

6. What type of mushroom should not be eaten? (line 3)

Passage upon which prequestions are based:

1 Mushrooms are often grown in deserted mines, caves, cellars, or sheds.

2 Poisonous mushrooms are called toadstools.

3 Be careful not to eat this type of mushroom.

4 Mushrooms can be fried, steamed, or breaded.

5 Some mushrooms are prepared by being stuffed and fried.

6 Puffballs, if white inside, are common types

7 of mushrooms that are frequently eaten.

8 Mushrooms are tasty delights and add to the flavor of any dinner.

FIGURE 12.3. *Prequestions.*

ers often find students more engaged if they discuss the reading while it is taking place (Smolkin & Donovan, 2002).

Teacher questioning is especially important for Catch-Up Readers. Through teacher modeling, students learn to pose their own questions when reading independently, a process known as self-generated questioning. Student recall of information is directly related to the type of questions asked during postreading instruction. If teachers focus only on literal-level questions, their students will come to develop the same focus, ignoring the important interpretive and applied levels of comprehension.

Learning Logs and Journals

Encouraging Catch-Up Readers to express themselves in writing is an important component of literacy development. Quite often, these readers have more difficulty with the decoding aspects of reading than the encoding aspects of writing, especially if they are encouraged to use invented spelling to express themselves. These Catch-Up Readers find a way around their difficulties in learning content material by carefully listening to the teacher, engaging in class discussions and small group discussions, listening to another person read the content material, and writing or drawing significant information.

Some Catch-Up Readers encounter difficulty using writing to organize the information that is to be learned. Direct teacher guidance and providing sentence stems (i.e., the teacher supplies the first part of a sentence and the child fills in the rest) might be necessary to help these readers, who may be able to identify the information needed but who cannot effectively communicate it in writing.

Learning logs can be important learning tools for Catch-Up Readers and a means by which they take charge of their learning. These logs provide a format for communicating the *what, how,* and *why* of the lesson. In writing in their learning logs, students are not required to decode a teacher's message and respond to it. Rather they can use their own discourse to explain what has been learned. Examples of sentence stems that can be used to scaffold the use of learning logs include:

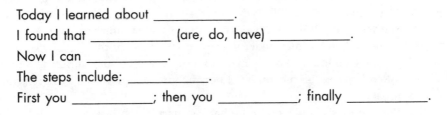

Today I learned about _____.

I found that _____ (are, do, have) _____.

Now I can _____.

The steps include: _____.

First you _____; then you _____; finally _____.

Students also can draw and caption the information that appears to be significant. If several students are engaging in the same project, their combined responses can be shared and discussed as a culminating activity.

Earlier we discussed use of journals with Catch-On Readers (see Chapter 5). Whereas learning log entries concern classroom content exclusively, journals offer space for personalized responses to reading and learning. Journals are powerful tools for Catch-Up Readers, as they are for *all* readers.

The "response journal" is the most familiar variety of journal in today's classrooms. Students are encouraged to record their personal responses to reading or class content. The teacher regularly reviews the journals and to writes brief responses. It is this personal response from the teacher that provides the response journal with much of its motivating power (Werderich, 2002).

Some Catch-Up Readers may find that writing in their journal is most meaningful to them if they are allowed to choose the type of written response. For the most part, however, especially in the first months of journal writing, most Catch-Up Readers experience more success if the teacher provides prompts. Such prompts can be specific to the reading material or more general:

What did you notice about what the author wrote?

Tell how you read this chapter, and why you read it that way?

What do you think will happen in the next chapter, and how is that related to what you read in this chapter?

What did the content of this chapter mean to you?

Why do you think the author wrote the chapter this way?

Journals serve as an important avenue of assessing student performance. At the same time, students are able to perform at their own achievement levels. More advanced students respond and write at more advanced levels, and struggling readers are able to find success at their own level of performance.

STRATEGIES USING GRAPHIC AIDS

Herringbone

The "herringbone" diagram is designed to help students locate the main idea of a selection. As a story or selection is read, they look for answers to the *wh* questions: *who, what, where, when, why,* and *how.* Students, with the help of the teacher, place the information they locate on a visual diagram shaped like a fish skeleton (see Figure 12.4). A summary is written along the central spine of the diagram. This visual diagram is useful for reviewing information and provides a visual structure for the selection that can be seen at a glance.

In a 1990 study, Weisberg and Balajthy reported that disabled readers at the intermediate grade level often found it impossible to construct good summaries, even after class discussion of the text. When an intermediary graphic organizer of the ideas was introduced, however, they were able to use the organizer to write effective summaries. In similar fashion, Catch-Up Readers can use a completed herringbone diagram as a visual organizer for writing a summary.

Writing the summary line is often the hardest part of the task for Catch-Up Readers. Barr and Johnson (1991) suggested that readers who are still learning to do the summary can identify the main idea of a selection by combining the information written on the *who, what,* and *how* bones. The summary is often a combination of the answers to those three *wh* questions.

The herringbone diagram is a highly successful aid for Catch-Up Readers who have comprehension difficulties, especially when used in a tutorial setting. Catch-Up Readers learn how to (1) look for facts within a selection, (2) determine the main idea, and (3) write a summarizing statement. Students gradually internalize the herringbone strategy and use it effectively on new material. It holds promise as an effective and engaging way to help struggling students locate and retain facts and details.

Graphic Organizers

The graphic organizer is a diagrammatic presentation of text concepts. It is designed, in part, to activate readers' prior knowledge. It is used before reading to help readers bridge

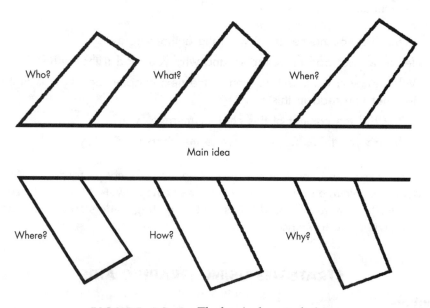

FIGURE 12.4. *The herringbone technique.*

the gap between what is already known and what is presented in text. Trabasso and Bouchard (2002) reviewed research on graphic organizers and concluded that they help students both understand and remember text content.

Graphic organizers exhibit the following characteristics:

1. Activate readers' prior knowledge.
2. Reflect a higher level of abstraction or generality than the selected material (Ausubel, 1968).
3. Present the relevant vocabulary from the selection.
4. Demonstrate the relationship between the vocabulary terms.
5. Provide a visual framework to help students organize and understand concepts.

In constructing and using a graphic organizer with Catch-Up Readers, we suggest several modifications that include teacher modeling and interaction with the students. Note that the teacher is highly involved in the preparation steps with our modifications. As the student becomes proficient in understanding the process, the teacher can and should withdraw from the activities that the student can complete independently.

1. Identify and list all the vocabulary and key concepts that students need in order to understand the major organization of the selection.
2. Choose an appropriate diagram (linear, branching, pictorial) to show the relationships between the various concepts and terms.
3. Add concepts and vocabulary that are already known by students to depict these relationships.
4. Evaluate the organizer by checking to see if all the major concepts are introduced and the relationships depicted.
5. Use the chalkboard or overhead projector to unfold the visual display as the concepts are being discussed. The visual array can be constructed with the students by leading them, via discussion, to the key terms and concepts.

Sometimes the organizer is presented in its entirety and the teacher discusses it with students, explaining how and why the terms are so arranged. A preferred model involving more student engagement is to gradually reveal the graphic organizer through discussion. Figure 12.5 illustrates a graphic organizer created around a lesson unit on types of energy.

SUMMARY

As mentioned in our consideration of story comprehension in Chapter 11, comprehension difficulties faced by Catch-Up Readers are usually secondary in nature. That is, the students' word-recognition or vocabulary struggles lead to difficulties in comprehension. Sometimes, however, the comprehension problems are primary. Students lack the strategies or engagement to understand and learn from text. These primary problems are especially evident with expository text, which is less familiar to elementary-grade students and which has a much wider range of text-organizational structures than do narratives.

In this chapter, we have examined a variety of methods to help Catch-Up Readers make use of the organization of expository text for understanding and learning. Some of these can also be just as useful with narratives. We have introduced reading and study

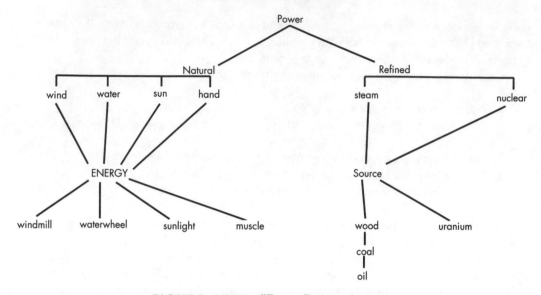

FIGURE 12.5. *"Energy" semantic map.*

methods whose purposes are to help readers link their existing knowledge to the new knowledge presented in text: advanced organizers, K-W-L, think-alouds, SQ3R, prequestioning and questioning, learning logs, and journals. We have also included two methods that highlight use of graphics for comprehension development, herringbones and graphic organizers.

Chapter 8 described Catch-Up Readers and gave suggestions for instruction. We also met one Catch-Up Reader in a case study. Chapters 9 through 12 provided details about possible instructional interventions. Next, in Chapter 13, we consider additional case studies representing the broad range of Catch-Up Readers. Chapter 14 completes our study of Catch-Up Readers with suggestions for additional resources.

Thinking through Case Studies of Catch-Up Readers

The following case studies were presented in Chapter 8.

THINKING THROUGH SARA'S STORY

Make a copy of the Monitoring Intervention Strategies chart from the appendix. Charts like this one can be used to (1) organize thinking and planning regarding the needs of individual students and (2) describe the overall effects of instruction and intervention.

Consider Sara's story and list the instructional goals for her in the chart's left-hand column titled Desired Outcomes. Include as many goals as you recognize in the story.

In the Assessment/Instructional Procedures column, briefly describe any assessment procedures that were used to acquire more information about the topic. Also describe the instructional plans that were implemented to facilitate achievement of the Desired Outcome.

Finally, in the right-hand column titled Actual Outcomes, briefly describe what actually happened as a result of each instructional plan that was implemented.

THINKING THROUGH JIMMY'S STORY

Make a copy of the form for Recording and Categorizing Reading/Literacy Needs in the appendix. Charts like this one can be used as a preliminary to planning instruction to track strengths and needs of individual students.

Consider Jimmy's story and make lists of his reading and literacy strengths and needs. Include observations of strengths and needs in areas other than reading and literacy, if they might add to your understanding of Jimmy's learning. When you are finished, compare your chart to the one we provide in Figure 13.1.

Next, brainstorm potential strategies for meeting Jimmy's needs and capitalizing on his strengths. Compare your ideas to the strategies described below, keeping in mind that different teachers can use a variety of methods to successfully address the same needs.

Jimmy's story in Chapter 8 ended with a consultation between the reading specialist, who had conducted an assessment of the boy, and Mrs. Jerome, his classroom teacher. In the consultation, the reading teacher focused on the development of Jimmy's sight-word performance and recommended the following strategies.

- Since Jimmy's running record showed that he has difficulty with basic sight words, the reading teacher recommended that Jimmy read from text that is at his independent or easy instructional level. He needs to see and use sight words repeatedly. Such repeated exposure to these words within easy text should strengthen his recall of them. To meet this need, the classroom teacher would manage Jimmy's instruction so that he would not waste time on third-grade-level reading, which would only frustrate him.

- A direct instruction approach also was recommended to improve his sight word recognition skills. The reading teacher explained that Jimmy needs not only to increase his stock of high-frequency sight words but also to acquire more general words that are recognized instantly. Prior to reading a selection, Mrs. Jerome should introduce sight words that are unknown to Jimmy. These words might be written on chart paper. Jimmy should be engaged in learning to recognize their distinctive features, and they should be discussed for meaning.

- The reading teacher also recommended that Jimmy keep the words he has learned in

Areas of need	Areas of strength
1. Incomplete written work—inattentive and distracted	1. Class discussion
2. Slow rate of reading	2. Social relationships
3. Dislikes oral reading	3. Above average aptitude
4. Poor spelling	
5. Word-recognition difficulties: —Poor letter–sound correspondence —Poor blending, vowel digraphs, diphthongs, r-controlled vowels	

FIGURE 13.1. *Thinking through Jimmy's story.*

his personal word book—a variation on the use of word boxes containing file cards. This is a notebook that has alphabetical separators, with one or two pages allotted per letter.

- Paired reading was suggested, so that Jimmy could have the support and social engagement provided by reading with another student in the classroom. Working with material at his instructional level, Jimmy and his partner would read aloud and help each other when either student comes across a word that is unknown.

- Two or three afternoons a week, Jimmy should read an easy book to a kindergartner. This experience would give him the extra practice he needs, provide motivation to succeed, and help him to feel like a real reader.

These strategies were put into practice during the first 4 months of the school year. Gradually, Jimmy began to build a sight-word vocabulary and feel comfortable reading books at his instructional level. He enjoyed reading to the kindergarten child, and his reading improved dramatically when he took on the teacher's role. Paired reading also proved to be very effective. Jimmy and another reader practiced reading for at least a half hour per day. Jimmy was well on his way to recognizing words and becoming a reader.

THINKING THROUGH KEVIN'S STORY

Kevin's story ended in Chapter 8 as Mrs. Swanson, his classroom teacher, and Mr. Hammond, the reading teacher, had decided to carry out diagnostic teaching experiences. They were interested in observing what would happen as they modeled appropriate comprehension strategies for Kevin.

Consider Kevin's difficulties by filling out a copy of the form for Recording and Categorizing Reading/Literacy Needs (in the appendix). Place the important assessment contrasts in the Areas of Need column. Are there other assessments that could shed light on Kevin's difficulties? Compare your results to the chart provided in Figure 13.2. Finally, consider what diagnostic teaching experiences might be appropriate to meet Mrs. Swanson and Mr. Hammond's objectives. Sidebar 13.1 provides some guidance in interpreting standardized test scores such as those provided for Kevin.

Mr. Hammond suggested that, although Kevin could decode words very well, he might be so intent on reading words that understanding text was not part of his reading agenda. Another possibility might be that Kevin lacked the world knowledge and related vocabulary to understand what he was reading. Mr. Hammond suggested that Mrs. Swanson assess Kevin's comprehension by reading segments of text to him and posing questions about the selections. If the task of word recognition is removed, does Kevin comprehend more of the selection?

Mrs. Swanson conducted informal listening comprehension tasks on several occasions and found that Kevin did not do well when listening. His comprehension difficulties did not seem to be limited to reading.

Mr. Hammond suggested that Kevin might need to activate his schema for the information he was going to read. By talking about the topic prior to reading, Kevin might better understand the text. Along these same lines, story mapping after reading might help Kevin recognize the various story episodes and how they are linked to the major problem in the story.

Mrs. Swanson used these prereading and postreading methods with Kevin. First, she

Sidebar 13.1. Interpreting Standardized Test Scores

Formal assessment refers to the use of standardized tests designed for administration under specified, controlled conditions. These tests may measure students' reading ability, general school achievement, aptitude, or other characteristics. Formal tests are often called "norm-referenced" because the norms by which the tests are scored are obtained from a reference sample population to whom the test has been administered. That is, the test publisher has administered the test to a sample of children (the *reference* or *norming sample*) and provided statistical information about the resulting range of scores (called "norms").

Although formal tests are designed for individual administration, most are developed for group administration. The scores obtained from formal tests are intended to be quantitative, nonbiased, and nonsubjective. Examiner judgment and other qualitative factors that might influence students' scores, such as attitude and interest, are minimized in these assessments.

In the scoring process, the students' *raw scores* (i.e., the number of answers that are counted as correct) are changed into different formats to facilitate interpretation. These formats are called *derived scores*, since they are derived from the raw score. Common derived scores include percentiles, grade equivalent scores, standard scores, stanines, and normal curve equivalents.

Percentiles. Percentile ranks are derived scores that show a student's position relative to the norming sample. The distribution of scores in the norming sample is divided into sections, each of which has 1/100 of the scores in the total distribution. Students with a percentile rank of 50 have scored at the median of the norming group, since 50/100 of the scores are above and 50/100 of the scores are below. A student with a percentile rank of 40 scored as well as or better than 40% of the norming sample and poorer than 60%.

Grade equivalent scores. These are derived scores that show a student's position relative to the norming sample, using a system that is based on the raw scores obtained by students at given grade levels in the norming sample population. The scores at the different grade levels are averaged, plotted, and mathematically extrapolated for each level of a published test. For example, if a reading test was given to a fourth-grade norming group, which produced an average raw score of 37, then any student taking the test and receiving a 37 would be scored at the fourth-grade equivalent.

Stanines. The word *stanine* is derived from the term *standard nine.* Stanines range from 1 (the lowest ability) to 9 (the highest). Scores of 1, 2, and 3 are considered low; scores of 4, 5, and 6 average; and scores of 7, 8, and 9 high.

Normal curve equivalents (NCEs). These are based on the basic concept underlying percentile ranks: that of dividing the scale of scores into 100 units. Like percentiles, NCEs range from 1 to 99, with a mean of 50. NCEs offer some advantages over percentiles in terms of interpretative clarity. NCEs have been mathematically transformed to represent equal units across the scale, a distinction not shared with percentiles. That is, the difference between two midrange NCE scores represents the same number of raw score units as an equal difference at the top or the bottom of the NCE scale.

introduced a basal reader story, provided some background for the setting of the story, and talked to Kevin about his experiences with the topic. Then she offered a prediction as to what she thought the story would be about and asked Kevin for a prediction of his own. She found that Kevin was initially reluctant to predict, though he did finally produce a prediction.

She proceeded by asking Kevin to read a section of the text to find out if either of their predictions were on the right track. Kevin read and—much to his surprise—he had predicted correctly what the story was about up to this point. Mrs. Swanson then talked to Kevin about remembering some of the important details in that part of the text. She modeled by saying, "I thought that _____ was very important to understanding what happened. What part of the story, so far, stays in your mind?" They talked back and forth until they had covered most of the important information. Mrs. Swanson then continued by modeling the next prediction and asking Kevin to make his. They proceeded in this manner throughout the story.

After Mrs. Swanson modeled these and other prediction-based strategies with Kevin for several weeks, he began to use them by himself, with her encouragement. His self-monitoring of what he read improved considerably, and he began to take pride in understanding what the text or story was about. Kevin was on his way to becoming a good reader.

THINKING THROUGH CLARA'S STORY

Clara's story, in Chapter 8, ended with Mrs. Dee, the reading teacher, conducting an assessment and consulting with Clara's teacher, Mrs. Prescott. Both teachers agreed that Clara was overusing context as a word-recognition strategy. Consider Clara's story and complete a copy of the Form for Recording and Categorizing Needs in the appendix.

Areas of need	Areas of strength
1. Poor comprehension of basal stories; poor recall; poor organization of story recall	1. IQ at normal range
	2. Word-recognition abilities

2. First grade:
    15%ile comprehension
    75%ile word recognition	

Second grade:
    12%ile comprehension
    70%ile word recognition	

3. Informal Reading Inventory results:
    Word recognition: 3rd grade
    Comprehension: early 2nd grade
    Difficulty with all levels of
        comprehension questions	

FIGURE 13.2. *Thinking through Kevin's story.*

- What conclusions can you draw about Clara's word-recognition difficulty?
- What word-recognition strategies would you suggest to the classroom teacher?
- What decisions would you make regarding enrolling Clara in a remedial reading program? Give your reasons.

Mrs. Dee recommended that Mrs. Prescott use chunking (see Chapter 9) as she reads with Clara. That is, Mrs. Prescott should read a line of text, using correct phrasing and intonation patterns; then Clara should read the line, using the same oral reading patterns as the teacher had modeled. Mrs. Prescott observed that Clara did not need to self-correct as much when this method was used. She read more slowly and seemed to be more confident about her word selections.

After reading a page of text in this manner, Mrs. Prescott asked Clara to reread the page orally while she listened. Although Clara's recitation maintained much of its original fluency, she again began to miscue and needed to self-correct some of the words. Mrs. Prescott made a list of the words that were self-corrected. After Clara completed the reading, they examined the words and discussed the ways in which they were confusing to Clara and what she might do to learn them. Mrs. Prescott asked Clara to point out the distinctive features of several of the words and discuss their meanings. Clara reread the page orally one more time, and this time, she was successful in reading fluently and accurately.

Clara is an example of a student whose major difficulties lie in an overly top-down approach to reading. That is, she is paying too little attention to the actual text. Compare your answers on the Form for Recording and Categorizing Needs with those shown in Figure 13.3.

Clara demonstrates good reading and listening comprehension. It may be that, in first grade, she found success with a word-recognition guessing strategy. When she encountered a word she did not immediately recognize, she was able to supply her own guess and still have the reading make sense. She understood that reading is comprehension, but she did not give much thought to individual word recognition. Now, in fourth grade, the reading

Areas of need	Areas of strength
1. Below grade level	1. Fourth grade reading level: on level but with word-recognition problems
2. Received remedial services grades 2 and 3	
3. Oral reading is halting	2. Good syntactic and semantic sense
4. Many self-corrections of miscues	3. Good comprehension and sequencing
5. Word recognition inconsistent—second-grade level	
6. Poor sight vocabulary, even with one- or two-syllable words	
7. Little or no use of decoding skills	
8. Overuse of context and guessing	

FIGURE 13.3. *Thinking through Clara's story.*

levels and vocabulary are more difficult, with a much wider range of possible vocabulary words than those in earlier years. Her word recognition problem is interfering with her fluency because her guessing now results in many miscues and self-corrections.

As an overly top-down reader, Clara is not using the appropriate strategies to identify words. She may have developed the habit of listening to new vocabulary the teacher introduced in class without examining the unfamiliar words closely for print features that would help her remember them. Drawing Clara's attention to the special features of words seemed to help her recall them when reading with Mrs. Prescott. The repeated reading procedure was also effective because Clara could concentrate on the meaning of the passage and, at the same time, hear the text being read with correct word identification and phrasing. This type of modeling helped Clara reread with more success. However, the teacher found that some of Clara's inattention to words reappeared when she read by herself, so Mrs. Prescott worked with her on the miscued words directly after the first reading had been completed. Before a second reading, Clara could be asked to locate those words in the text.

We would recommend that Clara receive her reading instruction within the classroom setting. Her reading needs can most likely be corrected with some sessions of teacher modeling.

THINKING THROUGH MARTIN'S STORY

In Chapter 8, our consideration of Martin's story ended with Mr. Zink expressing his concern about Martin's comprehension to the reading teacher and asking for additional assessment. Consider Martin's story and complete a copy of the sample Form for Recording and Categorizing Needs in the appendix.

- What have you learned about Martin that suggests he has a comprehension problem?
- What types of assessment would you conduct to learn more about this possible comprehension problem? Why?
- What teaching strategies would you recommend to Mr. Zink?

Compare your ideas with those in Figure 13.4.

Mr. Zink's observations suggest that Martin's difficulties lie in the area of higher-level comprehension and organizing information for writing. Previous testing suggested that Martin can identify words with ease.

In thinking through Martin's comprehension difficulties, there are many unanswered questions that can be addressed by further assessment. For example, we do not know whether Martin's comprehension is different when he reads orally from when he reads silently. His vocabulary, assessed at being in the low-to-mid range on the formal test, might be interfering with his comprehension. We would want to explore his organizational skills by asking him to retell stories. We would want to ask him direct questions about the story to identify where and at what level his comprehension breaks down.

We would take a story at the fifth- to sixth-grade readability level and engage Martin in a DR-TA (see Chapter 11), in which we would informally assess his ability to make predictions and discuss important aspects of the story. Several questions would be asked at each level to assess his literal, interpretive, and evaluative comprehension. If Martin had diffi-

Areas of need	Areas of strength
1. Receiving Title I since third grade	1. Spelling—average

2. Low standardized test scores
   Vocabulary: 38–41%ile
   Comprehension: 8–16%ile
	2. Literal-level comprehension

3. Poor classroom comprehension	
4. Not participating in literature circles	
5. Poor in interpretive-level questions that require integration of text content	
6. Poor recall	
7. Poor writing in response to reading	

FIGURE 13.4. *Thinking through Martin's story.*

culty answering our questions after silent reading, we would ask him to read selected pages aloud to determine if he had better recall of oral information.

We would also ask Martin to retell a narrative story after silent reading. A retelling assessment (such as those provided in the appendix under the comprehension category) can provide quantitative and qualitative information about Martin's ability to recall story content. We can pinpoint the areas of story grammar in which he does not respond (e.g., characters, theme, or episodes).

If Martin's answers to comprehension questions were limited to the literal level, there would be a strong possibility that the sentence patterns and vocabulary at this level might be too difficult for him. Recall that Mr. Zink reported that Martin seldom spoke in class or volunteered information. Perhaps he is delayed in language development and cannot yet handle the complex sentences and vocabulary used in some texts.

We would also ask Martin to read an expository section at the fifth- to sixth-grade level. We might introduce him to the K-W-L procedure, thereby tapping into his background experience and his ability to group words with similar meanings into categories. We would conduct diagnostic teaching with a K-W-L passage to determine the area(s) in which Martin had difficulty with the comprehension process (e.g., brainstorming, categorizing, forming questions, or answering questions). This information would help us determine how Martin approached text and organized his thoughts.

In Martin's actual case, further investigations indicated that his view of reading was bottom-up; that is, he considered word recognition to be his primary task as a reader. He recalled several episodes as he retold a narrative story, but he did not seem to understand the concepts of *theme*, *moral*, or *main idea*. When asked to reread certain passages and sentences, he would often remark, "I don't get it." Apparently he did not comprehend the gist of what he was reading.

Martin's silent and oral reading were about the same in regard to the amount of information he understood. His K-W-L indicated that he knew little about the topic we had selected for reading: famous presidents. He did not brainstorm many ideas, even though we participated with him by supplying several key terms that would normally trigger a student's recall of information. We did not see him making connections between terms as he tried to categorize the words, and he had difficulty thinking of what he wanted to learn. After reading the selection, he demonstrated poor recall of the information and difficulty answering his questions from the text material.

For Martin, future instruction would focus on encouraging his role as an active thinker. Martin needed direct instruction in how to read for meaning. His limited understanding of how to select important information from text and read between the lines to gain understanding, and his inability to recall and organize his thoughts so that he could report basic information about a story were contributing to his overall comprehension difficulties. The DR-TA, prequestioning techniques, and answering questions from his own language experience stories were recommended as the techniques that would best demonstrate to Martin how to respond the text.

The DR-TA was useful because of the prediction/verification element that is an essential part of the procedure. Martin would be guided by the teacher in narrowing the predictions he made as the story unfolded. Repeated direct modeling by the teacher would be needed to introduce this procedure to Martin.

Martin and several other students from his class with similar struggles were instructed in how to recognize story elements by identifying the characters, major episodes, problems and solutions. We recommended the use of story mapping (see Chapter 11) to help them understand the events, sequence, and solutions. After completing the story map, the story would be summarized in writing by using these events.

Martin dictated his own language experience stories and then answered, in writing, teacher-made questions based on that story. At first, the page and line number from the story on which the answer could be found were included to facilitate the process. As Martin gained proficiency in locating answers, line cueing was omitted.

THINKING THROUGH EMANUEL'S STORY

In Chapter 8, our consideration of Emanuel's story ended with Mr. Stevens, his teacher, conducting a running record (see the Running Record Summary Sheet in the appendix). Emanuel focused so strongly on recognizing each word that other aspects of oral reading, such as fluency and expression, were lacking. Considering Emanuel's story, fill out a copy of the Form for Recording and Categorizing Needs in the appendix. Compare your ideas with those in Figure 13.5.

Mr. Stevens decided to try some teaching techniques with Emanuel that could also serve diagnostic purposes, such as repeated reading chunking (see Chapter 9) and a language experience approach (see Chapter 4). Emanuel responded well to Mr. Stevens' modeling of the appropriate phrasing in the chunking procedure. He was able to reread the text parts using the same intonation patterns as had Mr. Stevens. However, on his own, Emanuel reverted back to his word-by-word reading. Mr. Stevens decided to forgo the repeated readings strategy and try a language experience approach as his next diagnostic teaching strategy.

At Mr. Stevens's request, Emanuel dictated a story to him. When the story was complete, Emanuel and Mr. Stevens read it aloud together. Then Mr. Stevens directed Emanuel to read the story by himself in the same way he had dictated it—as if he were talking to a

Areas of need	Areas of strength
1. Reads slowly	1. Good comprehension and recall
2. Uses finger to track	
3. Subvocalization	
4. Overuse of decoding	
5. Little expression; word-by-word reading	

FIGURE 13.5. *Thinking through Emanuel's story.*

friend. Emanuel read his story with more fluency than he had achieved using the other techniques. Mr. Stevens told Emanuel that he should not think about decoding words while he is reading but to look at the whole word and try to recall it. Emanuel read his story again, this time with increased fluency, and he began to feel pleased with his accomplishment.

Next, Mr. Stevens wrote the words from one of Emanuel's sentences in a column and asked him to read them as fast as he could. Emanuel immediately grasped the idea that these were the words in his dictated sentences, and he read the vertical sentence fluently. Then Emanuel selected some words from his story to write on cards and put in his word box for review. Emanuel and Mr. Stevens timed his reading of the language experience story and individual words from the word bank, and Emanuel kept a chart of his progress in speed of reading.

- What conclusions can you draw about Emanuel's fluency from the diagnostic teaching?
- Why did Mr. Stevens forgo using the chunking repeated readings? What additional information could he have gained about Emanuel?
- Why was Emanuel successful in reading his own story and the words in isolation?
- What other instructional techniques would you suggest to Mr. Stevens?

EXERCISES: EXAMINING READERS' MISCUES

Ask a student to read aloud from a book written at his/her instructional reading achievement level. (Photocopy the target section of the book prior to the session.) That is, the book should be challenging yet sufficiently easy to allow him/her to be successful with a bit of help from you.

Explain to the child that you will be writing on the copy as he/she reads from the book. As the reading proceeds, note the miscues that occur. For example, if the child cannot pronounce a word, simply draw a line through it on your copy. If the child mispronounces a word, write the mispronunciation above the target word on your copy. Jot a circled C next to any miscue that the child self-corrected without any help.

This procedure is a simplified version of several popular assessment methods, including the Running Record, the Informal Reading Inventory, and Reading Miscue Inventory.

Teachers often use oral reading miscues to help them understand the processes going on inside the minds of individual children during reading.

Afterward, create a chart of the miscues similar to the one in the appendix (Miscue Inventory Chart). Analyze the chart for any patterns the child may have displayed in his/her attempts to read. Discussing miscues with the child afterwards, a procedure called retrospective miscue analysis, can be a valuable instructional effort.

SUMMARY

The case studies of Catch-Up Readers are intended to provide you with examples of a broad range of students. In all cases, Catch-Up Readers have acquired the foundational principles of literacy, but they are falling behind their peers in reading achievement due to word-recognition, vocabulary, and/or comprehension difficulties. Teachers have the important responsibility of identifying the areas of struggle for individual Catch-Up Readers and providing appropriate, engaging intervention.

Chapter 14 provides a collection of resources that teachers may use to learn more about Catch-Up Readers and to provide them with effective instruction.

Additional Resources for Helping Catch-Up Readers

REVIEW OF PART TWO: THE CATCH-UP READER

Catch-Up Readers lag behind their peers in word recognition, vocabulary development, and/or comprehension. They understand the basics of reading and literacy, unlike Catch-On Readers. They do not suffer from neurological impairments or severe maturational delays, unlike some Stalled Readers.

The struggles experienced by a Catch-Up Reader can result from any number of factors. He/she may have experienced (1) a less successful start in reading acquisition, (2) a mismatch between learning strengths and the school's reading instructional program, (3) cultural or language differences, or (4) problematic home environmental conditions. Perhaps the student's general cognitive, social, or personal makeup has impeded the learning process. Classroom teachers can address the needs of Catch-Up Readers by providing individualized and small group instruction, and reading specialists can provide additional support and guidance.

All readers—those who struggle with reading and literacy and those who do not—benefit from effective and creative methods of teaching word recognition, vocabulary, narrative comprehension, and expository comprehension. These methods, modified for the needs of a struggling student, are imperative for the Catch-Up Reader. In addition, appropriate individualized attention and additional time-on-task in instruction and practice of reading and literacy are keys to helping these students achieve the performance levels appropriate for their age and grade.

KEY RESEARCH, THEORY, AND METHODS
RELATED TO CATCH-UP READERS

Allington, R. L. (2001). *What really matters for struggling readers: Designing research-based programs.* Boston, MA: Allyn & Bacon.

Richard "Dick" Allington has played a critical role in exposing the flaws of many regular education Title I and special education programs that attempt to meet the needs of Catch-Up Readers. His research found that such children are often placed in lower ability reading groups, where they typically remain throughout their schooling. Instruction in such groups is characterized all too frequently only by a slower pace of instruction, concrete learning with an emphasis on oral reading rather than silent, and increased repetition. Allington suggests that our schools today have the responsibility to use their knowledge and resources to provide children with a quality and amount of instruction that allows all of them to achieve literacy.

Carver, R. P. (2000). *The causes of high and low reading achievement.* Mahwah, NJ: Erlbaum.

Ronald Carver's primary contribution to the field of reading has been what he calls the rauding model, which is based on the idea that our best understanding of the reading process will come from examination of fluent reading—reading at a difficulty level where comprehension is successful. There are many models of reading within the field, but most remain almost completely unsubstantiated. Over many years, Carver has continued to develop a research base for his model and to modify it to meet new findings. His findings suggest that a variety of factors work together to allow fluent reading, but that only some of them are amenable to instruction. Word identification is a key factor that is critical to successful reading and that can be positively influenced by instruction.

Nagy, W. E., & Scott, J. A. (2000). Vocabulary processes. In M. Kamil, P. B. Mosenthal, P. D. Pearson, & R. Barr (Eds.). *The handbook of reading research* (Vol. III, pp. 269–284). Mahwah, NJ: Erlbaum.

This review of research on vocabulary instruction provides an overview of the complexity of vocabulary learning and its importance to reading achievement. Knowledge of the world, as reflected in the size of one's vocabulary, is an issue of special concern to children from culturally, socioeconomically, and linguistically different backgrounds. This review explains why traditional direct vocabulary instruction often fails and suggests contextual and definitional approaches that emphasize the learner's metacognitive awareness of the function of vocabulary in reading.

Stanovich, K. E. (2000). *Progress in understanding reading: Scientific foundations and new frontiers.* New York: Guilford Press.

Keith Stanovich is one of the most respected researchers in the field of reading. This text, which functions as a grand overview of his research and thinking over the past several decades, presents arguments supporting the critical importance of phonological awareness in early reading as well as word-recognition skill development. Several of his reading models have received widespread attention, though not always universal acceptance. The Matthew effect model, for example, suggests that "the rich get richer and the poor get poorer," as in the "Parable of the Talents" from the "Gospel of Matthew" in the Bible. In reading/literacy terms, students who have a strong start in reading acquisition make achievement gains that give them an increasing lead over students who have weaker foundations.

Stanovich's interactive–compensatory model of reading suggests that students who have poor word-recognition skills attempt to compensate by using less effective strategies and cueing systems. They may, for example, overly rely on top-down syntactic and semantic cues.

The phonological core deficit model attempts to distinguish between the most seriously impaired readers, whom we refer to as Stalled Readers (see Part Three of this text), and those whom Stanovich calls "garden-variety poor readers"—the Catch-Up Readers in this text. Stanovich suggests that an early language-processing deficit dealing with the sounds of language—that is, phonological awareness—creates the problems faced by Stalled Readers.

MATERIALS AND CURRICULA FOR CATCH-UP READERS

Series Books

The more teachers know about children's books, the better prepared they are to engage reluctant readers in spending the massive amount of time necessary to improve reading ability. Series books are popular with children, and by moving from one book to the next, Catch-Up Readers are often motivated to spend considerable time on the task.

Choose a series to introduce to your students. Read one of the early books in the series—the first is usually the best—to familiarize yourself with it. Then, in a class presentation or in a classroom display, provide information about the series to your class. You might want to read aloud a chosen selection from the book. Include information as to the typical plot content, the major characters, and other outstanding characteristics of the series. Provide a handout with information about the books in the series, the publisher, the author, and other resources (such as related Internet websites).

Publishers have recognized the financial implications of a successful series for children, and several new series appear each year. A classroom budget that allows purchase of the hot, new series is a big advantage. While having a single copy of some of the later books in the series will usually serve, it is best to purchase several copies of the first, second, and third books. Following is a list of popular series:

American Girls Collection, various authors (Readability: Grade 5)
American Girls History Mysteries, various authors (5)
Animorphs, K. A. Applegate (5)
Anne of Green Gables, L. M. Montgomery (5)
Arthur Chapter Books, Marc Brown (3)
Baby Sitters Little Sister, Ann M. Martin (3)
Bailey School Kids, Debbie Dadey & Marcia Thornton Jones (3)
Berenstain Bears, Stan & Jan Berenstain (2)
Berenstain Bear Chapter Books, S. & J. Berenstain (3)
Box Car Children, Gertrude Chandler Warner (4)
Cam Jansen, David A. Adler (2.5–3.0)
Choose Your Own Adventure, various authors (1.5–2.0)
Clifford, Norman Bridwell (2)

Encyclopedia Brown, Donald J. Sobol (4)

Franklin, Paulette Bourgeois & Brenda Clark (2)

Girls to the Rescue, Bruce Lansky (5.0–6.0)

Goosebumps, R. L. Stine (5)

Harry Potter, J. K. Rowling (6)

Henry and Mudge, Cynthia Rylant (2)

Indian in the Cupboard, Lynne Reid Banks (6)

Nancy Drew Mystery Stories, Carolyn Keene (5)

Nate the Great, Marjorie Weinman Sharmat (2.0–2.5)

New Kids at the Polk Street School, Patricia Reilly Giff (2)

Redwall, Brian Jacques (6)

The Royal Diaries, various authors (5)

Series of Unfortunate Events, Lemony Snicket (5)

Book Clubs

Book clubs serve an important purpose in encouraging children to develop their own personal libraries. These clubs make inexpensive editions of currently popular books readily available. Teachers must put in the substantial efforts necessary to send home forms, collect orders and money, tabulate the final order, and mail or fax it to the club headquarters. They are encouraged by a generous promotional policy that provides free books for the classroom and other classroom resources or personal gifts.

Trumpet Book Club, P.O. Box 7510, Jefferson City, MO 65102

Scholastic Book Club, P.O. Box 7503, Jefferson City, MO 65102

Sound Recordings of Books

Books read aloud on CDs and audiotapes can provide students with feedback and guidance during independent reading. Little or no reading improvement will result, however, if the child is not reading along with the recording. Careful monitoring by teachers or parents is necessary.

Books on Tape, P.O. Box 7900, Newport Beach, CA 92658, 800-626-3333. Online: *http://www.booksontape.com*

Listening Library (Random House), One Park Avenue, Old Greenwich, CT 06870, 800-243-4504. Online: *http://www.listeninglib.com*

Recorded Books, 270 Skipjack Road, Prince Frederick, MD 20678, 800-638-1304. Online: *http://www.recordedbooks.com*

Technology Resources for Catch-Up Readers

Inspiration, Inspiration Software

Graphic displays of textual material play a role in several reading methods for Catch-Up Readers. They are also useful for the prewriting stage in the writing process. *Inspiration* is application software for creating such graphic displays. The children's version, *Kidspiration*, is designed for use in elementary classrooms. These graphic displays can be used with semantic mapping (see Chapter 10), semantic webbing and story mapping (see Chapter 11), and graphic organizers (see Chapter 12).

Tenth Planet Word Identification Software, Sunburst

This software is the premiere series of word-identification software presently on the market for classroom use. The programs make effective use of voice and graphics, and the activities include up-to-date strategies, such as "making words." In *Consonant Blends and Digraphs*, for example, children drag and drop letters to manipulate word forms, making *room* into *groom* into *broom* and into *bloom* as the voiced instructions give guidance. These programs are structured according to typical reading skills taught in the classroom word-identification curriculum—a substantial advantage for classroom teachers.

Many other commercial software programs for word identification are available, but most offer instruction that is almost random. An exercise for a mid-year first grader, for example, might be followed by an exercise for a third grader. The usefulness of such software for instruction is limited. Programs in the Tenth Planet series include:

Consonant Blends and Digraphs
Letter Sounds
Roots, Prefixes and Suffixes
Vowel Patterns
Vowels: Short and Long
Word Parts

Evaluating Phonics Software

The checklist below is based on Michael McKenna's (2002) survey of phonics software issues.

Title of software _____

Publisher _____

Reviewed by _____ Date _____

	Excellent				Poor
1. Is instruction direct?	5	4	3	2	1
2. Is instruction systematic?	5	4	3	2	1
3. Does the software make it easy for the teacher to monitor progress?	5	4	3	2	1
4. Are students able to progress developmentally through the software?	5	4	3	2	1
5. Does the software include attention to onsets and rimes?	5	4	3	2	1
6. Do children use letter cards to form words and break them apart to form new words?	5	4	3	2	1
7. Does the software include multisyllabic words?	5	4	3	2	1
8. Do students spend an appropriate amount of time in learning, as opposed to playing games?	5	4	3	2	1

Commercial Curricula

Soar to Success—Houghton Mifflin, 222 Berkeley Street, Boston, MA 02116-3764, 800-733-2828. Online: *http://www.schooldirect.com*

This curriculum is designed to provide support to teachers who may not have extensive professional education in teaching reading. The accompanying teacher's manuals and staff development video present clear guidelines and instructions for daily work with students. Some educators call such curricula "turnkey" systems—turn the key and off you go. Everything is packaged for ease of use by most teachers, without extensive prior reading education and with a minimum of preparation time. Ease of use is an advantage; lack of flexibility and a possible sense of disempowerment on the part of professional teachers are disadvantages.

Separate sets of materials, including student workbooks and leveled paperbacks, are provided for each grade from third to eighth. Within each grade, the leveled paperbacks provide gradual increases in level of difficulty. The reading material includes both literature and factual books from social studies and science as well as a rich multicultural emphasis. Lesson plans include methods such as reciprocal teaching and use of graphic organizers.

"Four Blocks"—Carson–Dellosa Publishing Company: Cunningham, P. M., Hall, D. P., & Sigmon, C. M. (2000). *The teacher's guide to the Four Blocks: A multimethod, multilevel framework for grades 1–3*. Greensboro, NC: Carson Dellosa. Online: *http://www.fourblocks. com*

Developed by the well-known reading specialist Patricia Cunningham, this curriculum provides a framework for instruction of young readers up to grade 3. Unlike Soar to Success, which provides specific lesson plans, Four Blocks offers teachers a great deal of control over the content and structure of the curriculum. Four Blocks provides a general framework and suggested strategies, and teachers are responsible for applying that framework to their own materials and classrooms.

Cunningham incorporates a wide variety of strategies that can potentially be used in Four Blocks instruction, including word walls (see Chapter 3), making words (see Chapter 3), and teacher read-alouds. Instructional sessions are scheduled for 120–160 minutes per day. The sessions are divided into four components, hence the name of the programs: teacher-directed reading (Guided Reading), independent reading (Self-Selected Reading) that includes the teacher reading stories aloud, writing process workshop (Writing Block), and word recognition (Working with Words).

Read 180, Read XL—Scholastic, 2931 E. McCarty Street, Jefferson City, MO 65101, 800-724-6527. Online: *http://www.scholastic.com*

These programs are designed for upper-elementary and middle-school students who are struggling with reading. Instruction is based on leveled paperbacks and supported by software that provides additional drills on word recognition, comprehension, vocabulary, and spelling. Like Soar to Success, it is a turnkey curriculum that requires a minimum of professional teacher preparation but limits flexibility.

Scholastic Summer School—Scholastic, 2931 E. McCarty Street, Jefferson City, MO 65101, 800-724-6527. Online: *http://www.scholastic.com*

A turnkey curriculum packaged specifically for summer-school reading programs, this

6-week program provides instructions and materials for 3 hours of instruction per day. Materials include paperbacks, workbooks, and drill sheet masters. The curriculum heavily emphasizes drill and practice in a very traditional reading curriculum.

Success for All, Roots and Wings—Success for All, Johns Hopkins University, 3505 N. Charles St., Baltimore, MD 21218, 410-516-8800. Online: *http://www.successforall.com*

Success for All has gained high visibility in the national press in recent years. Several urban school districts, as well as many smaller districts, have adopted the curriculum. A good deal of research has been conducted to determine the program's impact, and Robert Slavin, the program's developer, has made much of positive results (Slavin, 2002). Other researchers have been more critical of the results (Pogrow, 2002).

The curriculum provides a basic structure that can be adapted to whatever reading materials a school might be using. Indeed, it is designed more for entire schools and districts than individual classrooms. It includes a heavy phonics component, cooperative learning experiences, tutorial and ability-grouped instruction, and independent reading.

Roots and Wings is a component that can be added to Success for All to extend instruction into mathematics, social studies, and science.

SUMMARY

In Part Two, we learned that Catch-Up Readers have acquired the basic print concepts and early word-recognition strategies that the Catch-On Readers in Part One failed to learn. These Catch-Up Readers have moved beyond the emergent reader level. However, they have begun to fall behind their peers in reading and writing achievement due to word-recognition, vocabulary, or comprehension difficulties. Teachers face the important tasks of observation and assessment to determine the literacy processes in which the Catch-Up Readers are struggling. Intervention follows upon the results of those assessments.

In Part Three, we introduce the third and last important group of struggling readers, the Stalled Readers. Like Catch-Up Readers, these students are past the struggles typical of Catch-On Readers. They have understood the basic functions of print and have begun to establish a successful foundational understanding of reading and literacy. Also like Catch-Up Readers, they have begun to fall behind their peers in achievement.

The difference between the Catch-Up Reader and the Stalled Reader lies in their different response to quality intervention. The Catch-Up Reader responds positively to appropriately targeted instruction, even though progress may be painfully slow. The Stalled Reader, on the other hand, appears to make no progress at all. Strategies learned one day seem to be forgotten the next. Stalled readers constitute a very small portion of the total population of struggling readers, but their needs are dramatic and challenging.

PART THREE

STALLED READERS

Who Are the Stalled Readers in Your Classroom?

MOLLY'S STORY

Molly was referred to the Reading and Literacy Center after completing first grade. Her mother reported that Molly could not recognize words; to cover for this inability, she had memorized stories all during first grade. Subsequently, the first-grade teacher was contacted and asked to find out if Molly could recognize words or if she really was memorizing the stories. Much to her teacher's surprise, Molly could only identify the words *is* and *a* out of context. Molly was enrolled in the center's summer reading program to help establish her sight-word base and to help her learn to recognize words in several different contexts.

Molly was very pleased to attend the Reading Center because she wanted to learn to read. We soon found out that Molly was indeed an exceptional child. She had a speaking vocabulary that paralleled that of many adults. Her concept formation, generalizations, and critical thinking abilities were far superior to other children her age. She handled her intellectual abilities quite well and, for the most part, enjoyed the same activities as her peers.

Molly's major learning problem was recalling sight words. Words taught one day were forgotten the next day. Words taught and identified early in the text were forgotten later in the text. We were working with a child of superior intellect. Psychological tests revealed that her IQ was in the 98th percentile. But she could not develop a sight-word vocabulary in spite of her interest and desire to learn words. The problem did not seem to be related to any difficulties with print concepts or phonemic awareness, as she did well on informal assessment tasks in these areas.

After working with several approaches to teaching sight words, such as preteaching during a directed reading–thinking activity (DR-TA; see Chapter 11) and asking Molly to dictate language experience stories, we were discouraged to find that she had not learned the words that had been taught. We decided to use a phonogram approach in which we would teach a pattern, such as -an (see Chapter 9). Molly was asked to supply rhyming words such as can, ran, and fan. Molly could supply many rhyming words and read them in lists, but she could not recognize these words when she read them in running text or when they were mixed with other sight words.

A synthetic phonics approach, in which letters within words were sound blended (see Chapter 9), was also introduced. Molly knew the consonant sounds but not the vowels. She typically became tongue-tied when she tried to use a phoneme-by-phoneme approach to word recognition. We also engaged Molly in a shared reading procedure (see Chapter 2), in which predictable books were read. Once Molly heard the teacher read a story, she could read it with near-perfect accuracy. However, when the words were taken out of context, or when she encountered them in another reading situation, she could not identify them.

Molly was very concerned about this problem. She was motivated to try to learn words and read connected text, but she could not remember the words for more than a short time. We decided to use a VAK (see Chapter 16) approach, in which two words a day would be taught in ways that involved the visual, auditory, and kinesthetic modalities of learning. Molly engaged vigorously in this activity—but to no avail. She still could not retain the words or recognize them in other contexts.

The Reading and Literacy Center's semester ended and Molly had not learned any words as sight words. We discussed the situation with her school principal, classroom teacher, and school psychologist. No specific disorders were evident from any psychological reports, school behaviors, or our clinic reports. One of our concerns was that Molly's anxiety about learning words might be interfering with her recall.

Molly's story is continued in Chapter 19. Think through her experiences and the instructional efforts that failed to succeed. What could possibly explain the difficulties Molly is facing? What are possible avenues for future instruction?

CHARACTERISTICS OF THE STALLED READER

Children like Molly are Stalled Readers: students who have achieved significantly lower reading levels than expected for their age and grade level, and despite consistent intervention instruction. Researchers and educators use a variety of terms to describe the problem faced by some of these students: dyslexia, deep dyslexia, surface dyslexia, learning disability, word blindness, and severe reading disability. These terms are used widely, loosely, and often incorrectly. In fact, most children who have been officially labeled with these terms by some form of a specialist are Catch-On or Catch-Up Readers, not Stalled Readers.

Stalled Readers are often blocked at the word-identification level of reading. While word identification seems to develop naturally for most of their peers, Stalled Readers typically have difficulty with decoding tasks such as sound blending of phonemes and syllables and sound to symbol associations. Sounds, word patterns, and syllables often become garbled as these students try to match letters to sounds and blend them to form words. Even if a word is blended correctly, Stalled Readers may have difficulty generalizing across sound patterns to recall the word in auditory or visual memory.

Stalled Readers also have difficulty developing a sight-word base, often forgetting words they have just practiced. Printed words that cannot be identified prohibit them from comprehending and appreciating print as a means of communication. Most Stalled Readers have serious problems learning to recognize the printed form of words, although comprehension difficulties can surface as the major form of reading difficulty in some cases. A slow rate of reading and/or slow internal processing of words may contribute to these comprehension difficulties. Students' self-reports might include statements about their need to re-read sentences and paragraphs over and over, until they understand the meaning. Some Stalled Readers have advanced beyond the beginning levels of reading, and their problems lie in the area of comprehension: They do not understand what they read.

How are Stalled Readers different from Catch-On and Catch-Up Readers? The key difference lies in the degree of their lack of positive response to effective interventional instruction. Catch-On Readers (see Chapter 1) have remained at the emergent level, despite consistent classroom instruction and opportunities to engage in early literacy activities. At a foundational level, they do not understand the nature of print experiences or the literacy processes in which readers engage. As they move through the kindergarten and first-grade years, they see their peers "catch-on" to the purpose and processes of reading and writing. The gap increases between their achievement levels and the level of classroom instruction. Once the teacher recognizes this increasing gap, however, instructional interventions through small group, tutorial, and/or pullout instruction begin to have an effect. Progress may be slow or it may be rapid, but an enriched literacy curriculum targeted to the child's appropriate performance levels does yield progress, and the child begins to understand how the reading and writing processes function.

Once Catch-On Readers have established a foundational knowledge of literacy processes, they may be able to rejoin their classmates in ordinary classroom reading programs. This is especially the case when their difficulties are noticed early—in kindergarten or first grade. They have not had the chance to fall significantly behind their peers. If the difficulty is not caught early enough, the Catch-On Reader becomes a Catch-Up Reader.

Catch-Up Readers (see Chapter 6) understand the foundational, emergent processes of literacy with which the Catch-On Reader is struggling. However, Catch-Up Readers continue to lag behind their peers in terms of reading and literacy achievement. As with Catch-On Readers, they exhibit progress when they are supplied with effective small group or individualized attention in the classroom or with pullout instruction. This progress may be slow. Some Catch-Up Readers, in fact, may not appear to be "catching up" to their peers. Sometimes the factors that created their problems in the first place are still present, slowing progress as their peers continue to move ahead in achievement. Yet progress is still discernible.

At some point in their primary-grade years, many children who are struggling with reading and literacy are identified by the classroom teacher and/or by a school-wide assessment as having difficulties and are referred to specialists for diagnostic evaluation. These may include a reading specialist, school psychologist, medical doctor, speech–language therapist, or other specialist. These specialists attempt to pinpoint the cause of the problem, locate relative processing strengths, and recommend instruction. The terminology used to identify causes of the reading difficulty and to classify the students according to their needs varies from specialist to specialist. Some specialists are very quick to label children as learning disabled or dyslexic, based on only one or two tests. In our experience, it is impossible to differentiate Stalled Readers from Catch-Up Readers at this point in the assessment process.

The key to this differentiation lies in what happens during interventional instruction. In a nutshell, Catch-Up Readers respond to instruction, but Stalled Readers do not. Lyon et al. (2001) noted: "The meaning of disability could change in the future . . . for children whose reading or other academic problems are severe and intractable (that is, for children who do not adequately respond to a variety of intervention approaches)" (p. 282).

It may seem odd to differentiate the less serious reading difficulties from the more serious simply in terms of instructional effectiveness. We have become used to classification systems that, in a sense, blame the student: He/she has some disability. A far more useful approach is to classify students in terms of the amount and kinds of intervention that are necessary. Allington (2002), for example, described the difference between these approaches in terms of those that focus on disabilities and those that focus on instructional programs for students with reading difficulties:

> What we now identify as reading/learning disability would, instead, be reconceptualized as a more comprehensive (and more expensive) instructional problem to be dealt with as part of the regular course of designing school programs, which would result in every child learning to read alongside his or her peers. Addressing the issue of reading difficulties would require school programs that were more comprehensive and flexible than most are today. These programs would focus on early intensive intervention but would acknowledge that some children will undoubtedly require long-term extraordinary instructional support—in some cases across the school career. (p. 280)

Years of experience with classroom and clinical reading instruction have shown us that making the differentiation is considerably more complex than our statement—"Catch-Up Readers respond to instruction, but Stalled Readers do not"—would suggest. How do we know whether a student is responding to effective instruction? How do we know that the instruction *is* effective in the first place?

We have found that many children who are diagnosed by specialists as being some form of what we would call a Stalled Reader are actually Catch-Up Readers. The common pattern works like this:

Mandy is in late second grade. She is having problems in her classroom, especially in learning to read and write. There may be some social and emotional difficulties as well. There are no other obvious reasons for the reading and literacy problems. The teacher or parents arrange for an assessment to be carried out by a reading specialist, school psychologist, medical doctor, or speech–language therapist. The assessment consists of one or more reading tests, an intelligence test, and perhaps some others. The tests indicate that Mandy has normal intelligence but is reading below her grade expectancy level. The assessment report that is sent to the school identifies her as learning disabled or dyslexic.

This is when we come on the scene. Mandy is enrolled in a university reading clinic, which provides her with one-on-one instruction carried out by a reading specialist. She immediately shows signs of progress. She is learning sight words and other word-recognition strategies. She enjoys and succeeds with the books that she is assigned, written at her instructional level. It is clear that she has a long road ahead of her, as she strives to learn the material that her peers have already mastered over the past 2 years, but the end goal is clearly achievable. Mandy is a Catch-Up Reader, not a Stalled Reader, despite any suggestions to the contrary by the specialists who examined her.

What has happened here? Why was such a diagnostic mistake made, despite 2 years of primary-grade instruction and expensive and extensive assessments? The key lies in our changing concept of diagnosis and assessment.

At one time, the dominant form of assessment in education was what might be called the medical model of assessment. In this model, which we see in action in the story of Mandy, the educational expert functions like a traditional medical doctor. When we go to a medical doctor because of a physical problem, he/she usually orders a battery of tests to find more about the problem. The remedy prescribed is based on those tests. You get your pills or injection or surgery, and then you get better.

When applying this medical model to education, the assessments are front-end-loaded, just as they are in the doctor's office. Mandy was sent to the educational expert because of an educational problem: falling behind in reading in her first 2 years of primary-grade instruction. A battery of tests was administered. The diagnosis—classification as learning disabled or dyslexic—was given, and the remedy—recommendations for instructional intervention—was prescribed.

There are serious flaws in applying the traditional medical model to educational assessment and intervention. (In fact, our friends in the medical profession tell us that this model is not really an accurate description of a high-quality practice of medicine, for that matter.) Assessment in reading and literacy is not a one-shot deal. There is no reliable battery of tests that can identify which readers are learning disabled (Allington, 2002). Assessment is an ongoing, multidimensional process—that is, it makes use of multiple measures. Those measures that can be administered in the context of authentic instruction (as opposed to tests administered under artificial circumstances removed from classroom realities) are the most powerful.

In order to make this important point, we have deviated somewhat from the major question we want to address. That question is, How can we differentiate a Catch-Up Reader from a Stalled Reader? We answered this question briefly above: The key to this differentiation lies in what happens during interventional instruction—the Catch-Up Reader responds to instruction, but the Stalled Reader does not. Since the only way we can determine whether a student responds to instruction is to actually instruct him/her, the observations and assessments carried out in actual instructional sessions provide the key (Broikou & Lipa, 1994; Lipa, 1996).

An important caveat: Even with careful observation in instructional sessions, it can be difficult to determine whether a child is truly a Stalled Reader. In the story above, for example, Mandy had two fine teachers in first and second grade, yet she was making no progress. We would suggest three contextual changes before making a determination:

1. *Vary the instructional setting.* Mandy failed to respond in a whole class instructional setting. A one-to-one setting, however, was successful. Perhaps a small group arrangement, in which Mandy was working with peers who were functioning at her reading level, would have worked. After 2 years of failure at her elementary school, a change of school might be another positive step to take in changing the instructional setting, though that might be quite hard to arrange.

2 *Vary the teacher.* Mandy had difficulty in two teachers' classrooms, in first and second grade. Perhaps the teacher factor was not an issue in her case. On the other hand, it may well be that both teachers shared a common instructional philosophy or a similar personality and approach to handling the classroom. Some children respond when there is a dramatic change between teachers.

3 *Vary the curriculum.* The curriculum provided by Mandy's school was not working. It may have been that her teachers tried alternatives, but perhaps they did not. Some children respond better to one approach to teaching reading than another.

Does all this seem like a lot of involved and complicated effort just to meet the needs of a single student? Sad to say, but some schools may find it easier and less expensive to pay an expert to administer a few tests and then warehouse the children in remedial or special education classes. Do we have a commitment to children to "leave no child behind"? If so, providing ongoing assessment as we vary instructional settings, teachers, and curricula allows the large number of Catch-Up Readers in our classrooms the maximum opportunity to acquire literacy and prosper in their future years of schooling and in life.

And what of those few students in every school who are true Stalled Readers—who, by definition, do not respond to instruction? Do we have to give up on them?

Well, as you have probably guessed, since this section of our book is devoted to helping Stalled Readers, we do not simply give up. We need to examine more closely what it is we mean when we say that Stalled Readers do not respond to instruction. We are, in fact, using a bit of hyperbole, exaggerating the situation for effect. Stalled Readers *can* learn to read when they are exposed to appropriate instruction.

Appropriate instruction for a Stalled Reader, however, is a quantum jump beyond anything we typically see in schools. As Lyon et al. (2001) noted: "Years of disappointing outcomes in special and compensatory education have taught us that mandated instructional/intervention programs (usually watered-down to allow rapid dissemination and a quick fix) ultimately cost more than a reasoned, systematic approach" (p. 280). Some 50 to 100 hours of the best quality instruction will be needed to help a Stalled Reader gain a single grade level in reading achievement (Carver, 2000). Reading and literacy instruction must be:

1. *Individualized*—with one-on-one tutorial (or largely so), with a longstanding commitment to the child on the part of a knowledgeable teacher
2. *Targeted*—based on careful and ongoing individual assessment, in which instructional time is directed toward the student's personal interests and needs
3. *Intensive*—involving a level of organization and repetition that makes maximum use of the key principles of learning
4. *Extensive*—moving beyond the one-hour-a-day reading time into all aspects of the curriculum and all content areas
5. *Motivational*—designed to creatively support the student in his/her desire to learn over the long haul of the child's academic career
6. *Supportive*—with the goal of helping the child not only achieve success in reading and literacy, but also in his/her personal and social life and vocation

Some Stalled Readers will experience difficulties in reading and literacy for the rest of their lives. Poor reading performance too often foreshadows overall poor academic performance and failure in career and life. Yet stories abound of children with reading difficulties who grow up to lead fulfilling and vocationally successful lives, sometimes even achieving national prominence (Morris, 2002), by compensating for their reading deficiencies with their positive attributes. Gaining that ability to compensate is a key goal we hold as we help the Stalled Reader develop strategies for success in reading and literacy.

For many Stalled Readers, however, their reading difficulties will not last their lives. They will eventually achieve average or even above-average reading performance. Once appropriate instruction has laid down a foundation for overcoming the difficulties in literacy development, these students can return to regular classroom reading and English instruction and keep pace with their peers.

REASONS FOR DIFFICULTY

As with Catch-On and Catch-Up Readers, the underlying causes of difficulty with Stalled Readers can be varied and complex: instructional practices, reading materials, general language skills, motivation, home environment, and so forth. There is a good deal of evidence, as well, that constitutional issues may be involved in the difficulties experienced by some Stalled Readers. A major presupposition in the ideas presented in this textbook is the principle that reading and literacy struggles can arise from a variety of causes (Wolf, 1999), a perspective often called the multiple causation viewpoint. Others in the field, however, may take the unitary causation viewpoint: that the one major common denominator among severely remedial students is a constitutional one—a learning disability specific to reading—dyslexia.

The Unitary Causation Viewpoint: Dyslexia

In practice, diagnostic procedures used by physicians, psychologists, and educational experts to determine whether a child is dyslexic—that is, learning disabled in reading—are often not very extensive or sophisticated. Leckliter (1994), for example, surveyed definitions of dyslexia to conclude that many specialists diagnose the condition based on the singular administration of a reading achievement test: If the child is 2 or more years below grade level, he/she is labeled dyslexic. Even more commonly, some specialists add an IQ test, then diagnose dyslexia if the child's reading achievement test score is significantly lower than the IQ test score.

When educational professionals or medical doctors identify a child as dyslexic or reading disabled, they usually are working under the assumption that the origin of the reading difficulty is constitutional in nature. A perceptual or neurological problem is believed to interfere with the child's ability to acquire long-term sight-word knowledge and/or to apply decoding skills to analyze words. Since most children easily acquire the word-recognition ability through regular classroom instruction, those who demonstrate extreme problems are thought to have differences in the way their brains process information—differences that interfere with word recognition (Lipa, 1983). This neurological problem is thought to be specific in the sense that the deficit is limited to performance of reading and reading-related tasks and does not affect other aspects of daily life.

The popular media leave little room for doubt but that constitutional problems are the root cause of difficulty for these most seriously affected readers. Dyslexia is seen as a neurological problem that is inherent in the individual and that cannot be cured. It supposedly has genetic attributes that can affect entire families, and especially the males in those families (Grigorenko et al., 1997; Lyon, 1995). This viewpoint became dominant in the mid- to late-20th century, as state and national funding agencies began to develop policies that provided extra money for instruction of children with such disabilities. School districts, psychologists, and physicians were thus encouraged to identify large numbers of students as having these subtle neurological problems, since schools would receive more funding. It is often estimated that 20% of students have neurologically related learning disabilities.

In fact, the great majority of Stalled Readers do not suffer from genetic, neurological dysfunctions. Gerald Coles (2000) extensively reviewed research in this area and concluded that such theories of reading dysfunctions are "bad science" (p. 1). Labeling a child as having a genetic flaw basically amounts to "blaming the child"—a reprehensible educational policy.

Researchers have hypothesized the existence of dyslexia subtypes. Reading professionals and parents need to be aware of the dangers of overconfidence in hypotheses and theories, no matter how self-assured the researchers and theorists may sound, and no matter how widespread the media attention they receive. Medical and educational research is nowhere near reaching consensus on either the causes or treatment of dyslexia, or even upon which children have dyslexia and which do not.

One typology of dyslexia that has attracted widespread attention differentiates "deep dyslexia" from "surface dyslexia." Children with surface dyslexia have difficulty recognizing whole words but have adequate phonological development for decoding words. Deep dyslexia is characterized by difficulty decoding words. Children with deep dyslexia must rely on a sight-word vocabulary to recognize words because of their difficulty sounding out words letter-by-letter.

Phonological Core Variable Difference Model

Keith Stanovich (2000), one of the foremost reading researchers and theorists, has offered the phonological core variable difference (PCVD) model. This model explains the causes of reading difficulty in terms of gaps or deficits in phonological awareness (see Chapter 3)—in understanding the constituent sounds of language and manipulating those sounds. This model suggests that "all poor readers have a phonological deficit"(p. 117). Stanovich explains that "phonological awareness facilitates decoding skill, which in turn determines word recognition ability" (p. 61). Other reading and literacy-related problems may develop, but all poor readers' problems begin with poor phonological awareness. This includes Catch-On and Catch-Up Readers, which Stanovich calls by "garden-variety poor readers" (p. 117).

Stanovich distinguishes between two types of dyslexia: phonological and surface. Phonological dyslexia is associated with decoding difficulties. The affected child would be unable to perform well on a word list that tested ability to identify and pronounce target words. The second type, which he calls the surface dyslexia, a different phenomenon from the construct of the same name cited above) creates difficulties related to general world knowledge. This child's problem would be less a reading difficulty and more a deficit in prior knowledge that could be applied to text in order to understand concepts being presented. Stanovich defines reading comprehension as an interaction between this general world knowledge (which he refers to as listening comprehension) and word-recognition ability. Instruction for children with phonological dyslexia would target phonological awareness and word recognition (see Chapters 2, 3, 9, and 16). Instruction for children with surface dyslexia would focus on increasing the child's knowledge about the world—that is, on general academic learning (see Chapters 10, 11, 12, and 18).

In his discussion of the implications of the PCVD model for teachers, Stanovich takes a hard line in favor of direct teaching of word-recognition subskills and against top-down cognitive models of reading and social constructivist models with their whole language curricular implications (see Chapter 8). He insists that scientific research is one-sided in its support of teaching word recognition directly: "I myself would like to know why [educational experts] in reading teach an outmoded, 30-year-old notion of a "psycholinguistic guessing game" that has been superseded by modern research (indeed, that was superseded some time ago" (p. 387).

He further argues that top-down and social constructivist advocates, in their attempt to create a more inclusive and validating perspective for disempowered and at-risk segments of our society, are actually doing more harm than good: "The primary casualties of the Reading Wars are disadvantaged children who are not immersed in a literate environment and who are not taught the alphabetic code—precisely the children that progressive forces most want to aid" (p. 363).

As with other theories that attempt to explain poor reading, the PCVD model stands in need of extensive further research. The importance of phonological awareness to reading is generally agreed upon; Stanovich seems to be extreme in his focus upon it. Carver (2001), for example, has critiqued the model and disagreed with its central focus on phonology for all struggling readers. Wolf (1999) agrees that the reading difficulties of some poor readers seem to come from other factors.

Rauding Theory

Ronald Carver has spent his professional life developing, researching, and refining the cognitive model of reading he calls rauding theory (combines *reading* and *auding*—listening for meaning). He identifies two types of dyslexia, mild and severe (Carver, 2000). Both types of dyslexia involve a deficit in phonological awareness (i.e., dealing with the sounds within spoken words) and an inability to learn phonics rules (i.e., associations of letter–sound relationships within words). Carver calls this latter inability a deficit in pronunciation aptitude. Children with either subtype will *not* have a general oral language deficit that limits the number of spoken words they can acquire.

The deficit suffered by children with mild dyslexia is limited to phonological awareness and phonics. Instruction should focus on word-level learning, such as word recognition, including phonics and spelling.

Children with severe dyslexia also have a deficit in what Carver calls cognitive speed aptitude, an attribute that can be measured by tests that time subjects' performance on tasks requiring them to name colors or digits. This additional deficit decelerates the child's learning process and makes it even more important for the family, school, and community to devote additional time monitoring the child's word-level studies as well as time spent in reading and in other forms of content area learning.

Our concept of a Stalled Reader differs considerably from the varied definitions of learning disability or dyslexia. Those definitions tend to focus on problems specific to individual words, to decoding and related cognitive processes. The label of Stalled Reader more closely conveys the issue of instructional response. Stalled Readers may indeed have decoding difficulties. Many of them do—and they may have other difficulties related to reading. They are identified in our model as Stalled Readers to reflect what we see as the core distinguishing characteristic: their poor response to excellent instruction.

INSTRUCTING THE STALLED READER

Instructional Assessment

The front line of assessment and instruction of at-risk students is the teacher. The teacher knows the students best and has most access to them. The teacher sees her students in action, performing literacy tasks in the various content areas, on a daily basis. This breadth of exposure affords him/her unique insight into individual students' strengths and weaknesses. It is one thing for an educational expert to analyze a student's test performances over one or several days. It is far more insightful and honoring to the "wholeness" of language development to observe the student's performance in real reading and writing tasks over a period of months. This principle is true for teachers of all at-risk students—indeed, of all students, even those without reading and literacy difficulties. For those who work with Stalled Readers, however, the role of insightful teacher who understands the individual child's thinking and processing as a result of long-term observation and interaction—a function we call instructional assessment—is critical.

We have emphasized the importance of instructional assessment as teachers work with Catch-On and Catch-Up Readers, but it is in this section on Stalled Readers that we focus on instructional assessment as the central core of teaching. The complexity and demanding nature of the challenges involved in teaching reading to Stalled Readers make it clear that a high-effort approach to teaching is necessary. This approach requires going beyond planning and implementation of curricula involving word-identification strategies, basal reader lessons, or managing a literature-based course of study. The teacher who practices instructional assessment develops a habit of reflecting on classroom events, observing and analyzing, working as a reflective practitioner. Without the engagement of such an approach, teaching becomes a dull, monotonous routine of following directions in a teacher's manual or presenting lessons unmodified from previous years, no matter what the individual needs of students may be.

"Kid watching"—close observation of the individual learner in action—adds life and vitality to the teaching enterprise over the course of one's professional life. A commitment to the belief that each child is a unique creation, with unique literacy-related attributes, makes daily teaching encounters continually new and vibrant.

Another great advantage of instructional assessment is its *immediacy*. In formal and most other informal approaches to assessment, specific times are set aside for assessment purposes. Usually there is a time lag between the onset of a reading difficulty in a child and the specific time allocated for either formal or informal assessment of that difficulty. In a classroom where assessment is carried out as a matter of course during instruction, difficulties can be identified quickly and appropriate instructional measures immediately instituted by the teacher.

Considerable challenges face the teacher who wishes to play an active role in planning individualized instruction for Stalled Readers:

1. *Teachers must have a personal and professional understanding of literacy processes.* Teachers should be both readers and writers, personally familiar with the internal processes involved in meaningful communication as well as the social aspects of sharing with others.

Teachers should have a comprehensive knowledge of the elements that comprise literacy acquisition—word identification, comprehension, writing, vocabulary, study strategies, and social and affective patterns—as well as the interactive relationships of these variables in the context of learning. Imagine both an expert teacher and a novice teacher observing a child's activities and responses during instruction. The novice might be able to discern whether the activities succeed or fail to meet the instructional objective. The expert, however, would be able to see beyond those easily measurable—but possibly superficial—criteria to discern patterns and relationships in the child's responses, and to construct meaning from the more subtle components of the literacy activities with which the child is interacting with his/her world.

Note that this principle does not suggest that teachers must directly teach and drill each skill and process, one by one, to every Stalled Reader. It has been said that there is only one person in the classroom who needs to know every skill rule: the teacher. Stalled Readers will learn many linguistic insights about reading and literacy through well-planned experiences with reading real stories and writing meaningful works rather than through interminable drills. But the teacher must know those subskills—what they are, how to assess them, and a wide variety of ways they can be taught and learned. In addition, teachers should have a clear understanding of both normal benchmarks of literacy development and abnormal patterns of development.

2. *Teachers must have a comprehensive understanding of the causes and effects of reading difficulties.* Collecting information on the background of Stalled Readers should be guided by this understanding, which gives purpose to the teacher's search for insight into the children's literacy development. Teachers should realize that the purpose of understanding these causes and effects has little to do with explaining a child's possible problems and more to do with gaining guidance for instruction. Some correlates of reading failure, for example, are beyond a teacher's control—social and economic disadvantage, neurological difficulties, or poor health in the early childhood years. To be helpful to the child, a teacher's emphasis in assessment should be placed on those factors that are amenable to instruction.

Some years back, an influential segment of educational experts advocated telling classroom teachers as little as possible about their students. This reasoning was based on the correct realization that teachers should have positive goals for their students, *and* on flawed conclusions from research investigating teacher expectations and self-fulfilling prophecies. Ultimately, these policies served only to hamper effective instruction: the less teachers know about their students, the less they will be able to modify instruction to meet their needs. It is certainly important, however, for teachers to set high goals that are realistic and to have positive expectations for their students, no matter what their gender, social status, race, or ethnic group may be.

3. *Teachers must recognize that instructional assessment requires high effort.* A low-effort teacher assumes that student progress is an automatic result of instruction. He/she assumes that students have the strategies necessary to succeed and that his/her job is simply to present information and manage instruction and evaluation. The high-effort teacher who provides differentiated instruction to Stalled Readers, on the other hand, recognizes that unique students will have unique needs, and that the only way to meet these unique needs is to individualize instruction. There is no doubt that reflective individualization of instruction requires an effort "above and beyond the call of duty" for teachers (see Teacher's Literacy Beliefs and Attitude Scale in the Appendix for a list of self-analysis questions about instructional beliefs and choices).

Initial lessons with a Stalled Reader can be thought of as trial lessons, a particularly high-intensity time in which the teacher carefully assesses the effectiveness of the methods used. However, the instructional assessment process is dynamic and ongoing throughout the school year, as the teacher observes each student and makes instructional decisions about how to best address his/her strengths and needs. Evaluation and its necessary accompanying record keeping are important parts of each day's literacy activities. Instructional assessment hypotheses are continually evaluated and revised, as necessary, to meet the Stalled Reader's needs.

Informal Assessments

Teachers can observe and interpret students' reading behaviors as clues to their strengths and weaknesses. Physical differences pertaining to vision, hearing, and attending ability (e.g., the book too near or too far from the eyes; repeated requests for oral directions; difficulty remaining on task for short periods of time) may be indicators of difficulty. Obviously, these behaviors do not necessarily identify students as Stalled Readers. They are simply signs that something might be interfering with reading.

Administration of a word-list test can be a first step in assessing the reading growth of a Stalled Reader (see Grouped High-Frequency Words and High-Frequency Words in the appendix). These lists can be helpful in estimating the number of words a student has acquired, and in determining the strategies a student uses to identify the words.

Typically, students first acquire a few sight words that they can identify in isolation. For example, words such as *I*, *me*, and *the* are among those that are learned early. Fry (2001a) identified the 20 most commonly occurring words in children's text:

1.	the	11.	he
2.	of	12.	was
3.	and	13.	for
4.	a	14.	on
5.	to	15.	are
6.	in	16.	as
7.	is	17.	with
8.	you	18.	his
9.	that	19.	they
10.	it	20.	I

The teacher should note whether students make random guesses for words on the list, use initial and final consonant cues, or do not respond to certain words ("I don't know that word"). Remember that a student who is just starting to acquire a sight vocabulary often reads words in lists better than in a story context. Listening to students read predictable text, their own language experience stories, or familiar text gives the teacher information about their ability to recognize familiar words in context, as well as their fluency and recall of text.

Comprehension can be informally assessed by asking students to retell a story or the relevant content of a selection (see Story Retelling in the appendix). Questioning and summarizing activities are also effective comprehension assessments. These informal observations during teaching can provide the teacher with information about *what* to teach and *how* to teach in order to effectively guide students to higher reading levels.

Instructional Goals for the Stalled Reader

Stalled Readers need to develop basic reading skills. These readers often have such a limited sight-word vocabulary and such poor decoding skills that they cannot read material independently no matter how low the readability level. Others have developed ability to read at the primer or first-grade level, or even higher, but have stopped in their growth. One specific goal is to develop an automatic sight-word vocabulary. A second goal is to develop decoding skills for unlocking unknown words (see Chapter 16).

Because they do not have a well-developed sight-word vocabulary or decoding skills, many Stalled Readers depend heavily on context for word recognition (Stanovich, 1992). Therefore, learning to use the context as a major word-recognition strategy is an important goal (see Chapter 17). Teachers should model how to use context as a word-recognition strategy and provide ample time for students to practice.

Another goal for Stalled Readers is to help them enjoy reading for recreational purposes: "At all times, developing children's interest and pleasure in reading must be as much a focus as developing their reading skills" (Learning First Alliance, 1998, p. 60). Too often, children who have difficulty learning to read grow into adults who dislike reading. Helping these readers become involved in literature and author groups, including them in story discussions, and providing them with books on tape (see Chapter 14) or other listening experiences are important goals that spark genuine interest and provide interaction with their peers. With the rise of the Harry Potter phenomenon in the late 1990s, many struggling readers made use of audio books to keep themselves abreast of events at Hogwarts School and make it possible for them to participate in discussions with their peers.

Stalled Readers need to learn how to circumvent their word-recognition difficulties to understand text. They need to become aware of comprehension as the important goal when reading. Activities that engage readers in contemplation about the author's purpose, the meaning of certain phrases, how stories unfold, and the message and/or moral of stories should be stressed (see Chapter 18).

It is also important for Stalled Readers to develop and maintain superior listening skills (Tunmer & Hoover, 1992) along with a well-developed vocabulary. They should know multiple meanings of words and continually monitor what they hear in terms of meaning, as they will often rely on these skills to ascertain the content information of schooling.

Principles of Instruction

Stalled Readers require direct instruction over time (Waddington, 1996), a large portion of which must occur in a tutorial setting. They need to be exposed repeatedly to the high-frequency words that are at the cutting edge of their learning, until these words become part of an automatic sight-word vocabulary (Moats, 1998). The issue of repetition and drill is a controversial one within the field of reading. No one would advocate the dull, rote drill-and-practice method, with no attempt at transferring the drilled material to real reading and writing, that is too often seen in classrooms. But intense, repeated exposure to the limited number of new words being targeted for learning *is* crucial for Stalled Readers. Repeated involvement in manipulating letters and sounds to develop decoding ability *is* crucial. Drill and practice provides an easy-to-manage and time-efficient means of providing those exposures. A developmentally on-target reader may learn a new sight word in three to five exposures. A Catch-Up Reader may need 15 to 25 exposures. The 75 to 100 exposures required by a Stalled Reader presents a supreme teaching challenge on three fronts: organization of material, sequencing of instruction, and maintaining student motivation.

Some readers stall in their achievement due to lack of underlying skill and strategy development. For example, students who cannot identify letter–sound correspondences or who demonstrate poor auditory discrimination ability might benefit from instruction in rudimentary auditory discrimination and phonemic awareness, such as identifying sounds and words that are the same or different, rhyming, and auditory segmentation. Similarly, those who have difficulty naming alphabet letters or who confuse letterforms should receive instruction in basic visual discrimination of those letters. Some students will demonstrate weaknesses in both visual and auditory processing areas. Try to find the achievement level at which the Stalled Reader breaks down. This is the point at which to begin teaching (Greene, 1998). Use a checklist of reading behaviors or benchmarks as a guide to identifying the pattern of acquisition (see the Observation Checklist of Response to Reading and Writing in the appendix).

It is important to work with Stalled Readers on a daily basis in frequent, short, meaningful instructional experiences. Teaching too many strategies or providing too many examples and applications during a single session will confuse students. Fifteen minutes per session of word-identification activities is often suggested as a maximum (Carver, 2000). If weekends or school holidays interfere with retention, parents can be given material to teach during those intervals.

A creative, rich language arts curriculum is a critical component of the Stalled Reader's instruction. Too often in schools struggling readers are intensively drilled in pullout instruction, then returned to the classroom in which the more creative, interesting language activities are utterly beyond their grasp. It is essential to provide Stalled Readers with successful reading experiences and help them maintain positive attitudes about their potential to become good readers (Pierson, 1999).

Stalled Readers need the commitment of a patient, forward-looking professional teacher over the long haul. Too often they are introduced to one reading program after another—or perhaps two different reading programs at the same time by the pullout teacher and the classroom teacher. When the program fails, the blame is simplistically placed on the program ("it didn't work") or the students ("they didn't learn"). Teachers should view the failure of a methodology to achieve its goals as an opportunity to learn more about the student. Why did it fail? What were its weaknesses? Are there other methods available that offer a better chance for success because they capitalize on students' strengths?

A method that has been ineffective in the past may have required reading achievement and knowledge of reading strategies that were inappropriate at the time. That is, the student may not have had the prerequisite abilities to learn the material that was being taught. Successful lessons require a developmental match with the needs of the individual Stalled Reader. Making this match requires knowing students' needs and the level at which they will learn successfully from instruction—the zone of proximal development (Vygotsky, 1934/1978). Provide ample opportunity for instruction, guided learning, and practice so that the student understands the task or strategy being taught (Beck, McKeown, Hamilton, & Kucan, 1998).

Stalled Readers have difficulty learning to use strategies taught to them. First, they have to learn to recognize the conditions under which each strategy will be effective. Thus they have to learn to be decision makers and to maintain their metacognitive alertness while they are reading. Instructional passages should be short so as not to overtax a student who is tense and who will become tired very quickly because of the mental energy needed to read. Teachers should go out of their way to make sure that they capitalize on students' interests. They must expect to reteach, as necessary, to help students gain better understanding of new strategies during subsequent lessons.

Proceed slowly, reteach whenever necessary, make sure each lesson provides the student with a sense of making progress in reading, and devote the time necessary to help the child make his/her way back into regular classroom instruction. Parents and school administrators must be led to recognize that there are no quick fixes, no golden bullets that will swiftly and inexpensively solve the Stalled Reader's problem. The stakes are high and well worth our best efforts.

Materials

Stalled Readers require materials that are written at easy levels. Unfortunately, such materials are often designed for children of younger ages, with pictures and content that older readers experience as demeaning. Some children just shrug their shoulders and keep on working with such materials. The older Stalled Readers may be so discouraged with their repeated failures in learning to read that they refuse to try materials that appear babyish or involve topics of little interest to them. Teachers are often at a loss as to how to respond to this reluctance or all-out refusal.

The difficulty level of published material can be adjusted in several ways for Stalled Readers. The teacher can read part of the selection to familiarize students with the content and style of language. Difficult words can be presented and their meanings discussed prior to reading. Several readings of the same material can provide practice in word recognition and comprehension. For example, students might read a selection the first time to locate specific information, then to prove a point, and then to identify a sequence of events or to identify character traits. After participating with the teacher in reading the printed article two or three times, the Stalled Reader is often able to read the whole article independently.

Six options for obtaining appropriate materials can be explored:

1. *Rewriting existing materials.* Whole-scale rewriting of text materials is prohibitively time consuming for any one individual teacher, but over the course of several years a group of teachers using the same material can share their rewrites with one another. Older proficient students can be enlisted to help; they should do their rewrites using word-processing software, so that teachers can later proofread and edit the materials before giving them out to their Stalled Readers.

2. *Actively searching out published materials.* The commercial market for Stalled Readers is not anywhere near as large as the general developmental reading market. Publishers tend to put their advertising dollars into pushing the materials that are geared toward the largest possible markets. Teachers need to take an active role in perusing publisher catalogs, skimming advertisements for materials in professional publications, and attending professional conferences where publishers display their wares.

3. *Materials designed for adult basic education (ABE).* A few publishers focus on the ABE market (see Chapter 20), providing educational materials and books written at very low readability levels but that have topics and pictures designed for older students.

4. *Predictable readings.* Many big books and other predictable books are designed for emergent readers of a young age. Song lyrics are an excellent alternative source of material

for Stalled Readers, because they contain the repetition and rhyming that function as clues to aid the struggling reader, especially useful in repeated reading methods.

5. *Poetry*. Poetry inherently contains the repetition and rhyming that contribute to predictability in text. As with song lyrics, books of poems can serve as important source material for Stalled Readers. The work of Shel Silverstein (1994) is filled with poems that are written with the insight and humor appreciated by Stalled Readers.

6. *Language experience approach and student writings (see Chapter 4)*. Teachers can make use of Stalled Readers' own language to encourage reading by using language experience stories, journal entries, poems and creative stories. Stalled Readers can usually "read" their own stories (as long as they do not get too long), but they will need other students or the teacher to act as scribe. Computers are useful for typing and publishing student work.

Commercial Reading Programs

Programs that are designed for Stalled Readers usually focus on the word identification component of reading, stressing sound–symbol relationships through multiple modalities (visual, auditory, kinesthetic, and tactile). They are usually phonics-based programs that require large amounts of drill and practice on letter–sound correspondence, sound blending techniques, phonic-based rules, and spelling.

Instructional methods in such programs are often surprisingly and outstandingly dull—little more than showing flash cards to children as they copy them into their workbooks. Innovation and creativity are left up to the teachers using the program. In some cases the programs defend their dull routines by suggesting that such tedium allows students to focus on the key elements of learning, and that creativity can result in off-task behaviors. Needless to say, we do not agree with this view.

The underlying purpose of the programs is to provide direct teaching experiences of the match between phonemes and graphemes for those students who have not developed, or are not able to effectively coordinate, their auditory processing skills with visual symbols, the alphabetic letters. One-to-one tutoring is the norm.

Published programs offer several advantages. They provide structure for the teacher—explicit directions for teaching, the sequence of skill instruction, tests to assess progress, phonic rules, and integration of spelling and writing with reading. Instruction manuals often tell the teacher exactly what to say at certain points in the lesson. The intensive nature of instruction forces novice teachers, who usually have trouble understanding the serious nature of the reading difficulties faced by their students, to slow down the pace of instruction, monitor learning, and reteach as often as necessary before moving on to further objectives.

The published programs have serious disadvantages as well. Unless the teacher exerts some creative bent, student attention span is severely limited. Some teachers feel comfortable with a highly structured program, but others prefer a more informal approach to reading instruction in which materials and strategies are changed to meet the ongoing needs of individual students. Published programs often use the same set methods for extended periods of instruction, perhaps years. The teacher reads exactly the same script, no matter whether the student is learning one-syllable words or four-syllable words. Students may well learn the strategies involved in the method long before all the instructional materials are covered. Once the strategies are learned—even if a lesson or two has been skipped—teachers should consider moving on to an alternative.

Published programs usually do not include provision for the rapid growth spurts some students make—or the persistent lack of growth that is not uncommon among Stalled Readers. When applying a 1- or 2-year program, teachers may find it difficult to recognize that a student has progressed to such an extent that the program is actually holding back him/her. On the other hand, if a program is not facilitating achievement, there may be a temptation to continue using it in hope that *something* will happen eventually. The key to making the decision as to whether to continue or discontinue can be found via the instructional assessment practiced by a reflective teacher.

SUMMARY

The major distinguishing characteristic of Stalled Readers is their failure to respond positively to high-quality instruction. They have mastered the basic functions of print; for example, they understand the function of a word or a sentence, and they recognize that print conveys a message. At some point, the Stalled Reader's parents or teacher recognized that the child was falling behind his or her peers in terms of ability to read, and determined that the child appeared to be a Catch-Up Reader. Teachers carried out observation and assessment and employed a variety of instructional strategies, which are described earlier as appropriate for Catch-Up Readers. None of these strategies resulted in signs of improvement.

A test of the difference between a Catch-Up Reader and a Stalled Reader contains three criteria. The student is a Stalled Reader if he/she demonstrates no improvement despite:

1. Use of a variety of instructional settings.
2. Attempts at intervention by multiple teachers.
3. Application of several different instructional curricula.

In this chapter, we described the extensive intervention efforts that are imperative if the Stalled Reader is to begin to make progress. These efforts require tutorial instruction that is specifically designed for the individual student and is intensive, extensive, motivational, and supportive in terms of academics, socialization, and vocation.

Chapters 16 through 18 examine key components of instruction for Stalled Readers. Chapter 16 focuses on word recognition, which is characteristically a foundational difficulty for Stalled Readers. Chapter 17 offers approaches that, in a sense, attempt to circumvent Stalled Readers' difficulties with word-level reading by emphasizing context and fluency. Chapter 18 presents methods for helping Stalled Readers who have been able to experience some degree of success with word recognition but who are experiencing serious comprehension difficulties.

CHAPTER 16

Helping Stalled Readers with Word Recognition

Not all Stalled Readers have difficulty with word recognition. Some exhibit problems related to comprehension. Others have successfully learned to mask decoding and sight-word difficulties by use of alternative means of word recognition (see Chapter 17). In fact, providing Stalled Readers with those alternative means can be a critical factor in facilitating their experience of success in school. But there is little doubt that the dominant problem experienced by Stalled Readers involves difficulties in word recognition. Sight-word and decoding development methods for Stalled Reader are discussed in this chapter, and alternative, context-based strategies are discussed in Chapter 17.

OVERCOMING SERIOUS SIGHT-WORD DIFFICULTIES

All emergent readers must first develop a sight-word base in order to efficiently process the information on a page. Fluent reading depends heavily on automatic word recognition. Some Stalled Readers have great difficulty recalling sight words; nonetheless, they need to develop a base of words on which they can rely. The approaches described below focus on a small number of sight words per lesson and provide multisensory experiences in which words are heard, seen, and written. Multisensory approaches to word recognition employ visual, auditory, tactile, and kinesthetic tasks. Engaging several sensory modalities sensitizes students so that they are able to recall words instantly—which means that the words have been incorporated into retrievable memory. Multisensory approaches are time consuming and demand a high degree teacher guidance with individual students, but such a commitment of resources is necessary if success is to be experienced by Stalled Readers.

When teaching sight words to Stalled Readers, it is very easy to lose track of the difficulties these students face. In an effort to achieve desired objectives, teachers may not realize that the Stalled Readers are not receiving the exposures necessary to ensure that new words are added to long-term memory. A monitoring device to aid in record keeping, such as the Sight-Word Monitoring Form in the appendix, can be helpful in tracking which words have been learned and which words need further study.

Sentence Approach

A direct instruction method, the sentence approach, is often successful with Stalled Readers. As noted, some of these readers need specific instruction with words that consistently elude retrieval, whether in or out of context. Teachers select the words with which the students are having the most difficulty (see step 6 below), and they remind students that one of the instructional goals is to recognize these words whenever they are encountered in print. The method below is described for small group instruction, but it can be easily adapted for tutorials.

1. *Introduce the word(s)*. Select one, two, or three target words for a lesson, depending on the student's ability to learn sight words. Print the words on the board or on chart paper. Discuss the word meanings and each word's structure in terms of its orthographic (spelling—"looks like") and phonological (pronunciation—"sounds like") features.

2. *Oral reading to print*. If working in a small group, ask each student to say a sentence using the word. Write the sentences on separate sheets of paper so that each student's sentence is recorded. Students then read aloud their sentences and point to each word while reading. Continue this procedure for each word that is presented.

3. *Test*. Present the words on file cards. Ask each student to read the words. Change the order of presentation for each student to reduce memorization effect.

4. *Practice*. Ask the students to trace each word and say it as it is traced. They can use tracing paper placed over the file cards. Then the file cards and traced versions of the word should be removed and each word should be written from memory. Compare each to the teacher's example. Practice continues until the words have been written correctly.

5. *Practice*. The teacher writes each word on a separate file card, with the student's sentence written on the reverse side of the card. These should be stored in a word bank (see Chapter 3) for daily review.

6. *Application*. Select a story from a basal reader or trade book in which the targeted words appear or from which the words were selected prior to reading. If students' reading skills are very limited, the teacher can write a short story in which the words are used. As the story is read, students should be expected to recognize the target words in context.

McNinch's Direct Instruction Method

McNinch (1981) proposed a direct instruction method consisting of six steps, for teaching sight words to students who have demonstrated difficulty in this aspect of reading. The small group lesson described below can be adapted for one-to-one tutorial instruction.

1. *Demonstration*. Write the word on the board or display a file card with the word, and say the word aloud to establish it as an aural unit..

2. *Demonstration*. Write the word in a different sentence for each child in the group. Either the teacher or the children can provide the sentences. Read the sentences aloud to the children and highlight the target word by underlining it.

3. *Interaction*. Choose a word from one of the sentences that is not the target word. Ask questions about the visual characteristics of this word:

> "Is it the same as the new word we are learning?"
> "What is the first letter? . . . the last letter? . . . the middle letter?"

4. *Clarification*. Have the children read the target word, the word chosen from the sentences, and the sentences themselves.

5. *Practice*. Have the children read the words in meaningful contexts for a purpose other than simply recognizing the words. They may read from a book, a printed story, or a language experience story.

6. *Practice for mastery*. Use games, puzzles, and worksheets to continue to draw students' attention to the distinctive features of the word.

Cunningham's Function Words

Many Stalled Readers have difficulty learning to read basic sight words, the function words commonly encountered in print (such as helping verbs, prepositions, and conjunctions) (see Chapter 9). Although miscueing these words does not always change the author's meaning and may not constitute a serious miscue, repeated confusion of words such as *were*, *with*, and *what* leads to frustration and inevitable comprehension difficulties. Cunningham (2000) proposed a method of direct instruction for teaching these function words:

1. *Print/meaning*.
   a. Introduce the word (or words—this lesson can be adapted to focus on more than one word, depending on students' abilities) in a meaningful context. Print the word on a card large enough for all the students to see. Have the students copy the word neatly on file cards of their own. Tell a simple story in which the word is used many times. (We usually choose a short story that is humorous or interesting about something that we have done in the past couple of days. It might be about a picnic, or a TV show we have seen, or something about one of our pets.) The story should be simple enough to tell so that the target word can be incorporated as often as possible.

      Students hold up their index cards each time the word is said in the story.
   b. Each student makes up a story using the targeted word. Each time the word is used, the other students hold up their cards.

2. *Visual discrimination*. Conduct visual discrimination exercises. Students make another file card with the word printed on it, then they cut the word into individual letters. Instruct students to mix up the letters, then to reconstruct word. Do this one or two times and monitor their progress. If students incorrectly arrange the letters, help them place the letters in correct order.

   Remind the students to look closely at the word. Place the letters and the first file card, the one with the word printed on it, in an envelope or clear plastic sandwich bag for later use. We usually have the students each keep a set of 10 sandwich bags for this purpose. As they master old words, their file cards are replaced by those with new words.

3. *Visual memory.*

   a. Write the word on the board or on chart paper. Tell students to "take a picture of the word," then to close their eyes and "see" the word, then open their eyes, look at the word, and compare to what they saw with their eyes closed.

   b. Give each student a piece of scrap paper. Do the "take a picture" procedure again. Erase the target word from the board or fold over the chart paper. Have the students write the word from memory, then write the word on the board. The students should compare your version with their written word. Do this three times.

4. *Context.*

   a. Write several sentences that contain the target word on the board or chart paper. The target word may be included, or the space where it should be can be left blank, depending on the students' progress. Each time a target word is the next word in the sentence to be read, one student comes to the board and writes the word.

   b. Give each student stories or books in which the target word is used frequently. Ask students to underline the target word each time they find it in the story.

Fernald Technique

This technique, developed by Grace Fernald (1943), was one of the first to employ a multisensory approach to word learning. Fernald described four stages of reading acquisition and emphasized the goal of increasing students' independence as they experience success in mastering word-recognition strategies. Most teachers associate the Fernald technique with only its first stage, in which students learn sight words through an integrated multisensory approach to word recognition.

Stage 1

Student: Selects a word to learn.

Teacher: Uses crayon or marker to write the word on a strip of paper. (Fernald suggested use of cursive writing because of the physical connection between letters; however, most teachers today use printing.) Says the word as it is being written but does not sound it out phoneme by phoneme. (In practice, teachers often write and say the word syllable by syllable but do not stop between syllables. Fernald stressed the importance of keeping the wholeness of the word intact.)

Student: Traces the word with one finger, pronouncing the word as it is being traced. Tracing continues until the student can write the word from memory. Writes the word from memory, then compares it to the teacher's version. If the word is incorrect, the student goes back to tracing and saying the word until it is written correctly.

After several words are taught by this method, story-writing activities are initiated to provide further practice with the new words and words learned in previous sessions. Language experience approach activities (see Chapter 4) work well.

As mentioned above, most reading teachers think of the procedure described in stage 1 as the Fernald technique. It is helpful to realize, however, that our objective is to move the student beyond this time-consuming procedure, toward increasing independence, as was Fernald's goal in developing the additional stages.

Stage 2

After some months of practice in tracing words, the procedure described in stage 1 can be eliminated. The student will be able to look at a new word that is introduced by the teacher and written on a strip of paper with crayon or marker, commit its features to memory, and write it from memory.

Stage 3

The student has learned to recognize a new word by seeing its printed form displayed. The writing step is eliminated and the student is able to recall the word from visual presentation alone.

Stage 4

This is the stage at which the student focuses on word analysis and learns to identify new words by examining familiar parts (phonograms, spelling patterns, syllables).

VAK Approach (Visual–Auditory–Kinesthetic)

The VAK approach, described below, is a simpler version of the Fernald technique. Although there are numerous variations and modifications of this procedure, the basic steps follow:

1. Select words (or a single word, depending on the students' abilities) for teaching.
2. Say a sentence for each word, introducing the word in context and discussing its meaning.
3. Present the word in a sentence that is written on the board or chart paper. Emphasize the word to be learned by underlining it or writing it in a different color.
4. Hold up large file cards with the words printed on them. Have students pronounce the words.
5. Hold up one of the file cards and tell the students to study the word visually. Next, with eyes closed, the students try to "see" the picture of the printed word (visual imagery).
6. Remove the word and have students print it from memory.
7. Show the word card and ask the students to compare the printed word with the one on the card.
8. Repeat Steps 5, 6, and 7 for each new word.
9. Repeat this lesson until the words can be written from memory.

OVERCOMING SERIOUS DECODING DIFFICULTIES

Stalled Readers often improve their word recognition by learning to use specific decoding strategies. A wide variety of intensive approaches to decoding instruction has been published; most of these approaches offer only minor variations on long-familiar themes of instruction. Since these approaches require a high degree of student attention, and since they are usually tedious, instruction is often limited to 15 minutes per session by necessity.

Advocates of using isolated letter and word drills for decoding instruction contend that isolation of the letters, sounds, and words helps the learner focus; too much context makes decoding too difficult at initial stages of instruction. In addition, some readers can mask their decoding difficulties by use of sentence and story context.

Decoding curriculum is only part of the integrated language arts curricula necessary to provide success for Stalled Readers. *All* students should spend most of their literacy instructional time engaging in authentic reading and writing.

This section describes two approaches that emphasize phonograms and one that emphasizes individual phonemes. A fourth approach, which can be used in combination with any of the preceding three, focuses on transferring decoding knowledge to actual reading tasks.

Glass-Analysis and Phonogram Approaches

Intensive phonogram approaches (see Chapter 9 for an introduction to phonogram approaches) are often successful with Stalled Readers, because these approaches do not require sound blending of individual phonemes. Usually tasks that require students to focus on individual phonemes are more difficult than tasks that allow manipulation of larger units (Ehri & Nunes, 2002; Liberman, Shankweiler, Fischer, & Carter, 1974). Finding a single phoneme in a word can be just as difficult as finding an entire phonogram.

Phonogram approaches (1) teach students to manipulate these larger units and (2) present decoding as an analogy strategy. The student, through repeated exposure, recognizes consistent letter patterns in words and learns the sound associated with these letters. Using a direct instruction analogy to word-recognition processes, students learn to look for and recognize familiar patterns in other words and then use these patterns as the principal means of accessing a word.

Glass-Analysis for Decoding Only (Glass & Glass, 1994) is a phonogram program that has been used for many years with various types of students, including developmental and English-as-a-second-language learners. Its structure and intensive nature make it particularly appropriate for Stalled Readers. Gerald Glass, the program's developer at Adelphi University, distinguished between decoding and reading, arguing that both are necessary in a beginning reading curriculum. He defined decoding as the act of correctly determining the accepted sounds associated with a particular word, and reading as the experience of finding meaning in print. Glass targets decoding aspects of instruction.

The central materials in Glass's program consist of a teacher's manual and several decoding kits of word cards (Starters, Mediums, Harders, and Completers). Drill books provide additional reinforcement and the opportunity to use the target words in context. Words with particular phonograms (also called word families or rimes; see High-Frequency Words in the appendix for samples of words with common phonograms) are included in each kit. These words are arranged by levels of difficulty (simple, average, difficult) within the kit. A phonogram cluster such as *am* might include simple words such as *dam* and *Sam*, average words such as *gram* and *sham*, and more difficult words such as *trample* and *stampede*. The student is taught to use each phonogram pattern to conduct further word analysis with new words. The Glass-Analysis program teaches 119 clusters.

Glass (1973) also developed a standard dialogue for teachers to use when presenting the words to students. He suggested that this dialogue provided both auditory and visual perceptual conditioning. The teacher conducts a discussion with the students about the letters that comprise the sound(s) within a sample word containing the target phonogram. Then the teacher says the word and asks the students to repeat it. (See Chapter 20 for a sample Teacher Dialogue for Phonogram Instruction.)

In the next step the teacher says the letter names from the targeted phonogram and asks students to reply with the sound(s) associated with the letter names.

Lessons should be carried out twice a day, 4 to 5 days a week. Short, distributed lessons provide more reinforcement than fewer, longer lessons. For Stalled Readers, a typical pattern might involve the introduction of a single phonogram family in two lessons, a third lesson that concentrates on another objective, such as review of past lessons or introduction of another phonogram, then a fourth lesson that refocuses on the first phonogram family.

An important aspect of Glass's program (and other phonogram approaches; see the following section) is that it requires less attention to sound blending techniques, analysis of words into syllables, or learning of phonic rules than do the synthetic phonics methods (see Chapter 9, and the Orton approaches described below). The strategic modeling in Glass's program is based on presenting the whole word as the unit of meaning. This along with focused attention to the letter cluster and other letter–sound associations direct the Stalled Reader toward purposeful word identification.

Another key aspect of the program is its emphasis on the *process* of word identification, as opposed to simply learning lists of phonograms and words. Teachers need to emphasize the visual and auditory components involved in the process of recognizing phonograms within words. The real breakthrough in word recognition occurs when students are able to apply this word-identification process *while* reading. Glass and Glass (1994) warned that the key words used to introduce the new phonogram are not

> considered complete or successful if the youngster can or is asked to merely identify the word at sight. A Glass-Analysis lesson must include those activities designed to help toward forming correct auditory and visual conditioned responses to the appropriate structures within the word. (pp. 5–6)

One concern about Glass's program is its transferability to authentic reading contexts. As is the case with all methods that focus on decoding, the teacher must play a strong role in providing additional practice with the Glass-Analysis target words in meaningful contexts. In addition, teachers can replace flash card drill work with more imaginative activities (see Sidebar 16.1).

Learning Word Identification through Analogy

All methods of teaching word identification use analogical thinking, to some extent. In word identification approaches that emphasize analogical thinking, students use words they already know as the key clues in determining the pronunciation of new words. For example:

> "If *w* plus *agon* is *wagon*, then *dr* plus *agon* must be *dragon*."

Readers use knowledge of a familiar word, such as *night*, to decode new words, such as *fight* and *fright*. Familiar letter patterns help readers make an analogy between the letters

Sidebar 16.1. Activities for Learning Phonograms

1. *Compose nonsense stories.* Use as many of the day's phonogram words as possible, plus phonograms families from previous days, to create nonsense stories. Using a computer and word-processing software often works best with this procedure. Write the first draft of the story, using as many of the day's phonogram pattern words as possible. Then give the students another phonogram family and have them add words and sentences to the story.

2. *Word cluster memory game.* Place cards representing several different phonogram patterns face down in columns and rows. The child tries to pick pairs that share the same cluster.

3. *Word cluster fishing game.* The deck should consist of several groups of four cards. Each group represents a different phonogram family. Each player is dealt five to seven cards. The players request word cards with a cluster: "Do you have a word with the /and/ word family?" If the player asked does not have such a card, the requesting player must take a card from the pool. When players assemble a complete group of four cards, the group is placed on the table. The first player to use up all cards wins.

4. *Killer card word cluster game.* Played like Old Maid, a deck is assembled of card pairs sharing the same phonograms. One odd card, the killer card, is also inserted. Players take single cards from one another in turn, placing any matched pairs on the table. At the end, the player left with the killer card loses.

5. *Write sentences using the phonograms.* Ask questions about the sentences. Students must write the answers in complete sentences.

The band had to stand with candles.

Who had to stand with candles? _____

With what did the band stand? _____

Each cow in the land had a brand.

What did each cow have? _____

Who had brands? _____

6. *Books with phonogram patterns.* Several major publishers sell sets of small books, each of which is composed largely of words using the same phonogram pattern.

and sounds in one word and those in the new word. The structure and regularity of this approach may provide Stalled Readers with a strategy for word identification that they can effectively use a large percentage of the time.

In Cunningham's Using Words You Know (2000; Cunningham & Cunningham, 2002) version of word identification through analogy, the teacher starts with four sight words that children can recognize. For example,

hit   Sam   rain   him

Words are listed on the board in four columns, and students copy the same word columns on their paper. Using Words You Know is based on rhyming, and students are reminded that words that rhyme often have the same spelling pattern. The spelling pattern (phonogram or word family) in one-syllable words starts with the vowel and goes to the end of the word. At this point, the teacher and students underline the phonograms in the target words:

hi<u>t</u>   S<u>am</u>   r<u>ain</u>   h<u>im</u>

The teacher provides sample rhyming words written on large index cards, and students copy them under the appropriate target word. A student at the board models the list-making activity. Teacher and students say the target words and the new words aloud to reinforce the rhyming connection.

In the next step, the teacher explains, "When we think of rhyming words, we are learning how to spell." He/she says words that rhyme with the targets, and the students discuss which target word is being rhymed and which phonogram to use in spelling the new word. The student at the board models writing the new words in the appropriate columns, and the rest of the class continues to copy the material on their own paper. Note that this approach provides extensive review of students' knowledge of initial letters (often called *onsets*).

hit	Sam	rain	him
bit	ham	pain	Tim
sit	Pam	main	dim
fit	ram	train	rim

Part of the usefulness of word identification through analogy lies in its use in longer or less familiar words. The next part of the lesson involves adding some of those longer words to the list and discussing with students how to use known words as keys to pronunciation of those longer words. This part of the lesson provides for differentiation of instruction, allowing more advanced students to apply the new strategies at their own levels.

fitness	Amtrack	remain	trim
pitbull	example	complain	limited

Words chosen for the lesson should emphasize the more commonly found words in printed text. One easy method of locating words with specific spelling patterns is to use the word-processing "find" function. Bring up any word processing document you might have available and carry out a "find" procedure for *am*. You will soon have a wide array of words at varying levels of difficulty. Cunningham and Cunningham (2002) recommended that teachers provide all the words for the lesson, because students will be confused by rhyming words that do not fit the target spelling patterns. Other teachers encourage students to join in the construction of the lists by offering their own ideas for rhyming words. The words that do not fit the spelling pattern are put in a separate list, and the teacher reminds students that there are usually several different ways to spell the same phonogram.

Common phonograms can be chosen from the lists of high-frequency words in the appendix. When working with Stalled Readers, it is not so important which phonograms you choose as it is to provide sufficient reinforcement exercises so that the phonograms are learned. In addition, ongoing review of the phonograms introduced over the next few weeks is essential.

Most methods that emphasize word identification through analogical thinking are designed for the average reader and fall far short of the rigorous instructional sequence needed for Stalled Readers. The Benchmark School is a private school for struggling readers near Philadelphia that has gained a high degree of visibility for its focus on word identification integrated with a rich language arts curriculum. Its word-identification curriculum uses analogy as its centerpiece. Teachers add additional repetition to the word-identification procedure, allowing students to focus more time and energy on the target words and phonograms in order to ensure learning.

For example, in order to improve students' ability to spot the phonograms in the context of reading, the teacher can provide sentences that use the target words but leave their spaces blank to encourage students to use context.

Sally gave the birthday present to _____ friend.

The batter _____ the ball toward right field.

Students can make up their own sentences to write on the board and engage the class or small group. Then the students can make up a group story using as many of the target words as possible, writing the story on the board and copying it on their papers.

As the list of target words with phonograms begins to get larger, making use of a word wall will allow students to regularly review and reference the words during reading (see Chapter 3 for word-wall activities). The target words (sometimes called key or clue words) serve as mnemonic devices for the students. During oral reading the teacher stops the class for a moment to discuss an unrecognized word in terms of the target words on the word wall:

"The story reads, 'Juana had made a _____, and she was going to keep her word.' Let's look at the unfamiliar word. It has *om*, as in our target word *Tom*. A *c* with *om* is *com*.

"It has *it*, as in our target word *hit*. With an *m*, that makes *mit*: *commit*.

"It has *ent*, as in our target word *tent*. With an *m*, that makes *ment*: *commitment*. Can anyone tell me what the word *commitment* means?"

Encouraging students to engage in the step-by-step word identification procedure is crucial. Ask the students to do their word-identification problem solving aloud during class reading. With time and review, each Stalled Reader should be able to explain his/her reasoning in a similar fashion and be able to use it independently when reading.

Orton Approaches

The Gillingham–Stillman Method and the Wilson Reading System are two of several methods known informally as Orton approaches. Samuel Orton (1937) suggested that in children who have specific learning disabilities, the normative pattern in which hemispheric dominance in the brain is established may have failed to occur. Orton hypothesized that printed word forms are stored in the dominant hemisphere of the brain, and that mirror images of the words are stored in the nondominant hemisphere. These mirror images may be expressed as reversals during reading (for example, *saw/was*).

This hypothesis has never been validated by research; in fact, it has long been known that disabled readers do not have more reversals than normal readers of the same ability. In spite of this research, parents and some teachers still view reversals as a symptom of dyslexia due to the media attention given Orton and his theories.

Orton approaches share the following characteristics:

1. *Instruction focuses on letter-by-letter decoding.* Letter sounds are then blended together (i.e., synthesized) to form words. This approach is more generally known as synthetic phonics (see Chapter 9).

2. *Instructional methods are multisensory.* That is, students are involved not only in seeing and hearing the letter sounds and words but in writing them as well. The now-commonplace addition of the tactile/kinesthetic modality to reading instruction was due, in large measure, to Orton's emphasis on multiple modalities.

3. *Instruction is structured and intensive.* A set curriculum is followed, in which certain phonics elements are introduced before others, and there is a large amount of repetition in the form of drills. The various commercial programs use somewhat different sequences of elements. Students overlearn material, demonstrate their mastery, and only then move on to different objectives.

The Gillingham–Stillman Method

The Gillingham–Stillman Method was developed by Anna Gillingham and Bessie Stillman, two followers of Orton (Gillingham & Stillman, 1973), to help students block out the nondominant hemisphere's mirror image through intensive multisensory training. The program emphasizes learning letter sounds and applying the sounds to letters within words through sound blending (synthetic phonics—see Chapter 9 for an overview of synthetic phonics methods). Although the dominance/mirroring aspect of Orton's theory has not been validated, the approaches themselves can be used effectively with Stalled Readers.

Several multisensory associations are systematically taught as part of this program:

Visual–auditory (V-A). Translation of visual symbols into sounds.

Auditory–visual (A-V). Translation of auditory symbols into visual images.

Auditory–kinesthetic (A-K). Translation of auditory symbols into the muscle responses associated with reading and writing.

Kinesthetic–auditory (K-A). Helping students produce a letter and say its name or sound.

Visual–kinesthetic (V-K). Translation of a visual symbol into the actions underlying speaking or writing it.

Kinesthetic–visual (K-V). Use of the muscular "feel" associated with vocalizing a sound or writing a letter to prompt the visualization.

The Gillingham–Stillman program also includes the development of three associations that include the above combinations:

Association I. Letter names to letter sounds
Association II. Letter sounds to letter names (orally)
Association III. Tracing and writing (copying sound representations)

The sequence of learning starts with letters and sounds, then words, and finally stories. The program attempts to develop the association of multisensory phonic relationships within the brain. The teaching emphasis in this program is primarily phonics with extensive drill activities. For example, the student is shown a letter and told its name. The student then repeats the letter name. The letter sound is introduced in the same lesson with the above steps repeated. The student is taught to sound blend individual phonemes to words. Advanced students practice syllabication, dictionary use, and recognition of irregularly spelled words. Materials for teaching include phonic drill cards, syllable concept cards, and very short stories in which the words are phonetically regular. Daily lessons last 1 hour.

The Gillingham–Stillman Method is a comprehensive program. All aspects of this program are sequenced and followed in a prescribed order. If students are instructed in this method, they are advised not to receive other reading instruction. The program emphasizes breaking the code and providing independence in word-attack. It is often used in schools for children who are dyslexic. Critics state that the program emphasizes the decoding aspects of reading, with special attention to phonics training but little attention to reading as a comprehension process.

The Wilson Reading System

Barbara Wilson created the Wilson Reading System as an Orton approach with some important updates (Wilson, 1996). The system includes making words activities using letter cards, phonemic segmentation activities, and a component in which the teacher reads aloud to the student and uses his/her retellings to focus attention on fluency and comprehension. In addition, the student spends some time reading, rather than focusing only on word-level instruction.

The Wilson Reading System provides a fast-paced, 10-step standard lesson plan that lasts about 1 hour. Wilson suggests that instruction be daily, but her system allows for a minimum of two lessons per week. Each lesson provides extensive review of phonics, affixes, syllables, and/or whole words, as well as introduces new language elements.

The first part of the standard lesson emphasizes decoding. The five quick steps of this section are:

1. *Drill with letter cards* for review, then ask students to identify the letter and its sound in a flashcard drill.
2. *Use letter cards or magnetic letters* to engage students in activities similar to those in Cunningham's making words activity (see Chapter 3). For more advanced students, cards with syllables and affixes are used.
3. *Drill with word cards.* Ask students to identify sight words in a flashcard drill.

4. *Drill with word lists.* The lists in the Wilson's Student Readers include words that contain the phonics and structural elements that have already been taught in the program.

5. *Drill with lists of sentences.* The sentences in the Student Readers contain only those phonics, structural elements, and sight words that have already been taught in the program.

The second part of the lesson plan emphasizes encoding. The first two components are very short, and the third component should take about 15 minutes.

6. *Drill with sounds.* The teacher says a sound and the students must repeat it and link it with a printed letter or letters. Depending on students' stages of development, they may either point to a letter card to identify the sound, write it, or trace the letter with a finger on the table or in sand.

7. *Spelling practice.* The teacher says a word containing elements that have been introduced previously. The students can use letter cards to form the word, or they can print the word on paper. Throughout this lesson, students are taught to tap out the individual phonemes as they say a word, to help them segment the word (or, at a later developmental stage, to segment syllables in a multisyllabic word).

8. *Dictation.* The teacher dictates and students write on paper. Depending on the level, this dictation is comprised of sounds, words, or sentences, the elements of which have already been taught. Phonics and structural analysis activities are included; the teacher, for example, might ask a student to circle the digraphs on the page. After the dictation, the teacher and students proofread the material together to ensure accuracy.

The third part of the lesson emphasizes fluency and comprehension. The first part lasts about 10 minutes, and the second part 10–30 minutes.

9. *Passage reading.* Students read from prescribed materials in the student readers, which contain only elements of language that have been taught. A series of workbook-like student readers provide material at varied levels. The students first read the passage silently. Then they retell the story, and the teacher asks comprehension questions. Then the students read the passage aloud. Repeated reading methods can be used, and students can take the passage home for more practice.

10. *Listening comprehension.* The teacher reads aloud to the student from material that is not limited to the language elements that have been taught. The students retell the story, and the teacher leads a discussion of the story contents.

Phonics for Decoding

Direct teaching and modeling of how to use phonics as a word-recognition technique are essential to help Stalled Readers gain control over the reading task. However, without the added objective of transferring the strategies learned in isolated, repetitive exercises to real text, Stalled Readers will not achieve the goal of real reading. "Phonics for decoding" focuses on this transfer of phonics knowledge to real world reading.

Step 1

Choose a text that is at an appropriate reading level and contains examples of the phonic elements that have been taught. Identify the words from the selection that contain the target phonic elements.

Step 2

This step has four options, providing a degree of flexibility. Your choice of which option to employ will depend on the difficulty of the text and the student's ability to attend to and sustain reading through a whole selection.

1. The teacher reads one paragraph, then the student rereads the same paragraph.
2. The teacher reads the whole selection, then the student rereads the same selection.
3. The teacher and student read one paragraph or parts of the selection together.
4. The teacher and student alternate reading paragraphs or pages.

Step 3

After the selection has been read, point out one of the words that has the phonic element you want to stress. Ask the student to reread the sentence containing the word and again point out the phonic element that is to be practiced.

Step 4

Write the word on a card, asking the student to underline the phonic element. Discuss the sounds and printed symbols that compose the phonic element, as well as other phonic elements in the word (e.g., the initial letter group or onset). Discuss the word's meaning.

Step 5

Tell the student that several other words in the selection have the same sound. Give clues to the location of the other words by stating the page and paragraph (or perhaps even the line) in which they can be found. Possibly supply a synonym or a definition as an additional clue.

Step 6

As the student locates each word, he/she writes it on a list. When all the words are located, the student reads the list. See the example below from a lesson on the /ea/ element.

treat

treason

cream

seat

teacher

meat

tease

seam

This procedure provides for context reading in conjunction with decoding instruction. Students should not lose sight of the primary purpose of reading, which is to comprehend the selection. In addition, practicing newly learned phonics strategies in context serves as a rehearsal for students' application of these strategies in authentic reading tasks.

SUMMARY

The dominant characteristic of most Stalled Readers is a serious difficulty with word recognition. Chapter 2 introduced the importance of foundational print concepts and phonemic awareness to the development of the word-recognition abilities of Catch-On Readers. Chapter 9 suggested a variety of methods for helping Catch-Up Readers acquire effective word-recognition abilities. Many of the methods provided in those chapters can be helpful for Stalled Readers as well.

This chapter has focused on intensive methods that direct the attention of Stalled Readers to word-level learning. The methods are discussed in the context of tutorial instruction, the only method of instruction that will satisfactorily overcome the serious challenges faced by the Stalled Reader. The chapter describes a two-pronged approach. Methods such as the Fernald technique and the VAK approach attempt to provide the Stalled Reader progress in sight-word vocabulary. Methods such as Orton approaches and Glass Analysis attempt to provide progress in decoding.

Chapter 17 offers insight into the instruction of Stalled Readers who have progressed a bit beyond the word-level stages of reading. They will benefit from reading sentences and longer passages in an effort to establish an improved level of fluency in reading.

Helping Stalled Readers Using Context-Based Approaches

We have frequently made reference to the importance of placing letter- and word-level instruction in the much broader context of a creative language arts curriculum that is integrated with the content area curriculum. Reading should not be limited to direct instruction and drills. All students—be they developmental, Catch-On, Catch-Up, or Stalled Readers—need to engage in large amounts of reading and writing in the context of a balanced curriculum that meets individual literacy needs and provides opportunities for practicing strategies and learning to enjoy authentic reading and writing (Cunningham & Stanovich, 1998).

What is the appropriate balance between direct, systematic instruction and authentic literacy experiences? The whole language movement of the 1980s and 1990s minimized direct instruction to the point of castigating any teacher using it as out-of-date and repressive. On the other hand, Richards and Morse (2002) described a special education classroom in which a commercial phonics curriculum is taught 1 hour a day, 5 days a week. Clearly that teacher will have no time left to provide authentic literacy activities for the students.

Answers to the question of appropriate balance vary with the program in place. The early intervention programs that follow the Reading Recovery pattern often balance 15 minutes of word-level studies with 15 minutes of reading. These programs, however, include writing as a part of the word-level study, and they assume that children return to the regular classroom to a rich language arts curriculum after the 30 minutes per day of tutorial instruction. Cunningham's Four Blocks curriculum (see Chapter 14) allots one-quarter of the literacy instruction time to word-level study and three-quarters to authentic learning. Traditional basal series would recommend that 50% of the reading program be devoted to recreational reading, and 50% to the basal lessons, which themselves contain significant amount of reading.

As a general rule of thumb, we would be very concerned if the daily time devoted to direct instruction and word-level study rises above 25% of the struggling reader's total reading and literacy time. Emergent readers would benefit from that balance as well, though in their case much of the word-level study can be smoothly integrated into such activities as language experience and shared reading lessons. Developing readers, whose abilities are growing normally, need a smaller—perhaps much smaller—amount of time on direct instruction.

Even readers with serious difficulties, such as Stalled Readers, need extensive exposure to reading experiences that are authentic and context-based. That is, instruction cannot be limited to phonics and word-level study. All too often, programs designed for the severely disabled reader ignore real reading and writing because of the difficulties these students have with word recognition. Although word identification is crucial to reading, isolated drill on word learning and decoding has little place in the real world of the reader, and Stalled Readers need to see how their efforts to acquire literacy fit into their real worlds.

MULTIPLE EXPOSURE/MULTIPLE CONTEXTS (ME/MC)

The ME/MC (multiple exposure/multiple contexts) method was developed to meet the needs of one severely disabled reader (McCormick, 1994). Peter was essentially a nonreader at the onset of the program. He progressed to the second-grade level after 56 hours of instruction using ME/MC. This approach has a major objective of improving word recognition, but it includes reading stories, practicing word recognition in context (as well as out of context), and listening to stories.

Step 1

The teacher and student select a series book (see Chapter 14) of high interest and low vocabulary (i.e., the interest level is for older students; the vocabulary used is for less able readers). A chapter book or a beginning reading book from a series is recommended.

Step 2

The student reads the first chapter of the book as a pretest. Record the words the student does not recognize on sight for use in the next session as words to be learned.

Step 3

In the next session, the teacher chooses a story or book to read aloud for 5–10 minutes. The selection should exemplify high-quality children's literature that will be of interest to the student.

Step 4

The teacher provides practice with the unknown words from the first chapter. The words from the pretest are written on cards and presented in isolation. The tutor says the word; the student uses the word. The tutor uses the word in an oral sentence; the student says the word in an oral sentence. The student traces each word. Games and activities are used to practice the words. The words are used in multiple contextual settings, such as short sentences or cloze activities.

As the lesson proceeds, the teacher creates charts or graphs of the new words learned by the student, demonstrating progress made. Another demonstration of student progress comes in occasional review sessions, when the student is asked to read the word cards of all the words he/she has learned.

Step 5

The student continues to study the words from the first chapter. When all the words have been learned, the chapter is reread. The teacher should not expect perfect reading. Rather, the student is ready to reread the chapter when he/she has learned the words sufficiently to get through the material fairly well. The goal is the student's realization that he/she can take control of reading. Waiting until the student is able to demonstrate perfect fluency in reading would bog down the process for too long a time.

It is clear from this step that the initial choice of book series is very important. The series should not present so many word-recognition problems that reading the first chapter would seem interminable to the student.

Step 6

This procedure is followed throughout the book. As the student's needs change, the games and context-based activities are modified.

Step 7

Finally the student rereads the entire book. The first run-through of this procedure may well mark the first book that a Stalled Reader has ever read.

This method has an advantage of consistency and structure. It is important to keep in mind that the words are usually practiced within some type of context. It is also important for the student to understand that reading involves not only word recognition but understanding the author's message as well.

NEUROLOGICAL IMPRESS METHOD (NIM)

Heckelman's (1969) neurological impress method uses longer units of discourse as the context for learning sight words, oral reading fluency, and correct phrasing. Heckelman hypothesized that the poor reader's oral reading errors lead to confusion regarding accurate word identification. He suggested that teacher modeling of correct patterns would allow those patterns to become impressed on the reader's mind and replace incorrect word identi-fication. NIM is often recommended as a method for improving fluency of reading (Johns & Lenski, 2001).

1. The teacher selects materials at the student's independent level—a level slightly eas-ier than the level at which the student is usually instructed. Materials should be interesting to the student. The student is told not to be overly concerned about accuracy of word recog-nition but to follow the line of print without rereading or trying to correct errors.

2. The teacher sits alongside the student, and both read from the same printed materi-als aloud at the same time. The teacher reads slightly louder and ahead of the student. Si-multaneously, the teacher tracks the reading; that is, his/her finger moves across the line of print as the words are spoken. This tracking is an essential component of the NIM, as it en-sures the integration of the aural and oral sensory modes.

Each session lasts about 15 minutes. It usually takes two or three sessions for the stu-dent and teacher to become accustomed to the procedure. As the student becomes more confident and successful with the approach, the teacher's lead during oral reading should decrease. The student can read louder and the teacher softer. The student can guide the pace of the lesson by moving his/her own finger across the print.

This method, while highly successful with some students, is very annoying and dis-tracting to others. Encouragement is important, but it will not always be worth the motiva-tional effort to continue with the method. Echo reading, described below, may be a useful alternative.

ECHO READING

Echo reading (Anderson, 1981), a variation on the neurological impress method, is also widely recognized as a method for developing reading fluency. Many students find it easier to accustom themselves to echo reading than to NIM.

The echo reading lesson starts with the teacher reading a phrase, line, or sentence of the story. The student rereads the same portion by echoing the teacher. This strategy is a form of direct modeling of how the text should be read in terms of speed, fluency, and word recog-nition.

As with all of the strategies described here for encouraging contextualized reading, teachers must choose passages that are at difficulty levels at which the Stalled Readers with whom they are working will succeed. We suggest that the teacher use selections in which the student would approximate 90% word recognition in an unpracticed first reading. As the teacher and student progress through the line-by-line reading, and as the student gains more ease with recognizing words and reading at an appropriate rate, the teacher can in-crease the length of the reading selections.

COMPREHENSION FOR DECODING

The comprehension for decoding method was developed by Sally Lipa (1990) to help the Stalled Reader who has very limited sight-word vocabulary and decoding strategies. Dis-abled readers need help in learning how to focus on significant cues for word recognition, and they need to learn how to use a variety of strategies based on the demands of the task and the situation. Low motivation and overwhelming anxiety about reading and learning are common behavioral traits of this reader. While reading running text, the student becomes so concerned with word recognition that the meaning conveyed by the print becomes less important than the arduous task of word recognition.

A first step in the comprehension for decoding method is to reduce the Stalled Reader's anxiety about reading so that various ways of understanding the story can be addressed and word identification can take place without concern about losing the comprehension.

Part I of the comprehension for decoding method emphasizes story reading.

1. *Predict and discuss* what will happen in the story by examining the pictures. This picture reading activity reduces the student's anxiety about the content of the text and it frees the student to use thinking/comprehension abilities by considering the meaning of the pictures.

2. *Teacher reads the story.* The student follows the text as the teacher reads aloud and tracks with a finger. The teacher stops at selected places and asks the student if the predictions from the earlier picture reading are supported or disproved by the text.

3. *Discussion of the story.* The teacher asks questions such as:

> "Did the events occur as we expected?"
> "Were our predictions accurate?"
> "What happened that surprised you?"

4. *Neurological impress method (NIM).* As described above in the section about the NIM, the teacher and student read the story aloud together. There are several variations to this procedure. If the story is long, only a portion is read as a NIM procedure. If there are several students in the group, each reads with the teacher one at a time.

5. *Student reads.* By this time both the content and specific words used in the story are well known to Stalled Readers who have had at least three opportunities to examine and use those words that are unknown. Word-recognition problems are reduced as the student gains control of the story content.

Part II of the comprehension for decoding method emphasizes word recognition. At this point the student has successfully read a whole story. Now strategies for identifying words can be taught.

6. *Teacher targets several words* considered necessary to comprehend the story. These words are printed on file cards, identified for the student, and examined together with the student for major identification cues, such as configuration, phonics, and structure. Target words are compared to other words that look or sound similar.

7. *Target words are framed.* The teacher and student locate and frame the target words within the text. In framing, the student outlines the configuration of the word with a pencil. The target word is read within the story context and its syntactical and semantic appropriateness discussed.

8. *Word-recognition strategies are practiced.* Several word-recognition strategies are presented, such as phonics, structural analysis, picture clues, prior knowledge, tapping the comprehension base of the story, and techniques for examining the special features of words. A word window and slide are used to move through the word, letter by letter.

The word window and slide can be easily constructed from a poster board. A 3-inch by 4-inch piece is cut from the poster board; using a utility knife, cut a rectangle out of the middle of the piece. The rectangle should be large enough to surround/display a typical word from the passage. The resulting hole forms the word window. Cut a slide that will be slightly larger than the window from the poster board. The slide is used to expose target words letter by letter.

Part III of the comprehension for decoding method provides additional practice for the Stalled Reader.

9. *Word location*. The student reads a list of target words, then locates them in the text by reading/scanning silently. Guide the student by revealing the page, paragraph number, or sentence number where the target word can be located. This scaffolding eliminates stress and reduces the amount of time needed to do the task.

10. *Summarizing*. The student writes a summary of the story by using as many of the target words as possible to complete sentence stems on a worksheet such as that seen in Figure 17.1, the story summary handout for the comprehension for decoding method. The teacher provides help, as necessary. Possible responses to the worksheet in Figure 17.1 might be similar to the following:

> <u>This story is about</u> a lake that becomes polluted and what a group of friends do to clean it.
>
> <u>The boys</u> were surprised when they saw a sign that said, "No swimming." The lake was filled with garbage, oil, and old tires.

Name _____ Date _____

Target Words

polluted	clean	newspaper
swimming	take	people
garbage	sign	surprised

The story is about

_____

_____

The boys

_____

_____

They told

_____

_____

Everyone

_____

_____

FIGURE 17.1. *Story summary handout for the comprehension for decoding method.*

Reading record of _____

Title of story: _____

Date: _____

Pages read: Start: _____   Finish: _____   Total: _____
Time: Start: _____   Finish: _____   Total: _____

This part of the story is about _____

_____

_____

_____

Title of story: _____

Date: _____

Pages read: Start: _____   Finish: _____   Total: _____
Time: Start: _____   Finish: _____   Total: _____

This part of the story is about _____

_____

_____

_____

FIGURE 17.2. *Time and page number chart for the comprehension for decoding method.*

They told the people about the lake with pictures in the newspaper.

Everyone in the town helped clean the lake.

11. *Mapping.* The student demonstrates retelling of the story by using the target words to make a story map (see Chapter 11).

12. *Rereading.* The student rereads the story silently, then uses a chart (see Figure 17.2) to record the number of minutes needed to read the story, the number of pages in the story, and at least one major idea about the story.

REPEATED READINGS

Too often the pace of instruction for Stalled Readers is too fast; they are never given the opportunity to achieve any level of success and fluency in their readings. One way that Stalled Readers can acquire sight words is by reading the same easy material repeatedly. A variety of methods uses the principle of repeated reading, including the ME/MC and comprehension for decoding methods described above, as well as the popular shared book experience described in Chapter 2. The purpose of such methods is to provide students with practice reading the same words over and over. The advantage to repeated reading approaches is that the words to be recognized on sight are presented over and over within the meaningful context of a story or a content selection. Repeated readings increase reading rate, reduce the number of word-recognition errors, and improve comprehension (Gerdes, 2001).

The National Reading Panel's (2000) thorough survey of comprehension methods found favorable results in studies that investigated repeated reading methods. The positive results spanned ability levels and affected both word recognition and comprehension. Apparently repeatedly reading text aids those readers who are having trouble attending to all the aspects of reading at the same time by giving them more time.

Samuels's Repeated Reading Method

S. Jay Samuels, a leading theorist and researcher in the study of the automatic processes of word recognition that occur during reading, developed the repeated reading method as a means of helping readers achieve fluency. In his version of repeated reading (Samuels, 1979, 2002) the selected text is read aloud a number of times until a satisfactory level of fluency is reached.

Short passages of 50 to 100 words or easy stories selected by students are used. The students practice reading until they feel comfortable with the material and are ready to read to an audience (usually, the teacher). Reading speed and word-recognition miscues are recorded and graphed by the teacher. Rereading continues (as does recording of speed and word recognition), until the preestablished fluency level is met. Samuels suggested 85 words per minute as a working definition of satisfactory fluency.

Emphasis is placed on reading speed rather than exact word identification. Samuels found that an overemphasis on exact word identification hindered students to such an extent that they could not reach the speed goal with reasonable effort.

The fact that the teacher records and graphs miscues provides motivation to make few miscues and helps Stalled Readers take charge of their own reading growth. The repeated exposure to the same words helps to develop a sight-word vocabulary. Most importantly, repeated reading provides Stalled Readers with opportunities to read successfully.

Samuels (2002) offered an adaptation of the repeated reading method that replaces the one-on-one tutorial component with greater independence on the part of the students. This adapted method is useful in classroom instruction, though not as powerful in terms of teacher supervision and input.

Students are paired, preferably one better reader with one poorer. The teacher reads the passage aloud first, with all the students reading along silently. Then the pairs take turns reading the passage aloud. While one student reads aloud, the other follows along with the printed text, reading silently. Since, in repeated reading methods, most growth in fluency occurs during the first four readings, each student reads the target passage four times.

Samuels warns that the teacher must first explain clearly to the students the purpose of repeated readings. In addition, the first several sessions need close supervision and a good deal of help from the teacher (as is the case with the introduction of any new educational strategy).

Chomsky's Repeated Reading Method

Carol Chomsky (1976) developed another closely related procedure that is also called repeated readings. Chomsky designed the method for struggling readers who have developed decoding skills but cannot transfer these skills to fluent oral reading. The method includes memorization of a book or story through repeated listening to a taped story. The students follow along in the text enough times until they can be read it aloud or silently with ease.

Step 1. Students listen to a short book or story on audiotape and follow along in their books. Some recordings can be purchased, but usually the teacher creates the recording. This step is repeated as many times as necessary for the whole book and/or for any difficult portions.

Step 2. The students read aloud along with the tape.

Step 3. The students record themselves reading the story on tape.

Step 4. The teacher evaluates the students' audiotapes.

Step 5. The teacher prepares follow-up work, such as games, sentence analysis activities, or writing, that will develop recognition of the words used in the story.

Step 6. The teacher selects several pages that the students can read fluently. Words that the students were not able to recognize independently are chosen from those pages. The teacher works with the students using a frame (such as a word window and slide, or by penciling the outline around the printed word) to examine the contextual clues to word identity.

MESSAGE WRITING

Message writing is an integrated reading–writing method best used in tutorial instruction. The method allows the teacher to see the students' literacy abilities in action, and it provides for a great deal of interaction and questioning about word recognition. The teacher can provide as much, or as little, scaffolding as necessary. The method is particularly useful with Stalled Readers, whose oral language abilities and understanding of their world outpace their literacy achievement. The method can be adapted for small groups or even for whole class use. In the latter case, it is useful if an aide circulates among the students to provide individual clues and help.

1. The teacher provides lined writing paper (or a blank writing book) in which each page is divided horizontally in half. The top half will be used for practice writing, and the bottom half for sentence writing.

2. Helped by the teacher, the students compose a brief message orally. This might be, for example, a summary of a story that has just been read.

3. The students attempt to write their message on the top half of their paper.

4. When students have problems with unfamiliar words, the teacher assists by drawing boxes on the practice half of the paper, one for each letter of the unfamiliar word (i.e., the word *their* would require five boxes).

5. The students use their phonemic segmentation abilities to slowly say the letter sounds of the word. They write the letters in the appropriate boxes.

6. The teacher monitors the word box activity, supplying any unknown letters in the correct boxes and giving explanations, if appropriate.

7. The teacher asks, "Does this look right?"
8. The students evaluate the finished word box and then print the word in their practice sentence.
9. Once the practice sentence is complete on the top of the page, the students copy it neatly onto the bottom half.
10. The teacher writes the sentence on sentence strip paper (a long, narrow strip of paper) and cuts it into separate words.
11. The students practice reconstructing the sentence using the word cards.
12. The sentence reconstruction activity is repeated in future lessons, as review.

SUMMARY

Serious word-recognition difficulty is the dominant characteristic of most Stalled Readers, as discussed in the previous chapter, Chapter 16. Even with Stalled Readers, however, instruction must not be limited to word-level drill and practice. All readers need the opportunity to employ their skills and strategies through authentic, context-based experiences to achieve fluent reading. Stalled Readers, however, need a great deal of scaffolding in order to succeed in these experiences. This chapter has presented a variety of such highly scaffolded strategies. A key ingredient to success in all these strategies has to do with careful teacher guidance in the choice of reading materials. Stalled Readers are often so far behind their peers in reading ability that text materials at an age-appropriate interest level need to be carefully chosen.

Our definition of the Stalled Reader is not limited to those whose problems have to do with word recognition. Methods in this chapter are also very appropriate for Stalled Readers who have made progress in word recognition but whose reading is stumbling and word by word. They have not been able to achieve a satisfactory level of fluency.

Some Stalled Readers have adequate word recognition, but they do not understand what they read. Chapter 18 will provide guidelines for intervention with these students.

Helping Stalled Readers with Reading Comprehension Difficulties

Some Stalled Readers appear to have adequate word recognition but do not understand what they read. Given the complexity of the human cognitive processing involved in comprehension, intervention for students with these problems can present more of a challenge than for students with word-recognition difficulties. Intervention procedures are often based on trial and error because of the difficulty in pinpointing the cause of the comprehension difficulty. The cause, for instance, may involve subtle word-recognition problems or stem from problems at a younger age in learning to read.

Models of comprehension development typically focus teachers' attention on several aspects of the reading process, all of which play a crucial role in the comprehension process:

1. *The text*. Text varies widely in its organization and structure, its reliability, and its appropriateness for target readers. Stalled Readers come in constant contact with text written for readers who are far more proficient than they.

2. *Background knowledge*. The reader's existing knowledge of relevant information about the text topics plays a key role in comprehension. A weak vocabulary may signal that some Stalled Readers lack sufficient knowledge about their world and are unable to bring key facts and understandings to bear in their readings.

3. *Strategies*. A fluent reader is able to apply a variety of learning strategies to text, in-

cluding the general monitoring of comprehension that we call *metacognition* (Narvaez, 2002). These strategies enhance understanding and retention and help the reader recognize the need for alternative strategies when comprehension is not occurring.

4. *Transaction.* In recent years, this fourth component of comprehension has received a good deal of attention. Transaction refers to the social nature of learning through collaborative activities. Teachers do provide comprehension instruction, but the emphasis is on students forming joint interpretations of the textual material through discussion.

The importance of the transactional nature of reading emerged when researchers began investigating such issues as students' zones of proximal development (Vygotsky, 1934/ 1978)—that is, the level of performance a student can reach unaided, and the level of participation he/she can accomplish when guided by another. "Expert scaffolding," another term used by Vygotsky, refers to the mediation by an expert to help another move from a given unaided level of performance to a higher level. A shift in educators' thinking about responsibility for comprehension occurred. The student as an isolated individual was no longer deemed primarily responsible for his/her poor comprehension of reading materials. Rather, comprehension development was seen as the product of teacher and student interactions with appropriate text and instructional activities within the social context of the learning environment.

A dominant set of transactional assumptions about how learning occurs and how reading and literacy are acquired are known today as constructivism or social constructivism. In actual classroom practice, constructivist approaches may be known as "integrated," "student-centered," "holistic," "literature-based," or "whole language" (though the latter term has taken on pejorative undertones and has been used infrequently in recent years). Cambourne (2002) lists three core presuppositions to the constructivist perspective:

1. Context is an integral part of the learning that takes place within it; learning is context-based.
2. Learners' purposes are central to the learning situation.
3. Learning is a socially constructed process involving transactions among learners.

Too often education consists of a mindless, repetitive effort to absorb and regurgitate information. The methods in this textbook could all be distorted by a nondynamic view of learning that fails to recognize that learning must make sense and have meaning to the learner. Learners make sense of what they are learning by placing it in a context in which they can make connections between new strategies and concepts and their world. Educational methods that attempt to teach content or skills in isolation, without connections to past learning or to authentic literacy experiences of reading and writing, will fail to make real differences in students' lives.

Constructivist theories have led to the development of strategies that include active teacher modeling, student involvement, and explanations of the thought processes and activities by which comprehension is developed. These thought processes and activities are very important for Stalled Readers, who may not know how to go about understanding an author's message.

It is important for the teacher of Stalled Readers to make extensive use of close observation to develop an understanding of each student's individual learning characteristics. The teacher should determine the following:

- Does the student's difficulty lie in dealing with long texts?
- Is the difficulty evident at the paragraph, sentence, or phrase level?

- Does the student understand narrative text better than expository text?
- Does the student understand well-formed stories better than poorly formed stories?
- Is the technical and specific vocabulary associated with some readings understood by the student?

In dealing with Stalled Readers, teachers must bear in mind the wide variety of textual materials and formats that students will encounter in real world reading (Duke, 2000). As a rule of thumb, start the teaching of comprehension strategies at the highest level at which the student demonstrates good comprehension but not so high that the student will be frustrated by the difficulty. For Stalled Readers, applying this guideline generally means (1) starting reading instruction at a level that is far below the level at which their peers are functioning, and (2) providing other means of instructional support to continue their engagement in classroom activities.

The activities presented below emphasize the principles of *transaction* and *strategy* in fostering the development of readers who take responsibility for their reading. Remember that many of the strategies are effective with normally developing readers and Catch-Up Readers as well as Stalled Readers. Duke and Pearson (2002), in an extensive examination of the characteristics of good readers, put "Good readers are *active* readers" (p. 205) at the top of their list. Many Stalled Readers have disengaged from the process as something that is taking place outside of their own control: something that someone else (the author or teacher) is doing *to* them, rather than something they are doing. Bear in mind, as you begin to reengage a Stalled Reader, that the disengagement is liable to be deep seated, a psychologically or socially self-protective avoidance of engagement due to years of discouraging failure in reading.

COMPREHENSION AT THE SENTENCE AND PARAGRAPH LEVEL

Question–Answer Relationships (QARs)

The QAR (question–answer relationships) procedure, developed and researched by Raphael (1986), is based on a well-recognized body of research that supports the value of self-generated questioning (Duke & Pearson, 2002). As noted, reading occurs through the interaction of the text being read and the reader's background knowledge. Information relevant to the specific reading task is a combination of text-explicit information (that can be found in the text), text-implicit information (that must be inferred by using background knowledge, but also requires the integration of text material), and script-implicit information (that is located in the reader's knowledge base).

QARs not only improve comprehension through use of an effective strategy, but also help Stalled Readers become aware of the metacognitive complexity of the reading task and take ownership of active reading. Students are taught to tell the difference between three types of questions, each of which targets a different aspect of comprehension:

1. "Right There QARs." These are text-explicit questions that address themselves to information that can be found by locating one or two sentences within the text; that is, the answers are presented explicitly in the text.
2. "Think and Search QARs." These questions deal with text-implicit information. The answers to the questions are in the text but they require the reader to integrate infor-

mation from more than one part of the text; that is, readers must search and make inferences.

3. "On My Own QARs." The answers to these questions are not in the story but in reader's past experiences and knowledge; the questions are derived from the text, but they cannot be answered by the text.

QAR instruction begins by demonstrating to students the two clearest categories, Right There and On My Own. A short passage, geared to the students' easy reading, independent level, is presented on an overhead projector. Students read the text aloud, and the teacher asks a Right There question. After a student answers, the teacher asks the student to show how he/she arrived at the answer and where it can be located in the text. Two or three more Right There questions are asked, then some On My Own questions. Through discussion, the students are guided to realize that some information relevant to the story is stated in the text and other information is in their heads. Later, Think and Search questions are provided and discussed.

Typically, instruction begins with modeling activities that involve strong teacher guidance. As students become familiar with the QAR terminology, they learn to collaboratively arrive at a determination as to which of the three levels a teacher-provided QAR is targeting. Next, students begin to develop questions collaboratively at all three levels. Finally, the teacher observes the students' individual comprehension in action during reading, confirming that each individual understands the QAR process (see Figure 18.1).

The direct instruction and modeling by the teacher in teaching about QARs make this procedure a valuable one for Stalled Readers. For these readers, however, it is necessary to limit the focus to the sentence or paragraph level of discourse. Length of text can be increased gradually during instruction. Bear in mind that emphasis on questioning tends to interrupt the reading session, which many students can find frustrating. QARs are best used as a regular but *intermittent* form of instruction. As students learn to generate their own questions during reading, their comprehension will improve.

In the following exercise, read the story and then examine each question and write whether the question is a *Right There*, *Think and Search*, or *On My Own* QAR.

> Some artists take minerals that come from the earth to make beautiful objects such as jewelry. Several kinds of stones and metals are taken from the earth. Semiprecious stones make beautiful jewelry. Metals are taken from the earth in ores.

1. _____ Who takes some of the minerals that come from the earth?
2. _____ How are some of the minerals that come from the earth used?
3. _____ What are some types of jewelry that can be made from minerals?
4. _____ How are the metals removed from the earth?
5. _____ Why are minerals valuable to people?
6. _____ What can be used to make beautiful jewelry?

FIGURE 18.1. *Identifying QARs.*

Reciprocal Questioning (ReQuest)

Similar to the QAR procedure, ReQuest (Manzo, 1969) is designed to help students monitor their own reading comprehension by learning to formulate questions about what has been read. This monitoring allows readers to develop the metacognitive abilities that allow them to control their own thinking processes during reading—an element that is crucial to comprehension (Baker, 2002; National Reading Panel, 2000). ReQuest's unique strengths lie in its game-like format and its externalization of thinking processes (teacher and students interacting with the text and with each other by posing questions and providing answers) that are usually invisible during reading.

ReQuest is introduced to the students as a game. Before actually keeping score, however, two or three practice trials help students understand the rules. The game aspects provide motivation for students, but the teacher's major purpose involves modeling fluent comprehension processes.

A copy of a short story or expository passage is given to each student. For many Stalled Readers, the ReQuest will proceed one sentence at a time. Depending on the difficulty level of the text, the sections may be longer. They should be clearly marked.

Both teacher and students begin by reading the first section aloud (or silently). The students have the first opportunity to ask the teacher whatever questions they want about the text. During ReQuest, the questioners may refer to the text, but the person or persons being questioned may not. The questions must be meaningful, not like "What is the third word on the fourth line?" A scorekeeper keeps track of how many questions are correctly answered or missed by the teacher.

After the students have completed their questioning, they close their books. The teacher now asks questions about the same segment of text, modeling the types of questions that will help students develop an understanding of the story at various levels of comprehension. The questions should include those that (1) set a purpose or bring focus to the selection, (2) build upon prior questions, (3) require students to integrate information, and (4) require relevant background knowledge.

At the end of the segment's questioning competition, the teacher should ask a prediction question, such as: "What do you think will happen next? Why do you think . . . ? Let's read and find out."

This process is carried out several times as the class moves on to new sections of the text. In many cases, ReQuest is carried out only on the first three or four segments of the passage, and then students are left to finish the passage in independent silent reading. The length of the entire text and of each segment within the text is determined by the teacher's judgment of the selection's level of difficulty and the complexity of the content in relation to the students' ability to comprehend. For Stalled Readers, the section is often very short, perhaps even a single sentence.

ReQuest is very successful with Stalled Readers. The detailed modeling of questions and predictions by the teacher provides these students with an established purpose for reading. Sentence by sentence, the story or content selection unfolds, providing opportunity for students to use prior information as well as new information to make hypotheses about what will happen next. In addition, the teacher's role is that of a collaborator, thus providing for a give-and-take game-like situation. The social interaction involved in activities such as ReQuest provide students with feedback about their reading and aid in their metacognitive development (Baker, 1996).

Reciprocal Teaching of Comprehension

Reciprocal teaching (Palincsar & Brown, 1984) was developed to provide process-based instruction to students whose reading difficulty is rooted in comprehending text. Expository text is usually selected for reciprocal teaching. In this procedure, the teacher acts as a model for students, demonstrating how one can interact with text by asking questions about it, summarizing small segments of it, initiating discussion, and posing a prediction question for the next segment of text.

As with QARs and ReQuest, the interaction and dialogue that ensue between teacher and student appear to be major factors in the success of this method. It is through this dialogue that personalized instruction and ongoing observation of student performance take place. In this procedure the teacher and the student take turns leading a dialogue about certain sections of a text. During this dialogue the participants (1) ask questions, (2) summarize, (3) clarify information, and (4) predict what will be presented in upcoming text.

In a reciprocal teaching lesson, a paragraph from expository text is read silently by both teacher and students. Then an assigned student leads a structured, four-step discussion:

1. Ask a question about the paragraph to the group.
2. Summarize the paragraph.
3. Ask a question about the paragraph for clarification, if necessary.
4. Predict the topic of the next paragraph.

The teacher provides as much support as is necessary. At the end, he/she provides feedback about students' performances as well as reminders about the purpose of the four strategies.

With all students, the procedure should be modeled repeatedly by the teacher prior to assigning students the leadership role. This is an excellent procedure to use with Stalled Readers. As they are with QARs and ReQuest, these struggling readers are given the opportunity to learn of the strategies needed to understand text from expert modeling. However, the teacher must be well prepared to model questions, clarifications, summaries and predictions. Reciprocal questioning requires prior reading and planning by the teacher.

Radio Reading

Radio reading (Green, 1979; Searfoss, 1975) is an interesting and motivating approach to oral reading comprehension. The purpose of radio reading is to communicate information to audience members, who in turn respond by asking questions for clarification. Skills related to both reading and listening comprehension are practiced with this method.

The reader takes the role of a radio announcer reading a script. The listeners act as the audience, listening to, reacting to, and restating what the reader has read. The listeners' responsibility in understanding the message is just as important as the reader's responsibility in delivering the message.

Step 1—Establishing the Ground Rules

1. Material is selected that is challenging and highly interesting but not too difficult for Stalled Readers. We have found that local newspapers often contain stories about people in the community who have interesting or odd hobbies or vocations; a local news event such

as an upcoming fair, can also be appropriate. These stories often are successful in holding students' interests (they may have to be rewritten to a lower readability level). Some students might read a portion of a short story, and others might read one or two paragraphs. Since the reader will be reading an unpracticed script aloud, teachers should err on the easier side in terms of selecting text difficulty.

2. The reader has the script (reading materials); listeners do not have the reading materials.

3. The listeners must try to understand the message from listening to the reader. If the information is confusing or does not make sense, the listeners should question the reader. They might ask, for example, about punctuation errors or word-recognition errors made during reading.

4. The reader is not given any help unless he/she asks for it.

Step 2—Communicating the Message

The reader takes charge of the activity by orally reading.

Step 3—Checking for Understanding

After the reader has completed the reading, a brief discussion follows. Retelling activities are excellent ways for the listeners to recount the reading. After discussion, the reader can continue reading, or the teacher can select another radio announcer.

Step 4—Clarifying an Unclear Message

Sometimes the reader does not deliver a clear message because of word-recognition errors, ignoring or incorrect use of punctuation, or fluency problems. If the passage chosen has proven to be too difficult—the oral reading problems are severe and the lesson seems to be breaking down—the teacher can step in with another method. For more typical oral reading problems, the reader returns to the story and rereads the parts that confused the audience. More frequently, the discussion shows that some listeners did not accurately interpret or recall the information that was read. The reader must clarify the misinformation by returning to the text and rereading unclear parts.

The teacher may have to help the reader and listeners focus on the content of what was read, especially as radio reading is first introduced in the classroom. After a few sessions of this approach, both readers and listeners begin to actively engage in the activity and enjoy the challenge. This procedure incorporates reading accuracy and fluency with comprehension.

COMPREHENSION OF LONGER DISCOURSE

Reading longer selections and whole text requires Stalled Readers to maintain a constant pattern of (1) hypothesis formation, (2) confirming or denying each hypothesis, and (3) making inferences and judgments about the information being read or heard. Readers must be actively involved in the text by recalling relevant information that can be included in the final analysis and interpretation of the selection. Grasping the main idea, making inferences, determining cause and effect, comparing and contrasting, and recalling information are some of the major patterns of thinking in which readers engage while reading expository text. Narrative text requires that readers make inferences about the theme and moral of the story, interpret characters' feelings and actions, predict upcoming events, and analyze the story for mood, effect, and emotional impact. Significant demands are made on readers' memory and cognitive abilities in analyzing, synthesizing, and interpreting information.

Stalled Readers who have difficulty comprehending text are likely to feel overwhelmed by such a daunting task. Thus the need for a high degree of structure and teacher instruction and modeling is evident.

Guided Reading Procedure (GRP)

The guided reading procedure (Manzo, 1975) is designed to help students remember what they have read, confirm that the information they have recalled is correct, and organize and identify relationships in the text. This is a time-consuming but powerful method for helping students focus on text that presents key content area concepts. The GRP was developed as a group activity but can be modified for use with individuals. For Stalled Readers at the primary-grade level, passages of about 100 words might be used to start.

1. *Student preparation.* The student should be prepared via discussing relevant background experiences, pertinent vocabulary, key concepts in the selected text, and purpose for reading. In the GRP the purpose is to remember as many of the details as possible. Explain that you will ask them what they recalled and record the information on the chalkboard. Setting this purpose is important, as it cues students to look for the details rather than concentrate only on the main ideas. Also warn the students that you will administer a test on the information.

2. *Silent reading and recall of information.* Students read the selection silently and place it face down on their desks when they are finished. Ask them to report what they recall without looking back in the text and record the information on the board or on chart paper.

3. *Rereading for additional facts and corrections.* After the students have supplied all the information they can recall, ask them to review the text and add or correct any information. Make the additions and changes on the board. Ask students to note inconsistencies in the information they have supplied and add information that they overlooked.

4. *Organize the remembered information.* Direct the students to organize the information into a modified outline form or a graphic organizer (see Chapter 12). Questions can be asked to help students organize the information based on the primary sequence and structure in the text (e.g., list, cause–effect factors, aspects that can be compared and contrasted, the time order, and main ideas).

5. *Questioning.* Ask questions that help the students integrate the information just read into a meaningful context. For example, ask how the information relates to an assignment read last week or to a preconceived idea about a topic. The purpose of this step is to help students synthesize new information with previously learned information.

6. *Evaluation.* A prepared test is administered to the students. Another possibility is to conduct a retelling that is evaluated in detail (see Chapter 11 and the comprehension section of the appendix). Give students feedback regarding the effectiveness of their learning. Usually, students are motivated to do better on the next GRP.

Guided Listening Procedure

The guided listening procedure (GLP) (Cunningham, Arthur, & Cunningham, 1977), a modification of the guided reading procedure, is useful for improving listening comprehension—a prerequisite for good reading comprehension.

After preparing students for the lesson by providing background information and predictions and setting a purpose for reading, the teacher orally reads the selection to the students and uses a tape recorder to make a record of the reading. Following this reading:

1. Students state information that they recall; teacher records the information on the board.
2. Students listen to the tape recording (or the teacher rereads aloud); students add and/or correct information on the board.
3. Students organize the material into an outline or graphic organizer; the teacher directs the students to use a suitable pattern of organization.
4. The teacher helps students synthesize new information with previous information. With younger students this step can be accomplished by asking them whether they ever had a similar experience or what they would do if they had the experiences of a character in the story.

Aided Story Retellings

Story retellings are useful comprehension measures for all readers (see Chapter 11) and provide observational information for the teacher as well as opportunities to model the thinking processes needed for understanding. Story retellings can be particularly difficult for Stalled Readers, as they often construct incomplete and/or partially incorrect information about the text. Teacher intervention and modeling are needed to help disabled readers recall, sequence, and organize information into a coherent retell. Aided story retelling provides the kind of structure that is important for Stalled Readers.

1. *Teacher preparation.* Select a picture book of high interest to the students. For older students, make sure that the picture book has a theme that is appropriate. Develop a response sheet to record student performance. A retelling assessment instrument, such as the General Analysis Checklist or the Specific Checklist (see the comprehension section of the appendix) will serve this purpose.

2. *The story.* Have the students read the title and look at the pictures on the cover and title page of the story. Ask the students to predict what will happen in the story.

Read the story to the students or have the students read it aloud. Use the format of a directed reading–thinking activity (DR-TA; see Chapter 11) or directed listening–thinking activity (DL-TA—a lesson for younger or less able children, similar to the DR-TA, in which the teacher reads the story aloud to the children), stopping the reading at preset points and asking students to recount the events and make a new prediction.

3. *The retell.* Ask the students to retell the story by using the pictures in the story. Clarify information that is incorrect or partially correct by rereading the sections of the text that would clarify the misconceptions. Discuss any persisting confusions.

Close the book and ask the students to retell the story from memory. Use the retelling checklist developed prior to the reading to determine which parts of the story the students recall and which parts are still unclear or incorrect.

4. *Summarize.* Model how to form a summary statement for the book. Sentence stems can be used like those in probable passages. (See Chapter 11. For example: This story is about _____, who _____. The problem starts when _____. It is solved when _____.)

Another possibility is to have students draw a summarizing picture from the story. After the drawing is complete, a summary statement can be written under the picture.

As students practice using picture clues to retell the story, their recall of the information improves along with their ability to provide accurate information rather than close approximations. Once students have become proficient with this technique, teachers can use unaided story retell procedures.

Herringbone Technique—Modified for the Stalled Reader

The herringbone technique was introduced in Chapter 12. Steps in modifying this strategy to meet the needs of Stalled Readers are as follows:

1. *Teacher preparation.* Select a story appropriate for the student—perhaps a chapter of a chapter book or an expository selection. Be sure that the *who, what, where, when, why,* and *how* questions can be answered by reading or listening to the selection.

Determine who should do the reading: the teacher, the teacher and student sharing the reading, or the student. Base your decision on the student's levels in reading words and comprehending text. If word identification interferes with comprehension, the teacher can do the reading the first time through a section of the text. The student can do the subsequent rereading to check responses, and so forth.

Construct a herringbone diagram (see Chapter 12). Have Post-its available to write the answers to the "wh" questions.

2. *Read the selection.* The teacher or student reads the selection and they discuss it, using the *wh* questions to structure the discussion. Answers to each question should be written on a Post-it.

3. *Complete the herringbone diagram.* Show the student the herringbone diagram you have constructed. After rereading the responses to the *wh* questions, the student should place the Post-its on the appropriate herringbone categories.

4. *Summarizing.* Help the student write a summary of the story by using sentence stems such as:

> This story takes place _____ (where). _____ (who) is a character in the story who _____ (did what) _____ (when) _____ (how). This happened because _____ (why).

Drawing a picture of the major events in the story and writing a caption below can serve as a viable summary for less advanced readers.

The teacher who works with disabled readers must be an active participant in the herringbone comprehension activities. Teacher support, guidance, and modeling are essential for these readers to develop independence in reading.

INTEGRATED APPROACH: READING AND WRITING

Modified Language Experience Approach

The language experience approach (LEA) is a strategy that can be used to enhance reading, writing, and comprehension development (see Chapter 4). Often Stalled Readers have difficulty reading another author's language. Responding to questions about a personally dictated story is relatively easy for the student and provides a model for answering questions about other selections, as the teacher helps the student transfer this comprehension ability to other authors' stories.

This modified language experience approach can be used as a tutorial lesson or a small group lesson with Stalled Readers who have word-recognition and comprehension difficulties. Used in its entirety, this procedure models the process of thinking about a topic, stating and writing ideas about the topic, and then responding to questions.

1. A language experience story is developed from a class trip, a class unit, a new story of interest, or a content reading selection. A sample language experience story is provided in Figure 11.6.

2. Once the story has been dictated by the student and printed by the teacher, it is reread by the student.

3. The teacher questions the student regarding the accuracy of facts, sequence of information, and the conclusions that are drawn. This information can be checked by looking back in a selection or redirecting the student's recollection of the experience.

4. The teacher then writes questions about the dictated story for the student to answer in writing. The resulting story, with the questions, is copied for the student. The teacher might need to provide hints to help the student locate the answers to the questions (see Figure 18.2).

SUMMARY

The strategies in this chapter are designed to be used with those Stalled Readers who have experienced success in word recognition and fluency, but who have serious difficulties understanding and learning from what they read. These strategies emphasize active teacher modeling and student engagement, as well as analysis of the thought processes by which comprehension successfully takes place. Stalled Readers suffering from comprehension difficulties often see reading as something that is outside of their control. They have become passive, disengaged readers. This passivity can be surprisingly deep-seated. The intervention methods described here involve engagement and close analysis of text at both the paragraph level and in longer discourse.

Chapter 15 introduced Stalled Readers, describing their characteristics and offering principles for intervention. We were introduced to one Stalled Reader in a case study. Chapters 16, 17, and 18 provided strategies about instructional interventions for Stalled Readers with differing needs. Next, in Chapter 19, we consider additional case studies representing the various types of Stalled Readers. Chapter 20 completes our study of Stalled Readers with suggestions for additional resources.

Space Shuttle OK and Well

1   The space shuttle went off Sunday. It went like

2   the speed of light. There were two astronauts on it.

3   The space shuttle was in space for two days.

4   It went around the earth in space. People thought it

5   might crash or blow up!

6   Around 1:14 it started to come down. It dropped

7   its wheels and hit the ground.

8   The space shuttle landed on the red X at the

9   airfield. The escape crew is checking the ship.

10   The astronauts are alive and O.K.

Questions

1. When did the space shuttle go off? (line 1)

2. How many people were on the space shuttle? (line 2)

3. What are the people called? (line 2)

4. How long did the space shuttle stay in space? (line 3)

5. Where did the space shuttle land? (line 9)

6. What is another name for a space shuttle? (line 9)

FIGURE 18.2. *Modified language experience approach story.*

CHAPTER 19

Thinking through Case Studies
of Stalled Readers

THINKING THROUGH MOLLY'S STORY

In Chapter 15, we read about Molly, a child who only learned two words during her entire first-grade experience. During a summer of intensive instruction targeted to sight-word recognition and phonics at the Reading and Literacy Center, her learning failed to produce observable results. Molly seemed unable to learn to recognize new words. Her anxiety level, reflecting her recognition that she was failing in a crucial task, was increasing. Her mom reported frequent crying sessions at home. Molly completely refused to attempt to read with her parents. During her assigned 20 minutes per day of parent–child reading, she would insist that her parents read aloud to her. She would not attempt any word recognition with them. Fortunately, by the end of the summer Molly was looking forward to coming back to the Reading Center for after-school sessions in the fall semester.

With concern for Molly's state of mind, her tutor in the fall decided to make the instructional sessions less intense. Objectives were scaled back significantly. In the summer, the pattern of instruction had involved presenting Molly with a number of new sight words every day. The day's lesson would focus on those sight words. Although the tutor recognized that Molly had not fully mastered the day's sight words (a concept called overlearning) by the end of the day's session, she wanted to avoid boring the girl with too much repetition. A vague understanding of the words on the first day would be reinforced in ensuing days with review. New words would be introduced the next day, and some review of the old words would take place. But at the end of the summer, it was apparent that Molly had been unable to master recognition of the words.

Molly's tutor took a new approach to setting objectives. Movement through the planned curriculum would be geared to a strict adherence to the principle of mastery: Molly would not move on to a new set of words until she was well able to recognize the old set of words. The tutor would attempt to offset any potential boredom and disengagement by planning a variety of creative activities involving word study. In addition, Molly was exposed to a rich language arts curriculum for at least half of each session at the center and in her school classroom.

We decided to capitalize on Molly's expressive language ability by having her use invented spelling, with the tutor's assistance, to write short language experience stories (see Chapter 4). The major purpose here was to develop an automatic sight word base. After writing and rereading her LEA story, Molly selected three words that she wanted to learn.

These words were then placed in her word bank. A variety of activities were carried out using the words, so that she would have the experience of actively participating in reading the words both in context and in isolation. She traced the words, wrote them from memory, and did a "making words" activity with them. Her tutor created several games that she used for teaching the sight words. To ensure Molly's success with the selected words, her language experience stories were bound together in a notebook so that she could read them repeatedly and they would always be available for her to reread and refresh her memory. Copies of the stories were also sent home to be read with her parents.

Gradually, Molly started to build her sight-word vocabulary. The process was very slow—so slow that her tutor had to be carefully supervised so as not to succumb to the temptation to push ahead before real learning had occurred. On the first day, she learned her three words, but she had forgotten them by the time she returned a few days later. The words were reviewed in the context of a variety of activities, which were interspersed with other reading and writing activities to avoid boredom and to space out the learning that required memory. (Distributed learning—distributing instruction in short spurts across a long period of time—is best for incorporation of new material into long-term memory.) On the third day, Molly was able to recognize the three words with a large degree of consistency. Two new words were added to her word bank on that day; three more words were added on the fifth day.

Once Molly started to learn how to discriminate between words, she was able to learn more words at a faster pace: two or three each session, mostly chosen from her language experience stories. The first two months of instruction, however, continued to be painfully slow.

At this point we wanted Molly to begin reading another author's writing (the tutor had been using an Arthur series book), so we introduced her to easy reading materials. We decided to use easy readers such as Arnold Lobel's *Frog and Toad* (Lobel, 1970/1999) series rather than predictable text because of her inclination to memorize text and not focus on individual words. Since Molly was still reading at the preprimer level, and Lobel's books are written at a second-grade level, Molly's tutor read the books to her. When she came to a word from Molly's word bank, she stopped reading, pointed to the word, and waited for Molly to fill in the word. Molly's parents followed a similar pattern of reading with her in her evening reading time.

Molly made steady progress, profiting from the extra time-on-task provided by the Reading and Literacy Center and by her parents' commitment to evening and weekend reading times. By the end of second grade, she had a substantial store of sight words and was reading at the late first-grade level. By the end of third grade she was reading at the same level as her peers. She would occasionally substitute her own words for the author's words, but her metacognitive strategies for monitoring text were excellent, as was her comprehension.

Working with Molly early in her school career was essential if she were to overcome her early reading difficulties. Without consistent tutoring geared toward her specific needs, Molly might have remained a Stalled Reader throughout her schooling.

THINKING THROUGH GEORGE'S STORY

George, a third grader from a disadvantaged neighborhood school in a large city school district, was referred to an after-school tutorial reading program by Mrs. Hauer, his classroom teacher, because of his comprehension difficulties. Mrs. Hauer, as well as George's first- and second-grade teachers, had recognized his comprehension problems. George seemed unable to join in class discussion of reading materials. The teachers had worked with him and monitored his work to make sure he completed the reading assignments. George seemed willing enough to do the reading, but he had little to show for his efforts when asked to respond by way of discussion or writing.

Comprehension difficulties are not unusual in disadvantaged children. As they reach the intermediate grades, their lack of world experiences may have negatively affected vocabulary development of words relevant to schooling and academics. These children may not have the background schemata that help students understand content area materials. George's comprehension problems, however, were more serious than the other children in his classes, and they seemed to have affected his performance much earlier than would be typical. In addition, comprehension difficulties due to lack of world knowledge are associated with a vocabulary deficits, and George's vocabulary test scores did not reflect such a deficit.

The school reported George's standardized test scores (Figure 19.1). The results of an informal reading inventory (IRI) administered at the after-school center supported the school information: George's reading difficulty seemed rooted in comprehending text. George read the word lists on the IRI through the sixth-grade level without any word-recognition or decoding difficulty. As he progressed through the word lists, his tentative tone of voice indicated to the examiner and tutor, Ms. Semanski, that he was not sure of many of the words' meanings.

As part of the IRI, Ms. Semanski asked George to read graded passages, both aloud and silently. His reading of the preprimer passage was at independent level, as was his compre-

First Grade, May: Stanford Achievement Test

Subtest	Percentile	Stanine
Word Study Skills	85	8
Word Reading	80	8
Comprehension	20	3

Second Grade, May: Stanford Achievement Test

Subtest	Percentile	Stanine
Word Study Skills	80	8
Word Reading	54	5
Comprehension	10	2

FIGURE 19.1. *George's standardized test scores.*

hension on both silent and oral measures. Beyond this point, George had difficulty responding accurately to the questions posed after his reading. Both his oral and silent reading levels were determined to be at the primer level due to comprehension problems. George was
further tested, using expository IRI passages to determine if there was a difference in his
reading of narrative versus expository text. Results indicated that George's instructional
level was preprimer on these passages.

Take a moment to consider George's status as a reader. What might lead you to suspect
that George is a Stalled Reader, as opposed to a Catch-Up Reader? What are his strengths
and needs? What possible route could his teachers take to help him acquire literacy?

Ms. Semanski began instruction by using narrative stories at a low first-grade level to
determine if George could comprehend when small units of text were read. She tried a strategy that was a modification of radio reading. First, George read a paragraph of text aloud
while the teacher listened. Then Ms. Semanski told George everything she remembered
from his reading. He confirmed or denied what she said. At first, she related only correct information from the reading, but later, when George had become accustomed to the procedure, she included information that was incorrect or distorted, to check his comprehension.

Next, she read a passage aloud in short sections. George listened to each section and
then recalled its content. Ms. Semanski concluded that George recalled basic facts, but he
could not make inferences or judgments about the selection. At this point the teacher knew
that George could understand literal information when he read short paragraphs. Further
evaluation of George's reading comprehension was conducted by using longer units of text.
As the material increased in length, George had more difficulty recalling the facts, and often
his recall distorted the information. Through these instructional assessment sessions, Ms.
Semanski concluded that George could comprehend short segments of text but had difficulty with longer units.

She wondered if George's meaning vocabulary might be interfering with his comprehension. Perhaps the standardized tests had not been accurate in reporting that his vocabulary was satisfactory. She chose several key words from the passages that had been read,
trying to choose words that would have interfered with George's comprehension if the
word meanings were not clear. For each word, she developed a semantic map (see Chapter
10). George and his tutor worked through the meaning of the word by mapping key elements with questions such as:

"What is it used for?"
"What do you do with it?"
"What does it look like?"

She found that George had vague ideas about the meanings of many of these words. His stated
meanings only approximated the meanings that were conveyed by the text. She concluded
that George's vocabulary weakness was contributing to his comprehension difficulties.

Having narrowed the parameters of the comprehension difficulty, Ms. Semanski was
now ready to provide George with direct instruction and guided experiences of recalling information in both narrative and expository text. She decided to preteach the vocabulary in
each selection they read by presenting key words in context and discussing their meanings.
Although some vocabulary strategies incorporate a step at which the student makes a prediction as to the meaning of a new word, she decided to eliminate this step with George.

Since he seemed to have already developed a strategy that involved partially defined vocabulary words, she did not want him to keep his guessed meaning in mind and forget to focus on what was intended by the author as the meaning of the word. The lessons used the context that was presented in the story as the basis of the vocabulary teaching.

Ms. Semanski then instructed George in how to use the ReQuest procedure. This procedure was selected because the teacher and George could focus on discerning the meaning from sentence-level text, and he could be instructed to use the information he already knew from previously read parts of the text. The ReQuest method would allow him to focus on both vocabulary and comprehension. She felt that this procedure would meet his present needs and guide him to the effective use of longer units of text. In addition, ReQuest could be used with both narrative and expository text.

George and Ms. Semanski used ReQuest during reading throughout the semester. He was also given guided practice in recalling information read by discussion and by writing. Progress was slow. There are so many words in the English language that discernible vocabulary improvement takes place over years rather than months. The method, however, seemed to be motivating for George, and they allowed Ms. Semanski to incorporate successful lessons on the principles of comprehension into authentic reading experiences.

THINKING THROUGH CATHY'S STORY

Cathy was referred to a reading specialist at the end of third grade. She had been identified in first grade as a child who was not acquiring reading at the same rate as her peers, and she had received a good deal of intervention instruction. Psychological evaluation indicated that she had a verbal IQ of 136, performance IQ of 132, and full-scale IQ of 135. Obviously a bright child, she had little difficulty describing her reading difficulties. School reports and testing revealed that she had difficulty sound blending phonemes and syllables into words and that she had not developed a reliable stock of sight words. One-to-one correspondence of consonants was established, but she was seldom sure of short, long, or double vowel sounds. This problem often caused her to distort sounds when she resorted to sound blending. When seeing a medial *e* in a word, for example, she would not reliably try a typical *e* sound; instead she might use the short *a* or *u* sound.

Cathy's word recognition was mid-first-grade level. Her reading comprehension was also at this level because of her difficulty with word recognition.

We decided to ask Cathy to dictate language experience stories. From these we would develop a stock of reliable sight words. We also decided to use a phonogram approach to teach common vowel–consonant patterns by using a modified Glass analysis approach.

Cathy enjoyed the story writing. She had a wonderful imagination and dictated long and very interesting stories that she published for others to read. However, she had difficulty rereading her own stories. After a few days, she would forget her exact word choices. She would then resort to a sound–symbol approach that did not work well for her, or ask her teacher to identify the unknown words. Each time she read her own story, it was as if she had never seen it before, no less composed it herself. LEA was not working well for her.

Her teacher talked to her about writing much briefer stories and shorter poems for LEA lessons, and she engaged in teaching Cathy sight words by the sentence approach. They could see gradual improvement, but constant reinforcement was needed to help Cathy maintain the sight words.

Cathy learned the sound-blending approach by using the phonograms. However, she often became tongue-tied by the syllables and sounds. She had great difficulty generalizing across the sounds to mentally make the connection to the word she wanted.

Nothing seemed to be working very well. Her instructor engaged her in a series of instructional assessment discussions. She wanted to know more about Cathy so that she could help her overcome these serious obstacles to reading.

Included below is some of the dialogue that occurred between the instructor and Cathy as they talked and as Cathy demonstrated her approaches to word recognition. Read the dialogue, think through what seems to be happening, and answer the questions that follow.

TEACHER: How could I find out what you do when you read?

CATHY: When I read—I read. I try to figure words out by sounding them out. When I don't know about something—I read a book to find out. Books are used for different things.

(*Teacher and Cathy look at a book.*)

TEACHER: Tell me what you mean. Here's the book we selected for reading.

CATHY: Some books—have lines and carry over to the next line. Easy books don't do that.

TEACHER: Show me what you mean.

CATHY: Well, see this word? (*She points to* remembered, *which is hyphenated after the first* e *and carried over to the next line.*) It's on this line (*she points to* re), then there's a line (*she points to the hyphen*) and the rest of the word is on the next line. (*She points to* membered.) That's hard. Easy books don't do that. When the word is split up, it's easier.

TEACHER: Show me what you mean by a word that is "split up."

CATHY: Words like *every-thing, grown-up, side-wall.* That's easy.

TEACHER: Those are compound words. Is that what you mean?

CATHY: Yes, compound words. Because I recognize each word.

TEACHER: What else is hard for you?

CATHY: It's harder when they have all those lines there (*she points to quotation marks*) that tell you they're talking. They distract me. It's hard when they use a line [dash] to say it's pausing. I can understand the dots [. . .] better.

TEACHER: So when they use lines instead of dots for pauses, it's harder.

CATHY: When there's one sentence on a page, it's easier to have the distractions. I like it when it's next to each other, not when there's one sentence on a page.

TEACHER: Tell me what you mean. You don't like to read one sentence at a time? You like to read several sentences? That's easier for you?

CATHY: If I don't know a word they [She apparently means the teacher or tutor.] tell me to go to the end of the sentence. They take the word out [that is, show the word without context]. But I don't know the word before or after. I try to sound it out. I like more sentences because with my mind I can read ahead. I can think about what it will say and some words that might be there.

TEACHER: Can you show me what you mean in this book? (*She shows one of Donald J. Sobol's* Encyclopedia Brown *books.*)

CATHY: This sentence says, "What was the _____? [Target sentence: "What was the clue?"] I'd say, it begins with *c*, /k/ sound, or /s/ or maybe it's a silent *c*, but I don't think so. I think back to the rest of the story and they had an aide, a trumpet, case, skirt, clue. When they say, read ahead, I have to sound it. And I can't sound out the *u* and *e* sound.

TEACHER: Look at this sentence. If someone told you to read ahead, what would you do?

CATHY: (*Attempts to read "'You don't have a clue,' replied Encyclopedia Brown."*) You don't have a ... re- ... po- ... hide, re-, re-po-hide, Encyclopedia. Is that *Encyclopedia*? Yes, that's *Encyclopedia*.

TEACHER: How do you know that's *Encyclopedia*?

CATHY: I go to the beginning of the book to look at the beginning [that is, the title]. They look alike. (*She shows the title* Encyclopedia Brown *and the word* Encyclopedia.] You don't have a re-po-lide Encyclopedia. Re-polide. Repol-ide.

TEACHER: Did you read ahead?

CATHY: Sometimes I don't know the meaning of the word. Sometimes I make up a name—they're hard.

TEACHER: Tell me about reading ahead.

CATHY: When I read ahead, I forget to go back. Today in school I read ahead, and I forgot to go back, and the word was very important. I like to go back and find the same word. I figure whether it's an object or name, if that's what I think it is. I'll read a paragraph.

TEACHER: Tell me how you go about it.

CATHY: (*Reading from the book.*) The case of the window _____ [The target word is *dresser*]. The case of the window _____ bull. It doesn't look like *bull*."

TEACHER: Why not?

CATHY: It doesn't start with the same letters. (*She attempts to read again.*) The case of the window dr-esss-orrs (*softly*) dr—ess—ors.

TEACHER: Have you seen the word *dresser* before?

CATHY: Yes, but it doesn't make sense. (*Still attempting to decode "dresser"*) d-di-is-s-a-pear, disappear?

TEACHER: *Dresser* is the word. Look ahead at the picture. Do you see mannequins in the window? They're dressing the mannequins.

CATHY: The disappears were shopping in _____department store?

You have seen some of Cathy's strategies and have probably recognized some of her frustrations. Answer the following questions based on this data and what you know about diagnosis and remediation.

1. What are Cathy's strategies for word recognition and comprehension?
2. What strategies would you use with her if you were her classroom teacher? What strategies would you use with her if you were her tutor?

THINKING THROUGH DOROTHY'S STORY

Dorothy's fourth-grade teacher referred her to the Reading and Literacy Center. At 10 years of age, she was still experiencing difficulty with word recognition, but her teachers felt that her comprehension was a more serious problem. She was identified as language delayed and learning disabled early in her school career and had received support services from a resource room teacher throughout her schooling.

Dorothy was expected to participate in and learn the curriculum that was established for fourth-grade students. Although her teachers read most of the material to her and planned learning experiences in which she could participate with her classmates, she was not learning the concepts nor was she interacting with her classmates. The teachers asked for help to better understand Dorothy's comprehension and learning difficulties.

Two questions based on her language impairment were raised:

1. Would presenting information auditorially, without accompanying visual information, be helpful?
2. Were the concepts in the fourth-grade classroom too abstract for her?

We decided to read a picture book to Dorothy and ask her to retell the story. We selected *The Mysterious Tadpole* (Kellogg, 1977) because of its interesting plot, and the degree of abstractness would allow us to determine if she could understand the theme and the problem to be solved. We would also be able to determine if the number of plot episodes was appropriate for her recall abilities. We used a retelling checklist (see Figure 19.2) based on the information in *The Mysterious Tadpole* to evaluate Dorothy's comprehension.

The story was read to Dorothy using a directed listening–thinking activity (DL-TA). This is conducted like a directed reading–thinking activity (see Chapter 11), except the L-listening step is substituted for the R-reading step. At several points in the story, Dorothy predicted events and the teacher read on to confirm or deny the predictions. After reading the story to Dorothy, she was asked to retell it in her own words. Part way through the story retell she opened the book to help her recall the details.

Examine Figure 19.2 to familiarize yourself with the story, and then read the teacher–student discussion below.

TEACHER: What is a tadpole?

DOROTHY: A frog? A baby frog?

TEACHER: Tell me about this story.

DOROTHY: I liked it.

TEACHER: Tell me what happened in the story. What happened first?

DOROTHY: A guy brought a toad, no—a tadpole—to the kid's house, and then he brought him to the school, and then he went in the water. He dropped the garbage can down to him and he got it. Then he went home to go to bed and sleep. Kids wanted to go to swim. They ran out and he splashed water to the gym. (*She then reaches for the book and opens it to look at the pictures.*)

TEACHER: What kinds of water did the tadpole go in?

DOROTHY: Sink, bathtub, school gym pool. He—the boy, Louis—met a librarian.

TEACHER: Where did he take her?

DOROTHY: To the gym; tadpole got her purse from the water.

TEACHER: What else did Louis and the librarian do?

Directions: Indicate with numbers (starting with 1) the order of the information in the child's retelling.

Name _____ Date _____

1. Setting
    _____ A. Louis's apartment
    _____ B. Characters
    Louis, Alphonse, Mother, Father, Mrs. Shelbert (teacher),
    Miss Seevers (librarian), swimming coach, Uncle McAllister

2. Initiating Event
    _____ Uncle McAllister sent Louis a tadpole for his birthday.

3. Problem
    _____ Uncle McAllister sent Louis a tadpole for his birthday. The tadpole grew
    larger and larger, but it didn't turn into a frog. Louis had to find bigger and
    bigger water areas for the tadpole to live.

4. Attempts to Solve the Problem; Episodes
    Episode 1
    _____ Every year Uncle McAllister sent Louis a birthday present for his nature
    collection.
    _____ He sent Louis a tadpole this year.
    _____ Louis took his collection to school for show and tell.
    _____ Mrs. Shelbert showed the tadpole to the class.
    _____ Mrs. Shelbert asked Louis to bring the tadpole to school often, so they could
    watch it turn into a frog.

    Episode 2
    _____ Louis named the tadpole Alphonse.
    _____ Alphonse ate several cheeseburgers every day.
    _____ Alphonse wanted to learn.
    _____ He became too big for a jar and was moved to the sink.
    _____ He became too big for the sink and was moved to the bathtub.

    Episode 3
    _____ Mrs. Shelbert said that he wasn't an ordinary tadpole; he wasn't turning
    into a frog.
    _____ Mother said he was too big for the bathtub.
    _____ Father said he was too big for the apartment.
    _____ Louis said he needed a swimming pool.
    _____ There was no place in the apartment for a swimming pool.

    Episode 4
    _____ Louis wanted to buy the parking lot next door and build a swimming pool.
    _____ Louis's parents did not have enough money to buy the parking lot.
    _____ Louis's parents wanted to give the tadpole to the zoo.
    _____ Louis was very sad.
    _____ Louis put Alphonse in the junior high school pool for the summer.

    (*cont.*)

FIGURE 19.2. *Retelling general checklist:* The Mysterious Tadpole (*Kellogg, 1977*).

FIGURE 19.2 (cont.)

Episode 5

____ Louis spent every morning training Alphonse.

____ Louis earned money for Alphonse's cheeseburgers by delivering newspapers.

____ School reopened and the swimming coach found Alphonse in the pool.

____ The coach thought Alphonse was a submarine from another planet.

____ Coach told Louis to get rid of Alphonse by tomorrow.

Episode 6

____ Louis met Miss Seevers, the librarian.

____ Miss Seevers went to the pool to see Alphonse.

____ Miss Severs dropped her purse and books into the pool.

____ Alphonse retrieved them.

____ Miss Seevers called Uncle McAllister.

Episode 7

____ Uncle McAllister said that he found Alphonse near Loch Ness Lake.

____ Miss Seevers thinks that Alphonse is a Loch Ness monster.

____ Louis didn't care if he was a monster. Alphonse was his pet.

____ Louis asks Miss Seevers to help him raise money for a swimming pool for Alphonse.

____ Miss Seevers had an idea for Alphonse and Louis.

Episode 8

____ Miss Seevers told Louis about sunken treasure in the city's harbor.

____ Miss Seevers and Louis rented a boat.

____ Louis showed Alphonse a picture of the treasure chest.

____ Alphonse dove and looked for the treasure.

____ Alphonse found the treasure.

Episode 9

____ Louis and Miss Seevers bought the parking lot.

____ They hired people to build the pool.

____ They let all the children in the city swim in the pool.

____ Alphonse lived in the pool.

____ Alphonse had a home.

Episode 10

____ A year passed.

____ Uncle McAllister thought of Louis's birthday.

____ Uncle McAllister found an unusual stone.

____ Uncle McAllister brought the stone to Louis.

____ A crack appeared in the stone.

5. Result

____ Problem solved; Louis found a place for his tadpole Alphonse to live.

6. Reaction

____ Reaction to the ending, in which Uncle McAllister gives Louis another gift that will provide him with new problem-solving experiences.

Teacher comments:

(Dorothy looks for the picture that would help her answer this question but she cannot find it.)

TEACHER: Let's look at this picture. What is it?

DOROTHY: A ship. Went there. He showed the tadpole to go down and he found the treasure.

TEACHER: What did they do with the treasure? How did they use the treasure?

(Dorothy doesn't know. She is confused about the parking lot turning into a swimming pool.)

The teacher and Dorothy talked about the story again. They talked about building a pool next to Louis's apartment, but she did not seem to understand the idea.

The teacher asked Dorothy to retell the story once more. The following is her dictated story after looking at the pictures and discussing the story with the teacher:

"I heard this book about a tadpole, and that the tadpole was little, in a jar, and he was feeding the tadpole and he got bigger and bigger. He went in the sink, bathtub, and in the gym pool. And then they decided to bring the tadpole to where was the ship, and he could swim in the place, a lake, because it was so huge. He went underwater and got the treasure. They took the treasure and were taking out the gold to look at it. They were using it to buy a huge pool so the tadpole could swim around where the boat was underwater. Then he got a bird. Now he has two pets, a bird and a tadpole."

Reread the record of Dorothy's retelling. Evaluate Dorothy's retelling using the following three tools:

Retelling General Checklist: *The Mysterious Tadpole* (Figure 11.8)
Scoring Guide for Story Retelling (see the appendix)
Story Retelling—General Analysis Checklist (see the appendix)
Story Grammar Elements Record Sheet (see the appendix)

1. How would you evaluate Dorothy's retellings of the story?

    a. first retelling?
    b. retelling after teacher prompting?
    c. retelling by looking at pictures?
    d. dictated final retelling?

2. Based on this information, what suggestions would you give Dorothy's teachers?

SUMMARY

The case studies in this chapter present a picture of a variety of Stalled Readers and the literacy challenges they and their teachers face. Stalled Readers can achieve success in literacy acquisition, but the resources necessary for such success cannot be underestimated. Success can be achieved by carefully scaffolded instruction that is engaging and intensive and that is based on a clear understanding of the students' individual needs.

Chapter 20 provides a collection of resources that can be used to learn more about Stalled Readers and how to provide them with effective instruction and support.

Additional Resources
for Helping Stalled Readers

REVIEW OF PART THREE: STALLED READERS

Stalled Readers continue to require major teacher support and modeling to make gains in reading, despite effective instruction. Some may suffer from neurological impairments or severe maturational delays, whereas others fail to engage in the reading process for other reasons or have difficulty because of issues related to sociocultural factors. The key factor in distinguishing Stalled Readers from what Stanovich (2000) calls "the garden-variety poor reader" (which includes Catch-On and Catch-Up Readers) is the individual's response to instruction. When instructing Stalled Readers, teachers feel almost as if the students are learning nothing. In fact, Stalled Readers *can* learn to read, but high-quality, structured tutorial instruction is required.

The concept of Stalled Reader presented in this text differs dramatically from the traditional concept of a dyslexic child. In the traditional concept in place in most schools, dyslexia is diagnosed when a child's IQ predicts significantly higher performance than is demonstrated in a standardized reading test. The reading problem is presumed to have a constitutional cause, usually either neurological or developmental in nature. The solution usually suggested is an intensive, commercially published word-recognition curriculum that emphasizes letter–sound relationships and phonics rules.

Our concept of the Stalled Reader recognizes that severe reading and literacy difficulties arise from a variety of causes. In our decision making, we emphasize instruction rather than presumed constitutional factors. Intensive instruction is indeed required for the Stalled Reader, but only through close observation of the child under a variety of learning conditions can we determine which form that instruction should take. Word recognition is the key focus of intervention for most Stalled Readers, but teaching phonics in isolation must be supplemented by a rich language arts program that includes efforts to help the student transfer his/her word-recognition learning to actual reading and writing of text. Other Stalled Readers do not have word-recognition problems but do need intensive help to build their comprehension abilities.

To foster success in the intensive reading instruction and, at the same time, make it possible for these students to maintain success in content area learning, teachers and parents must support Stalled Readers in a variety of ways. Motivation and support on personal, social, and vocational levels must be part of the plan of action.

KEY RESEARCH, THEORY, AND METHODS RELATED TO STALLED READERS

Carver, R. P. (2000). *The causes of high and low reading achievement*. Mahwah, NJ: Erlbaum.

Carver's work on the rauding theory is briefly explained in Chapter 8 and annotated in Chapter 14. His text includes a survey of research on the dyslexia subtypes that have been proposed by other researchers as well a detailed analysis of the matching subtypes in his own model. As is the case in other important research and theory on the topic, the categorization system is based on assessments. (In contrast, in this text we categorize students according to instructional focus; in the traditional field of special education, a presumed but hard-to-measure constitutional condition is seen as the major causative factor.)

According to Carver, students who score low on decoding assessments but do well on general language tests are "mild dyslexics." Severe dyslexics also do well on general language tests, but they score low both on decoding assessments and on aptitude tests related to cognitive speed (such as timed tasks that require speeded identification of colors or digits).

Stanovich, K. E. (2000). *Progress in understanding reading: Scientific foundations and new frontiers*. New York: Guilford Press.

Stanovich's work is described in Chapter 8 and annotated in Chapter 14. His chapter on "Explaining the Differences between the Dyslexic and the Garden-Variety Poor Reader: The Phonological-Core Variable-Difference Model" provides details on his survey of research on dyslexic readers:

> Many investigators have located the proximal locus of dyslexia at the word recognition level. . . . It is now well established that dyslexic children display deficits in various aspects of phonological processing. They have difficulty making explicit reports about sound segments at the phoneme level, they display naming difficulties, their utilization of phonological codes in short-term memory is inefficient, and their categorical perception of certain phonemes may be other than normal. . . . Presumably their lack of phonological sensitivity makes the learning of grapheme-to-phoneme correspondences very difficult. (p. 114)

Falk-Ross, F. C. (2002). *Classroom-based language and literacy intervention*. Boston: Allyn & Bacon.

This collection of detailed case studies focuses on three elementary-grade boys, each of whom is classified as learning disabled due to prolonged academic difficulties. In all three cases, the boys have expressive language difficulties in that they have serious trouble participating in such tasks as class discussion and answering teacher questions. When encountering words during oral reading, they frequently miscue, offering a substitute word instead of the target word. Expressive language deficits are associated with lack of academic progress in both reading and writing as well as with socialization difficulties.

This text provides detailed transcripts of discussions in which student difficulties with language are evident. The case studies follow the intervention procedures, which were carried out in the students' regular classrooms, with strong collaboration between the classroom teachers and the consulting teacher.

Oldfather, P. (Ed.). (2002). How and why should we learn from students about overcoming motivation problems in literacy learning? *Reading and Writing Quarterly, 18*(3).

Motivation is a central concern when working with Stalled Readers. This themed issue of *Reading and Writing Quarterly* focuses on motivating struggling readers. In the research studies presented, two themes appear to be consistently interwoven with the findings:

1. Relationships between teachers and struggling readers, and among the struggling readers themselves, play a central part in the learning culture.
2. Emphasis must be placed on helping struggling readers construct self-identities as engaged and successful literacy learners.

Lyon, G. R., Fletcher, J. M., Shaywitz, S. E., Shaywitz, B. A., Torgesen, J. K., Wood, F. B., Schulte, A., & Olson, R. (2001). Rethinking learning disabilities. In C. E. Finn, A. J. Rotherham, & C. R. Hokanson (Eds.), *Rethinking special education for a new century* (pp. 259–287). Washington, DC: Thomas B. Fordham Foundation.

The authors provide important perspectives on both the history of special education and current research that points in new directions for assessment and instruction of learning disabled students. They review research that suggests that there is no verifiable difference between the two major school populations of struggling readers: the students classified as learning disabled in reading, and the students who are also struggling readers but have not been classified (often called "compensatory students"). Differentiation of instruction between the two populations is not validated by research.

They suggest that early intervention reading programs could decrease the number of struggling readers by 70%. Reading programs for older struggling readers should be designed to provide intensive instruction and rapid improvement so that students can rejoin their peers in reading and studying content area material.

MATERIALS AND CURRICULA FOR STALLED READERS

Sample Teacher Dialogue for Phonogram Instruction

Glass-Analysis presented one of the first widely received instructional patterns for phonogram instruction (Glass & Glass, 1994), but these are widely available today. The dialogue below represents a sample standardized script for introducing new word families. The script can be adapted for older, more advanced students by taking out some components. Glass and Glass (1994) suggested that intensive phonogram instruction be carried out 5 days a week, for 2 daily sessions of 20 minutes each. At the beginning of instruction, teachers might plan to introduce a new phonogram family every fourth session, but this rhythm will vary with each child. Regular review is necessary.

The order of the script's components can be changed. For example, a teacher might find it more motivational to start with the list of words using the phonogram, so that the student recognizes the usefulness of the lesson in reading.

As with all scripted lesson patterns, the first few times through this lesson tend to be a bit awkward, since both the teacher (if the method is new to him/her) and the student are unused to it. After that, the lessons flow smoothly and quickly. Although instructional time is precious, do not hesitate to customize the lesson to reflect student interests and to respond to student comments. A relaxed, personal atmosphere will add to the lesson's power.

Phonemes and phoneme groups—the actual sounds—are represented with slashes.

Preparation

Choose a phonogram pattern to be introduced to the student. The choice can come from a suggested list (see Letter Clusters and Rimes in the appendix) but may be even more profitably chosen from a story that the child has read or has listened to read aloud.

Make a card with the word printed neatly. Choose other words that use the phonogram pattern and make cards for those as well. In addition, make a poster with words that use the phonogram pattern, with shorter words on the top and longer ones on the bottom. A good way to find words sharing the same phonogram is to use a word-processing "find" feature on several documents.

Write meaningful sentences that use the words on a poster or on sentence strip paper.

Method

1. Show the card and say, "This word is *sand*. Please say the word with me: *sand . . . sand . . . sand*."
2. Ask: "What letters are in this word?"
   Reply: "*S . . . a . . . n . . . d*"
3. Ask: "What letter makes the /s/ sound? /s/ . . . /s/ . . . /s/?
   Reply: "The letter *s*." (Note: If the onset is a blend or digraph, ask for the sound of the blend or digraph rather than the separate letter sounds.)
4. Ask: "What letters make the /and/ sound? /and/ . . . /and/ . . . /and/
   Reply: "The letters *a, n,* and *d*."
5. Instruction: "That's right. The letters *a, n,* and *d* make the /and/ sound. Today, we are going to study the /and/ sound that occurs in words." (Note: Since /and/ actually constitutes a word in itself, the teacher should point this out. Most phonograms do not constitute words in themselves.)
6. Ask: "What sounds does each of the letters in /and/ make?"
   Reply: "The *a* makes the /a/ sound, the *n* makes the /n/ sound, and the *d* makes the /d/ sound." (Note: Some phonogram approaches avoid stressing the separate phoneme sounds within the phonogram; this has been called "cluster busting." All, however, do emphasize the sound of the word's onset—in this case, /s/.)

7. Instruction: "In the word *sand*, the letter *s* makes the /s/ sound and the letters *a-n-d* make the /and/ sound."

8. Ask: "Can you say the word that we would get if we sound these two sounds together: /s/ . . . /and/, /s/ . . . /and/?
   Reply: "/S/ . . . /and/ makes *sand*."

9. Review by asking: "What is this word?" Show the card.
   Reply: "Sand."

10. Ask: "If I take away the /s/ sound, what sound do I have?"
    Reply: "/and/."

11. Review these preceding steps as many times as necessary, until the student can identify the word when shown the card.

12. Present a list of words using the phonogram, with the easiest on top and the more difficult toward the bottom. The teacher says each word aloud, as in:
    "*Band*. The *b* makes the /b/ sound and the *a, n, d* make the /and/ sound."
    (Note: The student may be able to read some of the words and word parts, if asked.)

band	land	hand	
grand	brand	stand	
candy	handy	sandwich	candle
bland	standardized	dander	pander

(Note: The less familiar words at the bottom would be omitted for most Stalled Readers.)

13. Present sentences using the phonogram words on poster paper or on sentence strip paper. The student reads the sentences. Provide help, as necessary. If the student is hesitant in reading the sentence, have him/her repeat the reading two or three times.

   The band had to stand with candles.

   Each cow in the land had a brand.

(Note: You may want to preview some words from the sentences, as review or new sight words, to help the student recognize them when they occur. For example, in the sentences above, the words *to, in,* and *the* might be reviewed and the word *had* introduced for the first time.)

14. When reading the sentences at this stage, or when reading a book later, follow the same procedure as introduced in the earlier steps if a word with the target phonogram cannot be decoded.

   "Where is the *a, n, d*? What sound do those letters make?"
   "What is the first letter? What sound does that letter make?"
   "Can you put them together?"

   Or

   "What sound do we have when we take the _____ off? What is the whole word?"

15. Use the word cards for the other words from the list. Follow the same procedures used above in steps 1–11.

16. As future phonograms are introduced, emphasize that students are learning a strategy for word recognition, not simply lists of words.

Sample Teacher Dialogue for Orton-Type Instruction

Samuel Orton (1937) suggested that a multisensory approach to reading was needed for struggling readers—an approach that emphasized sound–symbol relationships as well as sight-word development. Although the program is generally considered to be phonics-based, the ultimate goal is the development of automatic word recognition and comprehension. The instructional sequence starts with letters and sounds. The students progress to reading phonetically regular words and finally stories in which specific phonic elements are included.

Presently, there are several reading programs that utilize the approach originally pioneered by Orton. Most of these programs maintain the multisensory approach, with emphasis placed on learning sound–symbol relations, sound-blending techniques, and spelling rules. Additionally, scripted lessons are usually included to ensure uniformity of approach. The highly repetitive lesson formats introduce phonic elements in prescribed sequences, with mastery as the expected outcome.

Students learn consonants and vowel letter–sound relationships as they begin the program. Sound blending and spelling are introduced as soon as enough letter–sounds have been introduced to form phonetically regular words. More complex phonic elements, such as consonant blends and digraphs, long and short vowels, vowel digraphs and diphthongs, syllabication skills, and dictionary usage are taught in a prescribed sequence. Repetition and practice guide the development of a sight-word vocabulary of both phonetically regular and irregular words. Mastery of reading and spelling is a key element in the program. Spelling, spelling rules, and dictation are essential to all lessons.

Learning Letter Names and Sounds; Writing Letter Names

1. Show printed cards containing the consonants and vowels to be taught in the day's lesson. (Note: Letters can be written on the board by the teacher. Some programs provide large wall cards that can be seen by the whole class.)

   Holding up one card at a time, the teacher says, "What does this letter say? (or "What is this letter?"). What sound does it say?" All cards are presented in this way.

2. Say the sound associated with each card's letter. In this section of the lesson, the students do not see the cards:

   "What is the name of the letter that says /k/?"
   "What is the name of the letter that says /a/?"
   The students respond with the name of the letter.

3. Handwriting instruction helps students associate the name of the letter with its printed form:

   "Today we're going to learn to make the letter *b*. Watch as I make a straight line. Now I am attaching a circle after the line. Use my model to trace this letter *b* on your paper. Now copy the letter. (Note: If you are working in a group, you might have each student go to the board to individually copy the letter. Describe the printed strokes as each is made.) Next, write the letter without looking at the model. Finally, close your eyes and write the letter without looking at your paper."

4. Give students practice in writing the letters that have been introduced in the lesson.

> "Write the letter that says /k/."
> "Write the letter than says /a/."

Blending Sounds to Form Words

Once sufficient sounds have been introduced to the beginning students, the next step is to practice blending sounds.

1. Place letter cards on the table to spell a simple word, such as *bat*.
2. Instruction: "Say the sounds of the letters. Say the sounds again."
   Response: "/b/ /a/ /t/. /b/ /a/ /t/."
3. Ask: "What word are you saying?"
4. If the student does not respond correctly, say: "Try to put the first two letters together."
   Response: "/b/—/a/."
   As the child blends the sounds, move your hand, as a pointer, underneath the sounds. A sliding motion of the hand can be associated with blending.
5. Instruction: "Now add the third sound to the first two."

Spelling Words

1. Instruction: "Listen carefully. I am going to say a word very slowly: /b/- /a/ - /t/, /b/-/a/-/t/.
2. Ask: "What sound do you hear first?"
   Response: "/b/."
3. Say: "Yes, /b/. What letter says /b/?"
   Response: "*B*."
4. Say: "Yes. Find the *b* card and put it on your desk."
5. Ask: "What sound do you hear next?"
   Response: "/a/."
6. Say: "Yes, /a/. What letter says /a/?"
   Response: "*A*."
7. Say: "Yes. Find the *a* card and place it after the *b*."
8. Ask: "What is the last sound you hear?"
   Response: "/t/."
9. Say: "Yes, /t/. What letter says /t/?"
   Response: "*T*."
10. Say: "Yes. Place the *t* card after the *a*."
11. Say: "Write the word on your paper. As you write it, say the letters aloud."
12. Ask: "Now, can you read the word aloud for me?"
    Response: "/bat/."

Sentence and Story Reading

The student learns to read several three-letter, phonetically regular words with ease. Each of the words is composed of letters and sounds that have been taught in instructional sessions.

At this point, the words are combined into sentences and stories. The sentences and stories are not intended to entertain a reader or provide meaningful content. They are intended to provide practice in reading words that can be sounded out. Possible instruction:

"Read the sentence to yourself until you are ready to read it aloud. Remember to read the sentence as if you were talking to someone. Ask for help if you cannot figure out a word."

Dictation

Dictation should be a part of every lesson. The dictation can be a letter sound, a word, a phrase, or a sentence. Break sentences into word or phrase units to help students recall the message. Possible instruction:

"I am going to say a sentence. Write the words you hear. Think about the sounds in each word. Now, write this sentence: 'The pig sat on a mat.' What word should you write first? Yes, *The*. Write it now. What was the next word in the sentence? Yes, *pig*. Write it now."

Continue in this way until all of the words have been written.

Technology Resources for Stalled Readers

Internet Sites

International Reading Association—*http://www.reading.org*

The International Reading Association is one of the nation's largest and most influential professional teaching organizations. Its comprehensive website includes news articles on current events dealing with reading and literacy issues, conference information, and a listing of IRA's extensive publications. A topics and issues section includes material on, for example, urban education, assessment, and language and cultural diversity. A links section lists many websites that address issues such as readers with special needs and English as a second language.

International Dyslexia Association—*http://interdys.org*

The IDA is a professional organization that has long advocated the unitary causation viewpoints espoused originally by Samuel Orton. They suggest that some 15–20% of students suffer from a constitutional condition that interferes with word recognition, a condition they refer to as dyslexia, a specific learning disability in language. The organization advocates the use of Orton methods for remediation of dyslexia. IDA's policies and philosophies have long stood in contrast to those of the much larger International Reading Association, which promotes a more open viewpoint about reading and literacy instruction. IRA suggests that reading and literacy difficulties can arise from a variety of causes and that curricular choices should be made that lead to literacy-rich language arts experiences that are based on the individual needs of students.

Reading and Writing Quarterly—http://www.tandf.co.uk/journals/tf/10573569.html

This journal provides research that focuses on students with serious reading and literacy difficulties. Quarterly issues often have a thematic emphasis on a specific aspect of supplying instruction to at-risk learners, such as writing difficulties, parent communication, or assessment. Each issue of the journal includes a column, edited by Ernest Balajthy, dealing with "Issues in Technology." These columns can be accessed at the column's website: *http://www.geneseo.edu/~balajthy/publications/rwq.*

Commercial Curricula

"Glass-Analysis for Decoding Only"—Easier-To-Learn, P.O. Box 259, Blue Point, NY 11715, 631-475-7693. Online: *http://www.glassanalysis.com*

Glass-Analysis for Decoding Only is described in Chapter 16. It is a word recognition curriculum that focuses on the use of word families, or phonograms, to teach decoding. Glass-Analysis has been in use for many years as an alternative to most other decoding curricula, which emphasize individual letter sounds. The curriculum includes a teacher's manual (*Glass-Analysis for Decoding Only: Teacher Guide*, by Gerald G. Glass and Esther W. Glass. Blue Point, NY: Easier-To-Learn), workbooks, and kits of word cards that have been categorized into letter-cluster families. Materials for alphabet learning and for the very beginnings of decoding (*Easy Starts*) are also available.

"Gillingham–Stillman Method"—Educators Publishing Service, 31 Smith Place, Cambridge, MA 02138, 800-435-7728. Online: *http://www.epsbooks.com*

The Gillingham–Stillman Method is described in Chapter 16 as an Orton approach to reading instruction that emphasizes letter-by-letter decoding and synthesizing of sounds together to form words. Although the use of multiple modalities in teaching reading has become commonplace, Orton approaches (Orton,1937) pioneered the way for its use. The key resource for understanding the Gillingham–Stillman Method is *Remedial Training for Children with Specific Disability in Reading, Spelling, and Penmanship,* by Anna Gillingham and Bessie Stillman (Cambridge, MA: Educators Publishing Service, 1973).

Gillingham was an associate of Samuel Orton, working with him to develop educational materials and as a teacher educator. The approach they developed was called the Orton–Gillingham Method at one time. Later, Stillman played an important role in revising and updating the curriculum. In a sense, the Gillingham–Stillman method is the "official" Orton approach, though a variety of curricula based on Orton's ideas is on the market today. The Academy of Orton–Gillingham Practitioners and Educators maintains a website at *http://www.ortonacademy.org.*

"Slingerland Approach"—Educators Publishing Service, 31 Smith Place, Cambridge, MA 02138, 800-435-7728. Online: *http://www.epsbooks.com*

The Gillingham–Stillman method is designed for individual tutoring and small groups. Beth H. Slingerland carried out a major revision that adapted the basic principles of the curriculum for whole class instruction. The key resource is Slingerland's *A Multi-Sensory Ap-*

proach to Language Arts for Specific Learning Disabled Children: The Slingerland Approach (Cambridge, MA: Educators Publishing Service, 1976).

"Benchmark Reading"—Benchmark School, 2107 North Providence Road, Media PA 19063, 610-565-3741. Online: *http://www.benchmarkschool.org*

The Benchmark School, near Philadelphia, has established itself as a national leader in working with readers struggling with serious challenges. It is a private school dedicated to incorporating interventional reading instruction throughout the curriculum. Its founder, Irene Gaskins, has carried out extensive research and development on the word-recognition curriculum used at the school and marketed nationally. The approach emphasizes learning by analogy (see Chapter 16).

"Wilson Reading System"—Wilson Language Training Corporation, 175 West Main Street, Millbury, MA 01527, 508-865-5699. Online: *http://www.wilsonlanguage.com*

This approach updated the Orton method with making words, reading aloud to students at a level beyond their instructional comfort, and a heavy emphasis on reading actual text rather than words in isolation. The texts are provided by the publisher and are prescribed at each level to make sure that students are reading material that contains only language elements that have already been taught (commonly known as decodable text).

The Wilson system includes student workbooks and readers with words, sentences, and very short stories. A placement test can be administered to determine where individual students need to begin in the program. The key resource in the program is the *Wilson Reading System Instructor Manual*, by Barbara A. Wilson (Millbury, MA: Wilson Language Training Corporation, 1996).

SUMMARY

Stalled Readers have reading achievement levels that are well below those of their peers, despite consistent intervention instruction. Often they face tremendous difficulties in word-recognition, but some have advanced beyond the word recognition developmental level and have problems with fluency or with comprehension. They are the most seriously impaired of the three types of struggling readers we have studied in this book.

Most other approaches to classifying these seriously affected readers tend to place the blame on the students themselves, suggesting that they have some physiologically based disability that may be at least partially genetic in nature. In our text, however, we define the difference between Stalled Readers, the students most unlikely to succeed in standard interventions, and the less seriously affected Catch-On and Catch-Up Readers in terms of instruction. Stalled Readers require a degree of intervention that is, for most teachers and parents, startlingly more extensive than usual intervention and remediation programs offered by schools.

Assessment Devices

APPENDIX OUTLINE

Master Cover Sheet for Cumulative Record

A. Biographical Information

Name _____ Date of birth _____

Parents' names _____

_____

Address _____

_____

Phone _____

Place of birth _____ Age at school entrance _____

Parents' occupations:

Father _____ Place of work _____

_____ Phone _____

Mother _____ Place of work _____

_____ Phone _____

Parents' marital status and approximate dates:

Married _____ Separated _____ Single _____

Divorced _____ Mother or father remarried _____

Siblings:

Name	Date of birth	Sex

In case of emergency call:

Name _____ Address _____

_____ Phone _____

Is there a second language spoken in the home? _____

If so, what language? _____

Schools attended:

School	Address	Dates

(cont.)

Present school: _____

_____

B. Health Record

Vision:

Name of test	Date	Results

_____

_____

Hearing:

Name of test	Date	Results

_____

_____

_____

Allergy _____ Description _____
Special diet _____
Medication _____ Reason _____
Surgeries (describe in detail) _____

Serious illness or accidents

Date   Description

_____

_____

Comments (i.e., physical activity, playground, etc.): _____

_____

C. Academic Record:

Grade	1	2	3	4	5
Social Studies					
Science					
Arithmetic					
Reading					
Spelling					
Art					
Music					
Handwriting					
Physical Education					
Absences					

Code: S = Satisfactory, U = Unsatisfactory, NA = Not applicable

(cont.)

D. Testing and Assessment

Early reading/Emergent literacy:

Name of test	Date	Grade	Percentile rank	Stanine

Achievement:

Name of test	Date	Grade	Percentile rank	Stanine

Intelligence/Aptitude:

Name of test	Date	Grade	Percentile rank	Stanine

Special services:

Speech: Dates _____ Description _____

_____

Counseling: Dates _____ Description _____

_____

Special math: Dates _____ Description _____

_____

Special reading: Dates _____ Description _____

_____

Diagnosis/tutoring outside of school setting:_____

_____

Observations of Recreational Reading Form

Student name _____

Observed by _____ Dates _____

Occasions student observed reading recreationally:

Before school _____

Free periods/lunch periods _____

During instruction _____

After school _____

Recreational reading behaviors/attitudes:

	Not much		A great deal
Likes to read	1	2	3
Shares/recommends reading	1	2	3
Developing author/topic preferences	1	2	3

Recreational Reading Preferences (include authors, if possible)

Fiction series:

Humorous:

Newspapers/Magazines:

Instruction manuals/How-to-do-it:

Comic books:

Other fiction:

Other nonfiction:

Comments:

Checklist of Reading Behaviors

Student name _____

Observed by _____ Date _____

I. Word Recognition (words previously encountered)

Adequate recognition of basic sight words _____

Adequate recognition of sight words common to pupil's grade level _____

Analyzes words when necessary _____

Guesses at words based on:

- Initial letter _____
- Final letter _____
- Shape/configuration _____
- Preceding context _____
- Middle of word _____

Miscues include nonwords _____

II. Word Identification (unknown words)

Uses initial cue _____

Uses middle cues (e.g., vowels) _____

Uses final cue _____

Uses consonant blends and digraphs (e.g., *fl*, *sh*) _____

Uses short vowels _____

Uses long vowels, silent *e* _____

Blends individual sounds to form words _____

Blends sound units to form words (e.g., *an*, *est*, *op*) _____

Visually recognizes sound units _____

III. Language Cues

Uses context to figure out an unknown word (e.g., substitutes a word of similar meaning) _____

Substitutions make sense grammatically and semantically up to point of miscue _____

Substitutions make sense grammatically and semantically after miscue _____

Reads words correctly in passages that were miscued in word lists _____

Passages are read at higher level than word lists _____

Passages are read at lower level than word lists _____

Miscues affect comprehension of passage _____

(cont.)

IV. Rate and Fluency

Reads instructional-level passage at adequate rate (e.g., not too fast, not too slow, rhythmical) _____

Reads independent-level passage in conversational tones _____

Silent rate equal to or faster than oral (for students in grade 3 and above) _____

Reads at a very slow rate _____

Reads at a very fast rate _____

Uses punctuation appropriately _____

Ignores punctuation or inserts punctuation at inappropriate places _____

V. Mannerisms and Behaviors

Stops reading to discuss selection or an inappropriate topic _____

Reads in an unnatural voice tone _____

Shows signs of nervousness (e.g. leg shaking, head movement, whispering, other) _____

Finger pointing:

- Under words _____
- Above words _____
- Both under and above _____

Mumbling/slurring words (e.g., examiner can't understand pupil) _____

Reads in flat tones (i.e., little expression) _____

Obvious lip movement during silent reading _____

VI. Comprehension

Comprehension matches word-recognition levels _____

Comprehension higher than word-recognition levels _____

Comprehension lower than word-recognition levels _____

Comprehension higher for oral than silent reading _____

Comprehension higher for silent than oral reading _____

Comprehension shows difficulty with types of questions:

- Factual _____
- Inferential _____
- Vocabulary-related _____
- Evaluative _____
- About main idea _____
- About background experiences _____

Listening comprehension higher than reading comprehension _____

Listening comprehension lower than reading comprehension _____

Observation Checklist of Response to Reading and Writing

Student name _____

Observed by _____

	Always	Sometimes	Never
General			
Responses coincide with main contents of story	___	___	___
Responses deal adequately with literal-level story elements—plot, characters	___	___	___
Responses deal adequately with interpretive-level story elements—theme, tone	___	___	___
Responses deal adequately with applied-level story elements—judgment, appreciation	___	___	___
Appropriate emotional response to reading: laughing, crying	___	___	___
Uses personal experiences in interpreting text	___	___	___
Makes connections between present and past reading experiences	___	___	___
Makes text-based and reader-based predictions	___	___	___
Uses text to verify interpretations	___	___	___
Oral	___	___	___
Responses are vague/lacking richness, Few ideas included	___	___	___
Goes beyond "I liked it" type reactions	___	___	___
Generates questions and seeks help when needed	___	___	___
Teacher input required	___	___	___
Responses are animated, showing interest	___	___	___
Adequate security/self-image to conjecture and guess	___	___	___
Shares reading experience with peers	___	___	___
Written	___	___	___
Responses are vague/lacking richness; few ideas included	___	___	___
Writes in response to literature without prompting/enforcement	___	___	___
Connects personal experience to readings	___	___	___
Uses story structure in personal stories	___	___	___

From *Struggling Readers* by Ernest Balajthy and Sally Lipa-Wade. Copyright 2003 by The Guilford Press.

Monitoring Intervention Strategies

Student name _____ Grade _____

Clinician name _____ Date _____

Desired outcomes	Procedures	Actual outcomes

Recording and Categorizing
Reading/Literacy Needs

Student name _____ Grade _____

Clinician name _____ Date _____

Areas of need	Areas of strength

Checklist for Oral Language Assessment

Student name _____

Observed by _____ Date _____

	Yes	No
1. Does the child mimic adult utterances?	____	____
2. Does the child overuse nonverbal language such as pointing or gesturing?	____	____
3. Does the child construct utterances as the need arises?	____	____
4. Does the child respond to adult attempts to clarify or expand the child's utterances?	____	____
5. (a) Does the child speak in words or phrases?	____	____
(b) Does the child speak in sentences?	____	____
6. (a) Does the child name objects using ambiguous terms, such as "it," "the," "ya know"?	____	____
(b) Does the child name objects using specific, descriptive labels?	____	____
7. (a) Does the child mumble?	____	____
(b) Does the child speak clearly?	____	____

Grouped High-Frequency Words

Persons
father
mother
son
daughter
girl
boy
dad
mom
baby
child
aunt
uncle

Numbers
one
two
three
four
five
six
seven
eight
nine
ten

Vocations
teacher
police officer
nurse
doctor
mail carrier

Toys
toy
doll
ball
bat
game

Food
bread
jelly
cereal
meat
water
milk
juice
soda
pop

Meals
plate
fork
knife
spoon
bowl
cup
glass

Fruit
fruit
orange
grapes
peach
plum
apple
banana

Home
chair
sofa
bed
pillow
blanket
table
desk

Animals
cat
dog
bird
fish
horse
duck
chicken
cow
pig

School
pen
pencil
paper
notebook
computer
book
letter
word

Transportation
car
truck
plane
jet
boat
bus
ship

Neighborhood
house
home
street
bush
flower
grass
tree

High-Frequency Words

a	can	help
about	come	her
after	could	here
again	day	him
all	did	his
am	do	house
an	done	how
and	don't	hurt
any	down	I
animal	drink	if
are	each	in
as	eat	into
ask	eight	is
at	find	it
away	first	jump
be	five	just
because	fly	kind
been	for	know
before	found	like
best	four	line
big	from	little
black	get	live
blue	give	long
boy	go	look
brown	good	made
but	green	make
buy	had	many
by	has	may
call	have	me
came	he	more

(cont.)

mother	say	try
much	see	two
must	seven	up
my	she	us
name	show	use
new	six	very
no	small	want
not	so	was
now	some	way
of	stop	we
off	take	well
old	tell	went
on	ten	were
one	than	what
only	thank	when
or	that	where
other	the	which
our	their	white
out	them	who
over	then	why
people	there	will
play	these	with
pretty	they	work
put	thing	would
read	think	write
red	this	yellow
ride	those	you
right	three	your
run	time	
said	to	
saw	too	

Letter Clusters and Rimes

-ack	-ear	-is(s)
-ake	-eat	-it
-al (as in *pal*)	-el(l)	-ock
-al(l) (as in *tall*)	-en	-oke
-ale	-er	-ook
-ame	-est	-op
-an	-ice	-or
-ank	-ick	-ore
-ap	-ide	-ot
-ash	-ight	-ou (as in *shout*)
-as(s)	-il(l)	-uck
-at	-in	-ug
-ate	-ing	-un
-aw	-ink	
-ay	-ip	

Letter Name/Sound Test: Student Form

A. Upper Case Letter Names

Z   J   U   H   C   W

X   Q   K   V   Y   N

O   I   A   B   S   C

D   F   E   P   T   M

L   R

B. Lower Case Letter Names

r   o   h   l   m   y

t   v   k   p   z   i

a   j   u   s   v   b

c   q   w   d   f   x

g   e

(cont.)

C. Letter Sounds

b   n   s   f   h   k

l   t   m   g   c   p

y   r   d   w   j   v

z   y   a   e   l   o

u   q

Letter Name/Sound Test: Teacher Form

Student name _____

Administered by _____ Date _____

A. Upper Case Letter Names

Directions: Look at the letters that are printed here. Tell me the name of each letter.

Z ___   J ___   U ___   H ___   C ___   W ___

X ___   Q ___   K ___   V ___   Y ___   N ___

O ___   I ___   A ___   B ___   S ___   C ___

D ___   F ___   E ___   P ___   T ___   M ___

L ___   R ___

B. Lower Case Letter Names

Directions: Look at the letters that are printed here. Tell me the name of each letter.

r ___   o ___   h ___   l ___   m ___   y ___

t ___   v ___   k ___   p ___   z ___   i ___

a ___   j ___   u ___   s ___   v ___   b ___

c ___   q ___   w ___   d ___   f ___   x ___

g ___   e ___

C. Letter Sounds

Directions: These letters make sounds. Say the sound of the letter I point to, or say a word that starts with the same sound as the letter I point to.

b ___   n ___   s ___   f ___   h ___   k ___

l ___   t ___   m ___   g ___   c ___   p ___

y ___   r ___   d ___   w ___   j ___   v ___

z ___   y ___   a ___   e ___   l ___   o ___

u ___   q ___

Scoring Summary

	Correct/Possible
Letter names (upper case)	_____/26
Letter names (lower case)	_____/26
Letter sounds	_____/26

From *Struggling Readers* by Ernest Balajthy and Sally Lipa-Wade. Copyright 2003 by The Guilford Press.

Lipa Logo Test—Scoring Guide

Name _____ Birthdate: _____ Age:_____

Date of test: _____ School: _____

+ Correct response   − Incorrect response

	Logo		Word	
Item	Generic	Specific	Generic	Specific
1. Pepsi	_____	_____	_____	_____
2. M and M	_____	_____	_____	_____
3. McDonald's	_____	_____	_____	_____
4. Coke	_____	_____	_____	_____
5. Bubble Yum	_____	_____	_____	_____
6. Burger King	_____	_____	_____	_____
7. Kool Aid	_____	_____	_____	_____
8. Crayola	_____	_____	_____	_____
9. Spaghetti-O's	_____	_____	_____	_____
10. Play Doh	_____	_____	_____	_____
11. Hershey's	_____	_____	_____	_____
12. Fruit Loops	_____	_____	_____	_____
Totals	_____	_____	_____	_____

Teachers create this assessment with pictures from advertisements representing the different items (e.g., golden arches for McDonald's) that are pasted on file cards. The assessment can be updated by choosing alternative logos.

From *Struggling Readers* by Ernest Balajthy and Sally Lipa-Wade. Copyright 2003 by The Guilford Press.

Miscue Inventory Chart

Student name _____

Observed by _____ Date _____

Age _____ Grade _____

	Target word	Miscue	Graphophonemic	Syntactic	Semantic
1.					
2.					
3.					
4.					
5.					
6.					
7.					
8.					
9.					
10.					

Print Awareness Checklist

Student name _____ Age _____ Grade _____

Observed by _____ Date _____

The child . . .	Yes	No	Developing
1. Recognizes common logos and signs (e.g., cut-out logos and signs such as McDonald's, Pepsi, Play Doh) when asked, "What is this?"	___	___	___
2. Attends to and discusses pictures on a page.	___	___	___
3. Recognizes a "favorite" story book.	___	___	___
4. Identifies a "favorite" story by name.	___	___	___
5. Self-selects a story book to be read.	___	___	___
6. Points to objects in the pictures when asked (e.g., "Can you find the moon?")	___	___	___
7. Helps with page turning when asked.	___	___	___
8. Opens book at the beginning of story.	___	___	___
9. Shows the reader a favorite part of story.	___	___	___
10. Demonstrates knowledge of left-to-right progression of reading.	___	___	___
11. Follows print while story is read.			
• By pointing to words as they are read.	___	___	___
• With eyes	___	___	___
12. Joins in the reading by completing a phrase, saying a rhyming word, etc.	___	___	___
13. Demonstrates knowledge that words on a page represent the story that is being read.	___	___	___
14. "Reads" by saying the gist of the story after it becomes a "familiar" one.	___	___	___
15. Is aware of punctuation; recognizes			
• Period (.)	___	___	___
• Question mark (?)	___	___	___
• Exclamation point (!)	___	___	___
16. Understands the difference between letters and numbers.	___	___	___
17. Understands the difference between single letters and words.	___	___	___
18. Identifies capital and lowercase letters of those that have been taught.	___	___	___
19. Can retell stories by			
• Looking at the pictures	___	___	___
• Remembering	___	___	___
20. Retells story with a beginning/middle/end.	___	___	___
21. Recalls characters and episodes in stories.	___	___	___
22. Retells story, including several episodes, in correct sequence.	___	___	___

Running Record Summary Sheet

Name _____

Grade _____ Age _____

Observed by _____ Date _____

Type of text: Very familiar _____ Familiar (current)_____ Unfamiliar _____

Title of story: _____

Author _____

Reading level determined to be: Easy _____ Instructional _____ Hard _____

Oral reading: Examining particulars

1. Count the # of running words (RW)   _____

2. Count the # of miscues (M)   _____

3. Count the # of self-corrects (SC)   _____

4. Determine the rate of miscues (MR)   1:_____
      MR = RW/M

5. Determine the self-correct rate (SCR)   1:_____
      SCR = $\underline{M + SC}$
                SC

6. Determine the % of running text that is correctly read   _____%
      RW – M/RW x (100/1) = % correct

Comments:

Miscue patterns_____

Rate and fluency_____

Physical behaviors (sighing, pauses, finger pointing, etc.)_____

Sight-Word Monitoring Form

Student name _____

Date

Sight word													
1													
2													
3													
4													
5													
6													
7													
8													
9													
10													
11													
12													
13													
14													
15													
16													
17													
18													

Sample Cloze Assessment

Original Selection Used for Cloze Passage

The Horse

The origin of the horse can be traced back millions of years ago to a small animal who stood about 14 inches high. Fossils of what is known as the dawn horse have been found in North America and Europe. The horse changed gradually over the years until what is known as the primitive horse evolved. The primitive horse more closely resembled the horse we know today. Four types of primitive horses have been found. These include the Forest Horse, the Asian Wild Horse, the Tarpan, and the Tundra Horse. Horses have been a part of man's culture throughout the centuries. Early in their evolution, they were a source of food for man. As horses gained in size, they were used to carry man, and to pull vehicles, such as the Roman chariots. Because of their speed and endurance, they opened up communication with other tribes and groups who lived some distance away.

The horse is also known for taking man into battle. Genghis Khan's successful conquests throughout Asia were, in part, because of the horse. The Mongols became proficient horseback riders, learning to maneuver their horses through many obstacles and to effectively use weapons while riding. Horses continued to be used in battle throughout the centuries. The Holy Wars were fought on horseback as were many of Napoleon's conquests. Much later, the United States Cavalry and American Indians fought many of their battles on horseback.

Early in history, man found that horses could be tamed to work for them, to carry them swiftly across lands, and to provide them with food. Great leaders such as Alexander the Great often established special bonds with their horses. Bucephalus, Alexander the Great's horse, only allowed Alexander to ride him when he was outfitted with his harness and decorative coverings. Man's love of horse as a faithful companion and sturdy mount developed early in civilization.

Cloze Passage: The Horse

The origin of the horse can be traced back millions of years ago to a small animal who stood about 14 inches high. Fossils of what is ____1____ as the dawn horse ____2____ been found in North America ____3____ Europe. The horse changed ____4____ over the years until ____5____ is known as the ____6____ horse evolved. The primitive ____7____ more closely resembled the ____8____ we know today. Four ____9____ of primitive horses have ____10____ found. These include the ____11____ Horse, the Asian Wild ____12____, the Tarpan and the ____13____ Horse.

Horses have been ____14____ part of man's culture ____15____ the centuries. Early in ____16____ evolution, they were a ____17____ of food for man. ____18____ horses

(cont.)

gained in size, _____19_____ were used to carry _____20_____, and to pull vehicles, _____21_____ as the Roman Chariots. _____22_____ of their speed and _____23_____, they opened up communication _____24_____ other tribes and groups _____25_____ lived some distance away.

_____26_____ horse is also known _____27_____ taking man into battle. _____28_____ Khan's successful conquests throughout _____29_____ were, in part, because _____30_____ the horse. The Mongols _____31_____ proficient horseback riders, learning _____32_____ maneuver their horses through _____33_____ obstacles and to effectively _____34_____ weapons while riding. Horses _____35_____ to be used in _____36_____ throughout the centuries. The _____37_____ Wars were fought on _____38_____ as were many of _____39_____ conquests. Much later, the United _____40_____ Cavalry and American Indians _____41_____ many of their battles _____42_____ horseback.

Early in history, _____43_____ found that horses could _____44_____ tamed to work for _____45_____, to carry them swiftly _____46_____ lands, and to provide _____47_____ with food. Great leaders such as _____48_____ the Great often established _____49_____ bonds with their horses. _____50_____, Alexander the Great's horse, _____51_____ allowed Alexander to ride _____52_____ when he was outfitted _____53_____ his harness and decorative _____54_____. Man's love of horse as a faithful companion and a sturdy, dependable mount developed early in civilization.

Total number of words: _313_

Total number of blanks: _54_

Total number of exact replacements: _____

Cloze score: _____

Level: _____

Sample Story Retelling—General Checklist: "Three Ducks Went Wandering" (Roy, 1979)

Setting
One day three ducks went wandering _____

Characters
3 ducks, bull, grasshoppers, foxes, hawk, snake, butterfly, mother duck _____

Events
1. —ducks went wandering _____

    —a bull saw the ducks _____

    —bull charged at the ducks _____

    —ducks didn't notice the bull _____

2. —ducks saw grasshoppers _____

    —ducks scrambled under fence _____

    —bull crashed into fence _____

    —ducks ate grasshoppers _____

3. —ducks walked in front of a den of hungry foxes _____

    —foxes chased ducks _____

    —ducks didn't notice foxes _____

    —ducks went swimming _____

    —foxes left on bank of pond _____

4. —a hawk flew above ducks in the pond _____

    —hawk zoomed toward ducks _____

    —ducks didn't notice hawk _____

    —ducks saw bugs under the water _____

    —ducks dove under the water _____

    —hawk went away hungry _____

5. —ducks paddled ashore in front of a snake _____

    —snake wanted to eat ducks _____

    —ducks didn't see snake _____

    —snake slithered toward ducks _____

    —ducks leapt into the air toward butterflies _____

    —snake tied himself in knots _____

6. —ducks headed toward barnyard in front of mother _____

    —mother suggested they take a nap _____

    —mother duck spread her wings _____

    —ducks went to sleep _____

Theme
Young animals (children) are often in danger but are not aware of it. They escape harm through innocent acts.

From *Struggling Readers* by Ernest Balajthy and Sally Lipa-Wade. Copyright 2003 by The Guilford Press.

Sample Story Retelling—Specific Checklist:
Jack and the Beanstalk (Kellogg, 1991)

Child's name _____ Grade _____

Teacher _____ Date _____

	Unprompted	Prompted
Once upon a time (setting)	____	____
There was a poor widow (main character)	____	____
She had a son named Jack (main character)	____	____
She had a cow named Milky-white	____	____
All they had to live on was the milk	____	____
One morning, Milky-white gave no milk	____	____
They were poor and needed money (theme/goal)	____	____
Jack offered to get work	____	____
He hadn't been able to get work before	____	____
Mother said to sell Milky-white (initiating event)	____	____

Episode #1

Jack went off with the cow	____	____
Jack met a funny-looking old man (attempt)	____	____
The man offered to swap beans for the cow	____	____
He said the beans were magical	____	____
Jack swapped the cow for the beans	____	____
The mother was angry (consequence)	____	____
She threw the beans out the window	____	____
Jack went to his bedroom without supper	____	____
He fell asleep	____	____

Episode #2

He woke and saw a giant beanstalk	____	____
Jack climbed the beanstalk	____	____
He came to a big house	____	____
In front was a big woman (main character)	____	____
She said that her husband is an ogre	____	____
The ogre likes to eat boys	____	____
She gave him breakfast	____	____
The ogre came (main character)	____	____
She hid Jack in the oven	____	____

(cont.)

	Unprompted	Prompted
He smelled Jack	____	____
His wife told him that no one is there	____	____
Jack took a bag of gold and leaves (attempt)	____	____
He gave the gold to his mother (consequence)	____	____

Episode #3

	Unprompted	Prompted
They lived off the gold for some time	____	____
Jack went back up the beanstalk	____	____
He met the big woman	____	____
She fed him	____	____
The ogre came	____	____
The woman hid Jack	____	____
The ogre got his hen that lays golden eggs	____	____
Jack took the hen and left (attempt)	____	____
The ogre woke up, but Jack got away	____	____
Jack gave the hen to his mother (consequence)	____	____

Episode #4

	Unprompted	Prompted
Jack went back up the beanstalk	____	____
He hid from the big woman in the bread box	____	____
The ogre came	____	____
The ogre smelled Jack	____	____
The ogre and his wife searched	____	____
They did not find Jack	____	____
The ogre got his golden harp	____	____
The ogre fell asleep	____	____
Jack took the harp (attempt)	____	____
The harp called out for the ogre	____	____

Resolution

	Unprompted	Prompted
The ogre woke up and chased Jack	____	____
Jack's mother brought him an axe	____	____
He chopped down the beanstalk	____	____
The ogre crashed to the ground (resolution)	____	____
Jack and his mother became very rich	____	____
Jack married a princess	____	____
They lived happily ever after	____	____

Scoring Guide for Story Retelling

Child's name _____ Grade _____ Age _____

Story _____ Date _____

____ Read aloud to child
____ Read by child

Setting _____ (0 or 1 pts.)

Main characters _____ (0 or 1 pts.)

Theme/goal _____ (0 or 1 pts.)

Plot episodes _____ (0, 1, or 2 pts.)

Sequence _____ (0, 1, or 2 pts.)

Resolution _____ (0 or 1 pts.)

Child's score: _____

Story Grammar Elements Record Sheet

Child's name _____

Story title	Date	Setting	Initiating event	Major episodes	Ending	Personal reaction

Story Retelling—General Analysis Checklist

Directions: + for behaviors child has developed
/ for behaviors child is developing
– for behaviors child has not yet developed

Does the child . . .

_____1. Name the characters in the story.

_____2. Understand what happens to the main character.

_____3. State the problem in the story.

_____4. State how the problem is resolved.

_____5. Retell the major parts of the story from memory.

_____6. Use the pictures to retell the story.

_____7. Need prompting and/or questioning to recall story details.

_____8. State the "gist" of the story.

_____9. State the major events of the story.

_____10. Sequence story events.

_____11. Retell an accurate story.

_____12. Lose the meaning of the story during the retell.

_____13. Retell a story that is not related to the one that has been heard or read.

Student Guide for Independent Think-Alouds

Name _____ Date _____

Text _____ Pages _____

Think-Aloud Strategy	Did I use it?	What did I do?
Connecting my life to the text	_____	
Connecting my knowledge to the text	_____	
Visualizing: Making a picture in my mind	_____	
Connecting one part of the text to another part	_____	
Making a guess as to an unknown word, based on the context	_____	
Predicting what will happen based on something in the text	_____	
Confirming: Noting that one of my predictions came true (or didn't come true)	_____	

Using Think-Alouds for Recognizing Patterns
in Student Reading

Child's name _____ Grade _____

Observed by _____ Date _____

Nonintegrator	Non-Risk-Taker
Schema Imposer	Storyteller
Good Comprehender	

Attitude Inventory

Student's name _____ Grade _____

Date _____

I like _____

My favorite _____

Sometimes I feel _____

My friends _____

My mother _____

My father _____

Yesterday _____

Today _____

School is _____

Reading aloud _____

Writing stories _____

My teacher _____

My favorite story is _____

I have fun _____

I don't like _____

My best friend _____

I can't wait _____

Interest Inventory

Name _____ Grade _____ Date _____

1. Do you have a favorite book? What is it?

2. Do you like your teacher to read aloud to you and the class? Describe.

3. Do you read aloud in your class? How do you feel about this?

4. Do you have a favorite TV program? What is it?

5. Would you rather watch TV or read a story? Why?

6. What kinds of reading do you do at home? Do you read comic books, magazines, story books, or newspapers?

7. Do you belong to any clubs in school?

8. Do you have any special interests or hobbies outside of school? Describe.

9. Do you have a favorite sport that you play?

10. Do you have a favorite sports team?

From *Struggling Readers* by Ernest Balajthy and Sally Lipa-Wade. Copyright 2003 by The Guilford Press.

Parent Interview Guide

Child's name _____ Grade _____ Age _____

Date of birth _____

Parents' names _____

Address _____

Home phone # _____ Father's phone # during day _____

Mother's phone # during day _____

1. Describe your family.
   a. How many children do you have?
   b. How many children are living at home?
   c. What are the names and ages of your children?
   d. What is the father's occupation? the mother's occupation?
   e. How do your working hours correspond to your child's school hours?
   f. What is the primary language in your home?

2. Describe your family's interactions with each other.
   a. What activities do you usually do as a family?
   b. What does your child like to do with father? with mother?
   c. Describe any family traditions.
   d. How does your child respond to participating in family traditions?
   e. What is your child's favorite family activity?

3. Describe your family's home activities.
   a. How do you feel about watching TV?
   b. Do you have any guidelines for watching TV?
   c. How many hours a day does your child watch TV?
   d. What are your child's favorite TV programs?
   e. Do you watch TV with your child?
   f. Do you read to your child? How often?
   g. What is your child's favorite book?
   h. Is reading aloud to your child an enjoyable activity? Describe.
   i. Does your child have a home library?
   j. How have you acquired this library?
   k. Does your child read to you?
   l. How would you describe your times of reading aloud with your child? Are they enjoyable for both of you? Are the times stressful?
   m. Does your child read the sports page, comics, cereal boxes, TV guide in the home?
   n. Describe your child's attitude toward reading. Why do you think your child feels this way?

(cont.)

From *Struggling Readers* by Ernest Balajthy and Sally Lipa-Wade. Copyright 2003 by The Guilford Press.

o. Does your child like to write? Describe the writing that is done (e.g., grocery lists, thank-you notes, greeting cards, addressing envelopes).

p. Do you leave notes for your child? Does your child leave notes for you?

4. Describe your beliefs and attitudes.

a. How do you feel about reading?

b. What types of materials do you read (e.g., newspaper, magazines, novels, informational books)?

c. How do you feel when you are asked to help your child complete homework?

d. How do you think the school is handling your child's reading instruction? Describe.

e. When do you think your child's reading difficulty started?

f. How do you help your child complete homework?

g. What goals to you have for your child?

h. Did you have any reading or learning difficulty in school? Describe.

5. Describe your child's outside activities.

a. Describe what your child does after school.

b. Who are your child's best friends?

c. What activities do your child and his/her friends like to do?

d. Does your child invite a friend to stay overnight? Does your child stay overnight at a friend's house?

e. Does your child like to participate in sports? Describe.

f. What recreational activity does your child like best (e.g., playing an instrument, playing a sport)?

6. Describe your child's school activities.

a. Describe your child's attitude toward school.

b. What is your child's favorite school activity? least favorite?

c. How many schools has your child attended?

d. Does your child have a favorite teacher? Describe.

e. Has illness contributed to your child missing school days?

f. What does your child say about the reading instruction in school?

g. How would you describe your child's reading difficulty?

7. Describe your child's physical health.

a. Does your child have frequent colds and ear infections?

b. Has your child ever been hospitalized with a serious injury? Describe.

c. Does your child wear glasses or have any vision problems?

d. Does your child have any speech or hearing problems?

e. How much sleep does your child require?

f. Does your child have difficulty staying with one task or completing tasks?

g. Are there any physical problems that might be interfering with your child's school performance?

h. Is your child presently taking any medication?

Student Interview Guide—Elementary Level

1. Name _____ Age _____ Grade _____ Date of birth _____
2. School _____
3. Tell me about your family. How many brothers and sisters do you have? What are their names? Who lives in your house?
4. Do your mother and father work? What do they do?
5. Is someone home for you after school, or do you go to day care or to a babysitter? Describe.
6. What is your favorite activity to do with your family?
7. Do you watch TV? What is your favorite program?
8. Do you have a TV in your bedroom?
9. Do you have any special jobs or chores to do?
10. What time do you usually go to bed?
11. Do you have homework very often? Who helps you with your homework? Describe.
12. What is your favorite book?
13. Do you have your own books? If so, where do you keep them? Do you borrow books from the library?
14. Does someone in your family read to you? How do you feel about this?
15. Do you have any games that you play with your family? What's the name of your favorite game?
16. What is reading?
17. What does a good reader do?
18. How would you describe yourself as a reader?
19. Who is the best reader in your class? How do you know?
20. What is writing?
21. What does a good writer do?
22. How would you describe yourself as a writer?
23. Who is the best writer in your class? How do you know?
24. If you could learn to do one thing to be a better reader, what would it be?
25. If you could learn one thing to be a better writer, what would it be?
26. Do you have a best friend at school? What do you and your friend like to do?
27. Do you have a best friend at home? What do you and your friend like to do?
28. How do you feel about reading in school? What reading activities do you like best? least?
29. How do you feel about reading at home? What reading activities do you like best? least?
30. How do you feel about writing in school? What writing activities do you like best? least?
31. How do you feel about writing at home? What writing activities do you like best? least?

From *Struggling Readers* by Ernest Balajthy and Sally Lipa-Wade. Copyright 2003 by The Guilford Press.

Teacher's Literacy Beliefs and Attitudes Scale

1. How do you feel about reading as a recreational activity? Do you read for pleasure?

2. How do you feel about writing as a recreational activity? Do you write for pleasure?

3. What kinds of reading material do you prefer (e.g., magazines, novels, informational books)?

4. What literacy goals to you have for your children this school year?

5. How do you plan to accomplish these goals?

6. Describe the reading materials in your classroom.

7. How did you acquire these materials?

8. Do you set aside time during the school day when your children can read for pleasure? Describe how you set up this pleasure reading time in your classroom.

9. How much time do you set aside for pleasure reading in your classroom?

10. How important is recreational reading in your classroom?

11. Do you group your children into ability groups for reading instruction? How do you feel about this?

12. Do you teach reading to the whole group? How do you feel about this?

13. Do you use children's literature as part of your reading instructional program? Describe.

14. Do you use a basal reader? Describe.

15. What would be the material of your choice to teach reading? Describe.

16. What activities do you initiate in your classroom to motivate children to read and write?

17. Do you have a special technique or activity you do to motivate children to read and write? How did you learn about this?

18. How would you describe your children's motivation to read and write? Can you give an example?

19. How would you describe your influence in motivating your children to read and write?

20. Do you set a time each day for your children to write? Describe.

21. Describe the formal writing instruction you provide your students.

References

Adams, M. (1990). *Beginning to read: Thinking and learning about print*. Cambridge, MA: MIT Press.

Allen, R. V. (1976). *Language experiences in communication*. Boston: Houghton Mifflin.

Allington, R. (1983). The reading instruction provided readers of differing reading abilities. *Elementary School Journal, 83*, 548–558.

Allington, R. (1994). The schools we have. The schools we need. *The Reading Teacher, 48*, 14–28.

Allington, R. (2002). Research on reading/learning disability interventions. In A. E. Farstrup & S. J. Samuels (Eds.), *What research has to say about reading instruction* (3rd ed., pp. 261–290). Newark, DE: International Reading Association.

Allington, R. L. (2001). *What really matters for struggling readers: Designing research-based programs*. Boston, MA: Allyn & Bacon.

Anderson, B. (1981). The missing ingredient: Fluent oral reading. *Elementary School Journal, 81*, 173–177.

Ashton-Warner, S. (1963). *Teacher*. New York: Simon & Schuster.

Au, K. (1979). Using the experience-text-relationship method with minority children. *The Reading Teacher, 32*, 677–779.

Au, K. H. (1993). *Literacy instruction in multicultural settings*. New York: Harcourt Brace Jovanovich.

Au, K. H. (2002). Multicultural factors and the effective instruction of students of diverse backgrounds. In A. E. Farstrup & S. J. Samuels (Eds.), *What research has to say about reading instruction* (3rd ed., pp. 392–414). Newark, DE: International Reading Association.

Au, K. H., & Kawakami, A. J. (1994). Cultural congruence in instruction. In E. R. Hollins, J. E. King, & W. Hayman (Eds.), *Teaching diverse populations: Formulating a knowledge base* (pp. 5–23). Albany: State University of New York Press.

Aulls, M. (1982). *Developing readers in today's elementary school*. Boston: Allyn & Bacon.

Ausubel, D. P. (1968). *Educational psychology: A cognitive view*. New York: Holt, Rinehart & Winston.

Baker, L. (1996). Social influences on metacognitive development in reading. In C. Cornoldi & J. Oakhill (Eds.), *Reading comprehension difficulties: Processes and interventions* (pp. 331–351). Hillsdale, NJ: Erlbaum.

Baker, L. (2002). Metacognition in comprehension instruction. In C. C. Block & M. Pressley (Eds.), *Comprehension instruction: Research-based best practices* (pp. 77–95). New York: Guilford Press.

Balajthy, E. (1986). The relationship of training in self-generated questioning with passage difficulty and immediate and delayed retention. In J. Niles (Ed.), *Solving problems in literacy: Learners, teachers, and researchers. Thirty-fifth yearbook of the National Reading Conference* (pp. 41–46). Rochester, NY: National Reading Conference.

Balajthy, E. (1996). Commercial literacy software trends for 1996. *Reading and Writing Quarterly, 13*, 87–93.

Barr, R., Blachowicz, C. L. Z., & Wogman-Sadow, M. (1995). *Reading diagnosis for teachers: An instructional approach.* White Plains, NY: Longman.

Barr, R., & Johnson, B. (1991). *Teaching reading in elementary classrooms.* White Plains, NY: Longman.

Baumann, J. F., Edwards, E. C., Font, G., Tereshinski, C. A., Kame'enui, E. J., & Olejnik, S. (2002). Teaching morphemic and contextual analysis to fifth-grade students. *Reading Research Quarterly, 37,* 150–176.

Beck, I., McKeown, M., Hamilton, R., & Kucan, L. (1998). Getting at the meaning. *American Educator, 22,* 66–71, 85.

Berg, J. H. (1961). *The O'Leary's and friends.* Chicago: Follett.

Blachowicz, C. L. Z., & Fisher, P. (2000). Vocabulary instruction. In M. Kamil, P. B. Mosenthal, P. D. Pearson, & R. Barr (Eds.), *The handbook of reading research* (Vol. III, pp. 503–524). Mahwah, NJ: Erlbaum.

Block, C. C., Oakar, M., & Hurt, N. (2002). The expertise of literacy teachers: A continuum from preschool to grade 5. *Reading Research Quarterly, 37,* 178–206.

Breznitz, Z. (1997). Effects of accelerated reading rate on memory for text among dyslexic readers. *Journal of Educational Psychology, 89,* 289–297.

Broikou, K., & Lipa, S. (1994, April). *Developing profiles of disabled readers through dynamic assessment.* Paper presented at the annual meeting of the American Educational Research Association, New Orleans, LA.

Cambourne, B. (2001). Why do some students fail to learn to read? Ockham's razor and the conditions of learning. *The Reading Teacher, 54,* 784–786.

Cambourne, B. (2002). Holistic, integrated approaches to reading and language arts instruction: The constructivist framework of an instructional theory. In A. E. Farstrup & S. J. Samuels (Eds.), *What research has to say about reading instruction* (3rd ed., pp. 25–47). Newark, DE: International Reading Association.

Carver, R. P. (1994). Percentage of unknown vocabulary words in text as a function of the relative difficulty of the text: Implications for instruction. *Journal of Reading Behavior, 26,* 413–437.

Carver, R. P. (2000). *The causes of high and low reading achievement.* Mahwah, NJ: Erlbaum.

Carver, R. P. (2001). Book review: Progress in understanding reading from the viewpoints of Stanovich and rauding theory. *Journal of Literacy Research, 33,* 361–382.

Chomsky, C. (1976). After decoding, what? *Language Arts, 53,* 288–296.

Clay, M. (1985). *The early detection of reading difficulties* (3rd ed.). Portsmouth, NH: Heinemann.

Clay, M. (1993). *Reading recovery: A guidebook for teachers in training.* Portsmouth, NH: Heinemann.

Clay, M. (2001). *Change over time in children's literacy development.* Portsmouth, NH: Heinemann.

Coles, G. (2000). *Misreading reading: The bad science that hurts children.* Portsmouth, NH: Heinemann.

Cook-Gumperez, J. (1986). Literacy and schooling: An unchanging equation? In J. Cook-Gumperez (Ed.), *The social construction of literacy* (pp. 16–44). Cambridge, England: Cambridge University Press.

Cunningham, A., & Stanovich, K. (1998). What reading does for the mind. *American Educator, 22,* 8–15.

Cunningham, A., & Stanovich, K. (1991). Tracking the unique effects of print exposure in children: Associations with vocabulary, general knowledge, and spelling. *Journal of Educational Psychology, 83,* 264–274.

Cunningham, P. M. (2000). *Phonics they use: Words for reading and writing* (3rd ed.). New York: Longman.

Cunningham, P. M., & Allington, R. (1999). *Classrooms that work.* New York: Longman.

Cunningham, P. M., Arthur, S., & Cunningham, J. W. (1977). *Classroom reading instruction, K-5: Alternative approaches.* Lexington, MA: D.C. Heath.

Cunningham, P. M., & Cunningham, J. W. (1992). Making words: Enhancing the invented spelling–decoding connection. *The Reading Teacher, 46,* 106–115.

Cunningham, P. M., & Cunningham, J. W. (2002). What we know about how to teach phonics. In A. E. Farstrup & S. J. Samuels (Eds.), *What research has to say about reading instruction* (3rd ed., pp. 87–109). Newark, DE: International Reading Association.

Currie, J. (2000). *Early childhood intervention programs: What do we know?* Washington, DC: Brookings Roundtable on Children.

Dahl, K. L., & Scharer, P. L. (2000). Phonics teaching and learning in whole language classrooms: New evidence from research. *Reading Teacher, 53,* 584–594.

Dahl, K. L., Scharer, P. L., Lawson, L. L., & Grogan, P. R. (1999). Phonics instruction and student achievement in whole language first-grade classrooms. *Reading Research Quarterly, 34,* 312–341.

Dahl, P., & Samuels, S. J. (1977). Teaching children to read using hypothesis test strategies. *The Reading Teacher, 30,* 603–606.

Dolch, E. W. (1939). *A manual for remedial reading.* Champaign, IL: Garrard.

Duke, N. (2000). 3.6 minutes per day: The scarcity of informational texts in first grade. *Reading Research Quarterly, 35,* 202–204.

Duke, N., & Pearson, P. D. (2002). Effective practices for developing reading comprehension. In A. E. Farstrup & S. J. Samuels (Eds.), *What research has to say about reading instruction* (3rd ed., pp.205– 242). Newark, DE: International Reading Association.

Durkin, D. (1974–1975). A six year study of children who learned to read in school at the age of four. *Reading Research Quarterly, 10,* 9–61.

Duvoisin, R. (1973). *The crocodile in the tree.* New York: Knopf.

Ehri, L. (1991). Development of the ability to read words. In R. Barr, M. Kamil, P. Mosenthal, & P. D. Pearson (Eds.), *The handbook of reading research* (Vol. II, pp. 383–417). New York: Longman.

Ehri, L. & Nunes, S. R. (2002). The role of phonemic awareness in learning to read. In A. E. Farstrup & S. J. Samuels (Eds.), *What research has to say about reading instruction* (3rd ed., pp. 110–139). Newark, DE: International Reading Association.

Ehri, L., Nunes, S. R., Willows, D. M., Schuster, B. V., Yaghoub-Zadeh, Z., & Shanahan, T. (2001). Phonemic awareness instruction helps children learn to read: Evidence from the National Reading Panel's meta-analysis. *Reading Research Quarterly, 36,* 250–287.

Ehri, L., & Robbins, C. (1992). Beginners need some decoding skill to read words by analogy. *Reading Research Quarterly, 27,* 12–26.

Falk-Ross, F. C. (2002). *Classroom-based language and literacy intervention.* Boston: Allyn & Bacon.

Fernald, G. (1943). *Remedial techniques in basic school subjects.* New York: McGraw-Hill.

Fisher, M. P. (1994). *The country mouse and the city mouse.* New York: Random House.

Foster, M. L., & Peele, T. B. (2001). Ring my bell: Contextualizing home and school in an African American community. In E. McIntyre, A. Rosebery, & N. Gonzalez (Eds.), *Classroom diversity: Connecting curriculum to students' lives.* Portsmouth, NH: Heinemann.

Fowler, G. L. (1982). Developing comprehension skills in primary students through the use of story frames. *The Reading Teacher, 36,* 176–179.

Fry, E. (1999). *1,000 instant words: The most common words for teaching reading, writing, and spelling.* Westminster, CA: Teacher Created Materials.

Fry, E. (2001a). *Informal reading assessments, K–8.* Westminster, CA: Teacher Created Materials.

Fry, E. (2001b). *Instant word practice book, primary.* Westminster, CA: Teacher Created Materials.

Gambrell, L., & Chaser, S. (1991). Explicit story structure instruction and the narrative writing of fourth- and fifth-grade below-average readers. *Reading Research and Instruction, 31,* 54–62.

Garcia, G. E. (2000). Bilingual children's reading. In M. Kamil, P. B. Mosenthal, P. D. Pearson, & R. Barr (Eds.), *The handbook of reading research* (Vol. III, pp. 813–834). Mahwah, NJ: Erlbaum.

Gentry, J. R. (2000). A retrospective on invented spelling and a look forward. *The Reading Teacher, 54,* 318– 332.

Gerdes, S. (2001). Using repeated reading, paired reading, and demonstration to improve reading fluency. In W. M. Linek, E. G. Sturtevant, J. A. R. Dugan, & P. E. Linder (Eds.), *Celebrating the voices of literacy: The twenty-third yearbook* (pp. 55–78). Readyville, TN: College Reading Association.

Gillingham, A., & Stillman, B. (1973). *Remedial training for children with specific disability in reading, spelling, and penmanship* (7th ed.). Cambridge, MA: Educators Publishing Service.

Gipe, J. (1980). Use of relevant context helps kids learn new word meanings. *The Reading Teacher, 33,* 398–402.

Glass, G. (1973). *Teaching decoding as separate from reading.* Garden City, NY: Adelphi University Press.

Glass, G., & Glass, E. W. (1994). *Teacher guide: Glass-analysis for decoding only.* Garden City, NY: Easier to Learn.

Goodman, K. (1967). Reading: A psycholinguistic guessing game. *Journal of the Reading Specialist, 6,* 126–135.

Goodman, K. (1976). Behind the eye: What happens in reading. In H. Singer & R. B. Ruddell (Eds.), *Theoretical models and processes of reading* (2nd ed., pp. 470–496). Newark, DE: International Reading Association.

Goswami, U., & Bryant, P. (1992). Rhyme, analogy, and children's reading. In P. B. Gough, L. C. Ehri, & R. Treiman (Eds.), *Reading acquisition* (pp. 49–63). Hillsdale, NJ: Erlbaum.

Grant, C. A. (2001). Teachers and linking literacies of yesterday and today with literacies of tomorrow: The need for education that is multicultural and social reconstructionist. In J. V. Hoffman, D. L. Schallert, C. M. Fairbanks, J. Worthy, & B. Maloch (Eds.), *The 50th yearbook of the National Reading Conference* (pp. 63–81). Chicago: National Reading Conference.

Graves, M. F., & Watts-Taffe, S. M. (2002). The place of word consciousness in a research-based vocabulary program. In A. E. Farstrup & S. J. Samuels (Eds.), *What research has to say about reading instruction* (3rd ed., pp. 140–165). Newark, DE: International Reading Association.

Green, F. (1979). Radio reading. In C. Pennock (Ed.), *Reading comprehension at four linguistic levels.* Newark, DE: International Reading Association.

Greene, J. (1998). Another chance. *American Educator, 22,* 74–79.

Griffin, M. L. (2002). Why don't you use your finger? Paired reading in first grade. *The Reading Teacher, 55,* 766–774.

Grigorenko, E., Wood, F., Meyer, M., Hart, L., Speed, W., Shuster, A., & Paula, D. (1997). Susceptibility loci for distinct components of developmental dyslexia on chromosomes 6 and 15. *American Journal of Human Genetics, 60,* 27–39.

Guthrie, J. T. (2002). Preparing students for high- stakes test taking in reading. In A. E. Farstrup & S. J. Samuels (Eds.), *What research has to say about reading instruction* (3rd ed., pp. 370–391). Newark, DE: International Reading Association.

Harris, T. L., & Hodges, R. E. (1995). *The literacy dictionary: The vocabulary of reading and writing.* Newark, DE: International Reading Association.

Heckelman, R. G. (1969). A neurological impress method of remedial reading instruction. *Academic Therapy, 4,* 277–282.

Hiebert, E. H. (1994). Reading recovery in the United States: What difference does it make to an age cohort? *Educational Researcher, 23,* 15–25.

Hiebert, E. H., & Taylor, B. M. (2000). Beginning reading instruction: Research on early interventions. In M. Kamil, P. B. Mosenthal, P. D. Pearson, & R. Barr (Eds.), *The handbook of reading research* (Vol. III, pp. 455–482). Mahwah, NJ: Erlbaum.

Holdaway, D. (1979). *Foundations of literacy.* Portsmouth, NH: Heinemann.

Hoskisson, K. (1979). A response to "a critique of reading as a whole task venture." *The Reading Teacher, 32,* 653–659.

Huey, E. B. (1968). *The psychology and pedagogy of reading.* Cambridge, MA: MIT Press. (Original work published 1908)

Johns, J. L., & Lenski, S. D. (2001). *Improving reading: A handbook of strategies.* Dubuque, IA: Kendall/Hunt.

Johnson, D., & Pearson, P. D. (1984). *Teaching reading vocabulary* (2nd ed.) New York: Holt, Rinehart & Winston.

Johnston, F. R. (1999). The timing and teaching of word families. *The Reading Teacher, 53,* 64–75.

Juel, C. (1994). *Learning to read and write in one elementary school.* New York: Springer-Verlag.

Juel, C., & Minden-Cupp, C. (2000). Learning to read words: Linguistic units and instructional strategies. *Reading Research Quarterly, 35,* 458–492.

Kellogg, S. (1977). *The mysterious tadpole.* New York: Dial Press.

Kibby, M. (1989). Teaching sight vocabulary with and without context before silent reading: A field test of the "focus of attention" hypothesis. *Journal of Reading Behavior, 21*(3), 261–278.

Learning First Alliance. (1998). Every child reading: An action plan of the Learning First Alliance. *American Educator, 22,* 52–63.

Leckliter, I. N. (1994). Dyslexia. In R. J. Sternberg (Ed.), *Encyclopedia of human intelligence* (pp. 376–386). New York: Macmillan.

Leslie, L., & Thimke, B. (1986). The use of orthographic knowledge in beginning reading. *Journal of Reading Behavior, 18,* 229–241.

Liberman, I., Shankweiler, D., Fischer, F., & Carter, B. (1974). Explicit syllable and phoneme segmentation in the young child. *Journal of Experimental Child Psychology, 18,* 201–212.

Lipa, S. (1983). Reading disability: A new look at an old issue. *Journal of Learning Disabilities, 16,* 452–457.

Lipa, S. (1990). Comprehension for decoding. *Journal of Reading, Writing and Learning Disabilities International, 6,* 93–105.

Lipa, S. (1996, April). *Assessment decisions—instructional implications: Profiles of a disabled reader.* Paper presented at the Annual Meeting of the American Educational Research Association, New York.

Lipa, S., & Penney, N. (1989, October). *Whole language, early literacy, and the child with learning disabilities.* Paper presented at the 11th International Conference on Learning Disabilities, Denver, CO.

Lobel, A. (1999). *Frog and toad together.* New York: HarperFestival. (Original work published 1970)

Lyon, G. R. (1995). Research in learning disabilities: Contributions from scientists supported by the National Institute of Child Health and Human Development. *Journal of Child Neurology, 10,* 120–126.

Lyon, G. R., Fletcher, J. M., Shaywitz, S. E., Shaywitz, B. A., Torgesen, J. K., Wood, F. B., Schulte, A., & Olson, R. (2001). Rethinking learning disabilities. In C. E. Finn, A. J. Rotherham, & C. R. Hokanson (Eds.), *Rethinking special education for a new century* (pp. 259–287). Washington, DC: Thomas B. Fordham Foundation.

MacKenzie, K. K. (2001). Using literacy booster groups to maintain and extend reading recovery success in the primary grades. *The Reading Teacher, 55,* 222–234.

Manzo, A. (1969). The ReQuest procedure. *Journal of Reading, 13,* 123–126.

Manzo, A. (1975). Guided reading procedure. *Journal of Reading, 18,* 287–291.

Matanzo, J. B. (2001). Enhancing and reinforcing the concept knowledge of English language learners through children's literature. In W. M. Linek, E. G. Sturtevant, J. A. R. Dugan, & P. E. Linder (Eds.), *Celebrating the voices of literacy: The twenty-third yearbook* (pp. 162–178). Readyville, TN: College Reading Association.

McBride-Chang, C. (1995). What is phonological awareness? *Journal of Educational Psychology, 87,* 179–192.

McCormick, S. (1994). A nonreader becomes a reader: A case study of literacy acquisition by a severely disabled reader. *Reading Research Quarterly, 29,* 156–176.

McElveen, S. A., & Dierking, C. C. (2001). Children's books as models to teach writing skills. *The Reading Teacher, 54,* 362–364.

McKenna, M. (2002). Phonics software for a new millennium. *Reading and Writing Quarterly, 18,* 93–96.

McNinch, G. (1981). A method for teaching sight words to disabled readers. *The Reading Teacher, 35*(3), 269–272.

Meyer, L., & Wardhop, J. (1994). Home and school influences on learning to read in kindergarten through second grade. In F. Lehr & J. Osborn (Eds.), *Reading, language and literacy for the twenty-first century* (pp. 165–184). Hillsdale, NJ: Erlbaum.

Mike, D. G. (2001). Computer mediated word recognition: Poised to make a difference? *Reading and Writing Quarterly, 17,* 99–102.

Moats, L. (1998). Teaching decoding. *American Educator, 22,* 42–49, 95–96.

Morris, B. (2002). Overcoming dyslexia. *Fortune Magazine* [Online], *115.*

Nagy, W. E., & Scott, J. A. (2000). Vocabulary processes. In M. Kamil, P. B. Mosenthal, P. D. Pearson, & R. Barr (Eds.), *The handbook of reading research* (Vol. III, pp. 269–284). Mahwah, NJ: Erlbaum.

Nagy, W. E., Winsor, P., Osborn, J., & O'Flahavan, J. (1994). Structural analysis: Some guidelines for instruction. In F. Lehr & J. Osborn (Eds.), *Reading, language and literacy* (pp. 45–58). Hillsdale, NJ: Erlbaum.

Narvaez, D. (2002). Individual differences that influence reading comprehension. In C. C. Block & M. Pressley (Eds.), *Comprehension instruction: Research-based best practices* (pp. 158–175). New York: Guilford Press.

National Reading Panel. (2000). *Report of the National Reading Panel: Reports of the subgroups.* Washington, DC: National Institute of Child Health and Human Development Clearinghouse.

Neal, J. C., & Kelly, P. R. (2002). Delivering the promise of academic success through late intervention. *Reading and Writing Quarterly, 18,* 101–118.

Neuman, S. B. (2001). The role of knowledge in early literacy. *Reading Research Quarterly, 36,* 468–475.

Neuman, S. B., & Celano, D. (2001). Access to print in low-income and middle-income communities: An ecological study of four neighborhoods. *Reading Research Quarterly, 36,* 8–26.

Neuman, S. B., & Roskos, K. (1993). Access to print for children of poverty: Differential effects of adult mediation and literacy enriched play settings on environmental and functional print tasks. *American Educational Research Journal, 30,* 95–102.

Numeroff, L. (1994). *If you give a mouse a cookie.* New York: Scholastic.

Numeroff, L. (1996). *If you give a moose a muffin.* New York: Scholastic.

Numeroff, L. (1998). *If you give a pig a pancake.* New York: Scholastic.

Ogle, D. (1986). K-W-L: A teaching model that develops active reading of expository text. *The Reading Teacher, 39,* 564–570.

Oldfather, P. (Ed.). (2002). How and why should we learn from students about overcoming motivation problems in literacy learning? *Reading and Writing Quarterly, 18*(3).

Orton, S. (1937). *Reading, writing and speech problems in children.* New York: Norton.

Palincsar, A., & Brown, A. (1984). Reciprocal teaching of comprehension-fostering and comprehension-monitoring activities. *Cognition and Instruction, 1,* 117–175.

Paris, S. G. (2002). Measuring children's reading development using leveled texts. *The Reading Teacher, 56,* 168–170.

Pierson, J. (1999). Transforming engagement in literacy instruction: The role of student genuine interest and ability. *Annals of Dyslexia, 49,* 307–329.

Pikulski, J. J. (1994). Preventing reading failure: A review of five effective programs. *The Reading Teacher, 48,* 30–39.

Pinnell, G. S. (1989). Reading recovery: Helping at-risk children learn to read. *The Elementary School Journal, 90,* 161–183.

Pinnell, G. S., & Fountas, I. (1998). *Word matters: Teaching phonics and spelling in the reading/writing classroom.* Portsmouth, NH: Heinemann.

Pinnell, G. S., Lyons, C., Deford, D., Bryk, A., & Seltzer, M. (1994). Comparing instructional models for the literacy education of high-risk first graders. *Reading Research Quarterly, 29,* 8–39.

Pogrow, S. (2002). Success for All is a failure. *Phi Delta Kappan, 83,* 463–468.

Pressley, M. (2000). What should comprehension instruction be the instruction of? In M. Kamil, P. B. Mosenthal, P. D. Pearson, & R. Barr (Eds.), *The handbook of reading research* (Vol. III, pp. 545–562). Mahwah, NJ: Erlbaum.

Pressley, M. (2002). Metacognition and self-regulated comprehension. In A. E. Farstrup & S. J. Samuels (Eds.), *What research has to say about reading instruction* (3rd ed., pp. 291–309). Newark, DE: International Reading Association.

Raphael, T. (1986). Teaching question–answer relationships, revisited. *The Reading Teacher, 39,* 516–523.

Rhoder, C., & Huerster, P. (2002). Standpoints and voices: Use dictionaries for word learning with caution. *Journal of Adolescent and Adult Literacy, 45,* 730–735.

Richards, J. C., & Morse, T. E. (2002). One preservice teacher's experience teaching literacy to regular and special education students. *Reading Online, 5*. Retrieved June 7, 2002: *http://www.readingonline. org*.

Richards, M. (2000). Be a good detective. Solve the case of oral reading fluency. *The Reading Teacher, 53*, 534–539.

Richgels, D. (1995). Invented spelling ability and printed word learning in kindergarten. *Reading Research Quarterly, 30*, 96–109.

Richgels, D. (2001). Phonemic awareness. *The Reading Teacher, 55*, 274–278.

Robinson, F. (1970). *Effective reading* (4th ed.). New York: Harper & Row.

Rosenbaum, C. (2001). A word map for middle school: A tool for effective vocabulary instruction. *Journal of Adolescent and Adult Literacy, 45*, 44–49.

Roy, R. (1979). *Three ducks went wandering*. New York: Seabury Press.

Ruddell, M. R., & Shearer, B. A. (2002). "Extraordinary," "tremendous," "exhilarating," "magnificent": Middle school at-risk students become avid word learners with the Vocabulary Self-Collection Strategy (VSS). *Journal of Adolescent and Adult Literacy, 45*, 352–363.

Rylant, C. (1982). *When I was young in the mountains*. New York: Dial Press.

Samuels, S. J. (1979). The method of repeated readings. *The Reading Teacher, 32*, 403–408.

Samuels, S. J. (2002). Reading fluency: Its development and assessment. In A. E. Farstrup & S. J. Samuels (Eds.), *What research has to say about reading instruction* (3rd ed., pp. 166–183). Newark, DE: International Reading Association.

Scharer, P. L., Lehman, B. A., & Peters, D. (2001). Pondering the significance of big and little or saving the whales: Discussions of narrative and expository text in fourth- and fifth-grade classrooms. *Reading Research and Instruction, 40*, 297–314.

Searfoss, L. (1975). Radio reading. *The Reading Teacher, 29*, 295–296.

Shanahan, T., & Barr, R. (1995). Reading recovery: An independent evaluation of the effects of an early instructional intervention for at risk learners. *Reading Research Quarterly, 30*, 958–996.

Silverstein, S. (1994). *Falling up*. New York: Harper Collins.

Singer, H., Samuels, S. J., & Spiroff, J. (1973–74). The effects of pictures and contextual conditions on learning responses to printed words. *Reading Research Quarterly, 9*, 555–567.

Sipe, L. R. (2001). Invention, convention, and intervention: Invented spelling and the teacher's role. *The Reading Teacher, 55*, 264–273.

Slavin, R. E. (2002). Mounting evidence supports the achievement effects of Success for All. *Phi Delta Kappan, 83*, 469–471.

Slingerland, B. (1976). *A multi-sensory approach to language arts for specific language disability children: A guide for primary teachers*. Cambridge, MA: Educators Publishing Service.

Smolkin, L. B., & Donovan, C. A. (2002). "Oh excellent, excellent question!" Developmental differences and comprehension acquisition. In C. C. Block & M. Pressley (Eds.), *Comprehension instruction: Research-based best practices* (pp. 140–157). New York: Guilford Press.

Snider, V. (1995). A primer on phonemic awareness: What it is, why it's important, and how to teach it. *School Psychological Review, 24*, 443–455.

Snow, C., Burns, M. S., & Griffin, P. (1998). *Preventing reading difficulties in young children*. Washington, DC: National Academy Press.

Stahl, S. A., & Murray, B. A. (1994). Defining phonological awareness and its relationship to early reading. *Journal of Educational Psychology, 86*, 221–234.

Stanovich, K. (1988). Explaining the differences between the dyslexic and the garden variety poor reader: The phonological core variable–difference model. *Journal of Learning Disabilities, 21*, 590–612.

Stanovich, K. (1992). Speculations on the causes and consequences of individual differences in early reading acquisition. In P. Gough, L. Ehri, & R. Treiman (Eds.), *Reading acquisition* (pp. 307–332). Hillsdale, NJ: Erlbaum.

Stanovich, K. (2000). *Progress in understanding reading: Scientific foundations and new frontiers*. New York: Guilford Press.

Stauffer, R. (1975). *Directing the reading–thinking process*. New York: Harper & Row.

Stine, R. L. (1993). *Be careful what you wish for*. New York: Scholastic.

Tan, A., & Nicholson, T. (1997). Flashcards revisited: Training poor readers to read words faster improves their comprehension of text. *Journal of Educational Psychology, 89*, 289–297.

Torgesen, J. K., & Mathes, P. G. (2000). *A basic guide to understanding, assessing, and teaching phonemic awareness*. Austin, TX: Pro-Ed.

Trabasso, T., & Bouchard, E. (2002). Teaching readers how to comprehend text strategically. In C. C. Block & M. Pressley (Eds.), *Comprehension instruction: Research-based best practices* (pp. 176–200). New York: Guilford Press.

Tunmer, W., & Hoover, W. (1992). Cognitive and linguistic factors in learning to read. In P. Gough, L. Ehri, & R. Treiman (Eds.), *Reading acquisition* (pp. 175–214). Hillsdale, NJ: Erlbaum.

Vacca, R. T. (2002). Making a difference in adolescents' school lives: Visible and invisible aspects of content area reading. In A. E. Farstrup & S. J. Samuels (Eds.), *What research has to say about reading instruction* (3rd ed., pp. 184–204). Newark, DE: International Reading Association.

Veatch, J., Sawichi, F., Elliott, G., Barnette, E., & Blakey, J. (1973). *Key words for reading: The language experience approach begins*. Columbus, OH: Merrill.

Vellutino, F. (1977). Has the perceptual deficit theory led us astray? *Journal of Learning Disabilities, 10*, 375–384.

Vellutino, F., & Scanlon, D. (1982). Verbal processing in poor and normal readers. In C. Brainerd & M. Pressley (Eds.), *Verbal processing in children: Progress in cognitive development research* (pp. 189–264). New York: Springer-Verlag.

Vygotsky, L. S. (1978). *Mind in society: The development of higher psychological processes* (M. Cole, V. John-Steiner, S. Scribner, & E. Souberman, Eds., & Trans.). Cambridge, MA: Harvard University Press. (Original work published 1934)

Waddington, E. (1996). Teaching students with dyslexia in the regular classroom. *Childhood Education, 73*, 2–5.

Wade, S. (1990). Using think-alouds to assess comprehension. *Reading Teacher, 43*, 442–451.

Wagner, L., Nott, J. G., & Agnew, A. T. (2001). The nuts and bolts of teaching first-grade writing through a journal workshop. *The Reading Teacher, 55*, 120–125.

Weisberg, R., & Balajthy, E. (1990). Improving disabled readers' summarization and recognition of expository text. In N. D. Padak, T. V. Rasinski, & J. Logan (Eds.), *Challenges in reading: Twelfth Yearbook of the College Reading Association* (pp. 141–151). Provo, UT: College Reading Association.

Werderich, D. E. (2002). Individualized responses: Using journal letters as a vehicle for differentiated reading instruction. *Journal of Adolescent and Adult Literacy, 45*, 746–754.

Wilson, B. A. (1996). *The Wilson Reading System instructor manual*. Millbury, MA: Wilson Language Training Corporation.

Wolf, M. (1999). What time may tell: Towards a new conceptualization of developmental dyslexia. *Annals of Dyslexia, 49*, 3–28.

Wollman-Bonilla, J. (2000). *Family message journals: Teaching writing through family involvement*. Urbana, IL: National Council of Teachers of English.

Wood, K. (1984). Probable passages: A writing strategy. *The Reading Teacher, 37*, 496–499.

Worthy, J., Patterson, E., Salas, R., Prater, S., & Turner, M. (2002). "More than just reading": The human factor in reaching resistant readers. *Reading Research and Instruction, 41*, 177–202.

Yopp, H. (1992). Developing phonemic awareness in young children. *The Reading Teacher, 45*, 696–703.

Yopp, H., & Yopp, R. (2000). Supporting phonemic awareness development in the classroom. *The Reading Teacher, 54*, 130–141.

Zutell, J., & Rasinski, T. (1991). Training teachers to attend to their students' oral reading fluency. *Theory into Practice, 30*, 211–217.

Index